THE ASSASSIN'S ACCOMPLICE

THE

ASSASSIN'S ACCOMPLICE

MARY SURRATT AND
THE PLOT TO KILL
ABRAHAM LINCOLN

KATE CLIFFORD LARSON

BASIC
BOOKS

A MEMBER OF THE PERSEUS BOOKS GROUP
NEW YORK

Hardcover first published in 2008 by Basic Books,
A Member of the Perseus Books Group
Paperback first published in 2010 by Basic Books

Books published by Basic Books are available at special discounts for bulk purchases in the
United States by corporations, institutions, and other organizations. For more information,
please contact the Special Markets Department at the Perseus Books Group, 2300 Chestnut
Street, Suite 200, Philadelphia, PA 19103, or call (800) 810-4145, ext. 5000, or e-mail
special.markets@perseusbooks.com.

Designed by Timm Bryson

The Library of Congress has cataloged the hardcover as follows:
Larson, Kate Clifford.
The assassin's accomplice : Mary Surratt and the plot to kill Abraham Lincoln / Kate Clifford
Larson.
p. cm.
Includes bibliographical references and index.
ISBN 978-0-465-03815-2 (alk. paper)
1. Surratt, Mary E. (Mary Elizabeth), 1823–1865. 2. Lincoln, Abraham, 1809–1865—
Assassination. 3. Conspiracies—Washington (D.C.) 4. Trials (Assassination)—Washington
(D.C.) I. Title.
E457.5.L33 2008
973.7'092—dc22
                                                        2008001060
Paperback ISBN: 978-0-465-01893-2

10 9 8 7 6 5 4 3 2 1

For Spencer, Rebecca, and Trevor.
With all my love.

CONTENTS

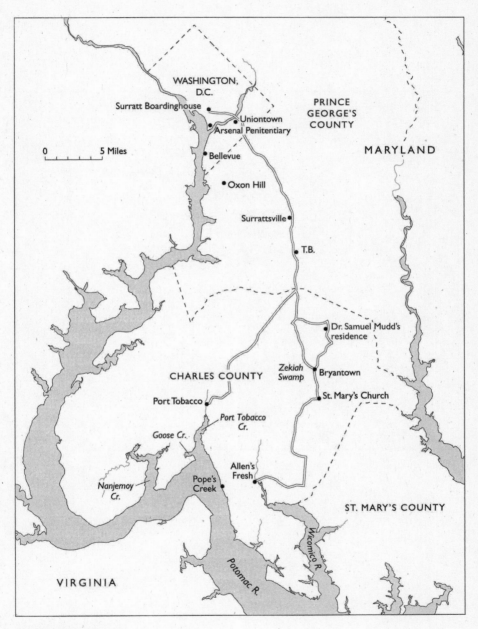

Southern Maryland.

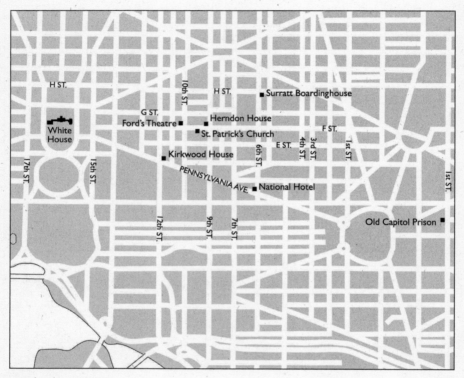

H ST.

10th ST.

H ST.

■ Surratt Boardinghouse

G ST.

Ford's Theatre ■

Herndon House

White
House

St. Patrick's Church

F ST.

E ST.

4th ST.

3rd ST.

1st ST.

6th ST.

■ Kirkwood House

17th ST.

15th ST.

PENNSYLVANIA AVE.

1st ST.

■ National Hotel

12th ST.

9th ST.

7th ST.

Old Capitol Prison ■

Washington, D.C.

INTRODUCTION

At 1:22 P.M. on July 7, 1865, forty-two-year-old Mary Elizabeth Jenkins Surratt was hanged for conspiring with John Wilkes Booth to murder President Abraham Lincoln. She would be the first woman ever executed by the United States government.

By the summer of 1865, practically every American knew who Mary Surratt was. To them she was either a hard-hearted, manipulative co-conspirator who aided in the plan to assassinate President Abraham Lincoln, or an innocent woman trapped in Booth's murderous web and subjected to a vengeful and bloodthirsty military tribunal. Hanged with three male co-conspirators beside her, Mary's fatal punishment sent shock waves around the nation. Today, nearly 150 years later, few Americans know her story and still fewer recognize her name.

Mother, widow, businesswoman, and a deeply pious Catholic, Mary Surratt seemed an unlikely assassin's accomplice. Until now, the reasons behind her choice to participate in such a deadly scheme have gone relatively unexplored. Looking back into Mary's past, however, one might find the seeds of rebelliousness and disloyalty nurtured in a fertile rebel community.

From her birth and upbringing in a modest slaveholding family in a small Maryland town, to her conversion to Catholicism (made much of during and after her trial) and her early marriage to an alcoholic ten years her senior, Mary's life story seems unremarkable in its detail. But clues to her fateful decision to befriend and support Lincoln's murderer may be found in the deep disruptions brought on by the Civil War and her husband's sudden death in 1862. Left with his massive debts to pay off, Mary may have discovered a strategy for survival: providing a safe haven for Confederate couriers, spies, and ultimately, assassins.

On the day of her hanging, Mary Surratt was the most reviled woman in America. But public opinion shifted again and again from the time of her arrest through the century and a half since her execution.

During the unseasonably hot weeks of May and June 1865, dramatic newspaper reports of Mary's trial fed a growing public appetite for revenge and retribution for Lincoln's assassination. During the four-week trial, which included the simultaneous prosecution of seven other Booth accomplices, daily news reports from the courtroom exposed the public to the depth of the conspiracy to kill Lincoln and Mary's central role in the plot. By the middle of June, when the trial was winding down, most Americans believed Mary was guilty, convinced that the cold, beguiling woman had aided John Wilkes Booth and his co-conspirators.

The Northern press had little sympathy for Mary Surratt during the highly publicized trial. At first, she was portrayed as a willing accomplice in the conspiracy. Some papers described Surratt in almost caricature fashion. An "Amazon" (she was about five feet, four inches tall and of medium build), they wrote, with black eyes and a small mouth—both attributes, according to the press, of a criminal face. Many of the leading newspapers of the day heartily supported the military tribunal's verdict of guilty. The Union had long suffered from the skillful spying perpetrated by cunning and seductive female Confederate agents, leaving little room for empathy for Surratt. To Northerners, her sex and mature age only amplified the perceived depravity of the Southern character.

But Surratt's punishment shocked the nation. Within hours of her hanging, people all across the country expressed horror and revulsion over her death. Days later, public sentiment began to dramatically change. For some Americans, Mary Surratt had been wrongfully sub-jected to a vindictive federal military tribunal. Her supporters accused the military court that tried her and the other co-conspirators with ille-gally prosecuting civilians. Eager news reporters featured these accu-sations in their papers, claiming the court suppressed exculpatory evidence and allowed false testimony given by government witnesses against Mary to go unchallenged.

Sympathy for Mary increased dramatically in the weeks after her ex-ecution, bolstering what would become a decades-long campaign to re-store her reputation and prove her innocence. Though many Northerners believed in her guilt, most apparently never expected she would actually be executed. The outcry was so great it would ad-versely affect political careers and spark years of scrutiny by those who believed deeply in her innocence. Vilified during the trial of the assassi-nation conspirators, Mary's wicked persona was recast into the sor-rowful victim, a perfect Victorian mother murdered by immoral and unrestrained powerful men.

Pro-Southern sympathizers saw the trial and execution differently than most Northern citizens, and it is through those sentiments that Mary's historic role in the conspiracy has most frequently been retold. The solidarity and determination of Mary's supporters helped reimag-ine and distort the historical record, bolstering strongly held beliefs that a gross miscarriage of justice took the life of an innocent woman.

As a result, the depth of Mary Surratt's complicity in the assassina-tion of Lincoln, the fairness of her trial, and the justness of her punish-ment have been debated since the day of her arrest on April 17, 1865, three days after John Wilkes Booth murdered Lincoln as he sat watch-ing a play at Ford's Theatre.

The Assassin's Accomplice confronts this historical controversy, detail-ing Mary's role in the assassination, and the chain of events that drove the court's and the President's decision to execute her. Thus, *The Assassin's Accomplice* will recover a little-known chapter in American history: the full and dramatic account of the life and trial of Mary Surratt, the woman who nurtured and helped cultivate the conspiracy to kill President Abraham Lincoln.

This biography was begun with the supposition that Mary Surratt was far more innocent of the charges against her than the original trial had determined, and that her unjust hanging was the result of a frenzy of revenge bolstered by a stunned federal government determined to exert its power. Even a woman would not escape the government's single-minded goal to avenge Lincoln's murder. But the research itself led to an altogether surprising conclusion: Mary Surratt was not only guilty, but was far more involved in the plot than many historians have given her credit for.

Most contemporary historians of the Lincoln assassination now generally agree that Mary Surratt was involved in the conspiracy to some degree. They have, however, failed to examine her specific actions, her motives, and the broader historical implications of her role in the scheme. This is, in some ways, understandable. The plot to kidnap Lincoln and, later, to assassinate him and other members of his cabinet was enormously complex and involved many accomplices. There were scores of major and minor characters, mostly male. It is the stuff historians love to research and decipher.

Nevertheless, most assassination scholarship focuses almost exclusively on the men who dominated the conspiracy. Telling the story of the male conspirators reinforces long-held notions of criminality. Their lives reflect devious and evil intent, personified through their careers as spies and petty criminals, and finally, assassins. Those images do not fit the profile of a middle-class mother and widow. Mary has remained marginalized, a shadowy figure whose goals and intentions have not been carefully explored. She is the only assassination accomplice whose story has not been fully told.

Highlighting Mary's role and placing it at the center of the narrative of the assassination conspiracy reveals strong evidence of her participation and her implicit contributions to the success of Booth's plans. Set within the context of a bitter Civil War, Mary's life as a widowed Southern slaveholding woman, struggling to raise her children and maintain her household independently, foreshadows the evolution of an insurgent who nurtured and helped cultivate the conspiracy to kill President Abraham Lincoln.

As Southern slaveholders, Mary and her neighbors were dependent upon the unpaid labor of enslaved African Americans. By midcentury, however, the abolition of slavery had become a major political issue for the growing nation. For Southerners, the preservation of slavery was deemed vital to the region's future. But threats to the slave-based social and economic order that defined Mary's status grew ever greater during the 1850s (the pressures from abolitionists were becoming more powerful), and Mary and her neighbors felt increasingly powerless to protect their way of life. The Civil War, fought in great part over the future of slavery in the United States, tested personal and community loyalties, pitting families and neighbors against one another. Maryland remained in the Union, but some of its citizens fled and joined Confederate forces in Virginia and elsewhere. Others remained in Maryland and operated clandestine networks supporting the rebel cause. Unlike the many Marylanders who chose to support the Confederacy through blockade-running, spying, and smuggling, Mary's fateful choice to aid in illegal rebel activities would draw her into the heart of one of the most shocking events in American history.

Throughout the Civil War, Mary and her family were deeply embedded in the regional network of illegal safe houses for Confederate spies and agents. Her son John Surratt, Jr., was already a seasoned spy and illegal rebel courier by the time he met John Wilkes Booth.

Booth's complex road to assassination evolved over several months and involved elaborate planning, substantial funding, and a large number of helpers. A devout Southerner determined to advance Confederate interests during the Civil War, Booth devised a scheme to kidnap President Lincoln and ransom his life for the release of Confederate prisoners of war being held in Union prisons. A popular actor, Booth spent months planning every aspect of the scheme, recruiting accomplices, and organizing support networks of Confederate sympathizers in Maryland, New York, and Canada.

John Surratt helped recruit several men to assist Booth in executing his plan. As Booth's right-hand man, John organized and conducted several meetings with co-conspirators at Mary's boardinghouse in Washington, D.C., with his mother's full knowledge. Booth visited the home frequently, not only for meetings with his accomplices, but to confer with Mary privately in the absence of the others. Mary's association with a number of the conspirators, many of whom stayed at her boardinghouse, sealed her fate that day on the gallows.

After intense preparation throughout the winter of 1865, Booth's original attempts to kidnap Lincoln failed. But when it became apparent that the Confederacy was in shambles and the war was rapidly coming to a close during the first days of April 1865, Booth suddenly struck upon a new plan: to kill the President instead, striking what he hoped would be a fatal blow to Union victory.

When Mary became aware of Booth's new plan is unknown. Booth may not have told her, but that seems unlikely. At least two times during the day of the assassination Booth met privately with Mary, and, perhaps most significantly, during the afternoon of April 14, Booth instructed Mary to bring a package to a predestinated location known to both of them in the Maryland countryside. Driving swiftly to the site late that afternoon, Mary delivered the package and a message to Booth's contact: that he was to have guns and other items ready, as Booth would need them as he fled Washington, D.C., that night. One hour before he killed Lincoln at Ford's Theatre, Booth met with Mary one last time. What they discussed remains unknown to this day.

Why did Mary willingly participate in such a vicious plot, risking her life and the lives of her children? Her strong Southern sympathies do not adequately explain her dangerous level of involvement. Some have suggested she was in love with Booth; her daughter Anna most certainly was, and this may account for the family's intimate and loyal bond with him. Or perhaps she was simply protecting her son John's interests as a Confederate secret operative. Nevertheless, she was a willing and supportive accomplice to Booth and his band of conspirators.

Tragically, Mary's son John probably could have saved his mother's life. Though he did not participate in the actual murder of Lincoln, his role as Booth's main supporter and the one who organized many of the details for Booth's various plans placed him at the center of the assassination plot. Immediately after the assassination, he fled to Canada, where he remained hidden by local Canadian Confederate sympathizers, eluding capture by federal marshals chasing him. Detectives attempted to negotiate with Mary for information about her son's whereabouts, but she claimed ignorance of his location.

When John learned of his mother's arrest, he did not come forward. When she was found guilty and sentenced to hang, he did not come to his mother's defense. Had John surrendered, the government probably would have lessened the charges against Mary. But he refused to give himself up, leaving many to believe that he let his mother die for his own treasonous deeds.

Part of the dilemma in understanding the passions elicited by Mary's execution lies somewhere in the mid-nineteenth-century popular imagination. Unable to completely embrace the notion of a woman's total and unforgivable guilt, the public's emotional transition to regret and nostalgia after Mary's hanging reveals complicated perceptions of femininity and piety wrapped up in war-torn attitudes about loyalty, virtue, and Southern womanhood. Mid-nineteenth-century conceptions of motherhood and widowhood played significant roles in arguments defending her innocence and later efforts to stop her execution.

Mary Surratt was part of a new breed of "troublesome women" who emerged during the Civil War period. As such, she presented problems for her contemporaries and historians alike. The nontraditional, "unladylike" behavior of some women during this period—which included spying, soldiering, and participating in politics, wearing pants and disguises, and holding, and voicing, unpopular views—all challenged mid-nineteenth-century gender conventions. Criminal activity by women tested those boundaries as well. Female rebel spies, couriers, and espionage agents posed a dilemma for Union soldiers and federal officials charged with tracking them down, stopping their work, and arresting and punishing them.[1]

For these reasons and more, Mary's arrest and trial seemed to fascinate Northern journalists and the reading public. The need for revenge against this special class of criminal quickly took on monumental proportions. But a strange thing happened on the way to the gallows. The disgust over Mary's hanging swept across the nation, and suddenly, her conviction based on solid evidence became "judicial murder."[2] Mary's execution firmly tested Victorian-era notions of gender norms; most were ultimately unwilling to accept that a woman like Mary could have participated in the achievement of such a horrific crime.[3]

Was Mary Surratt's role in the assassination plot so significant that the military court found no alternative but to order her hanged, the first such federally sanctioned execution in the nation's history? Or was she irresponsibly hanged by a court packed with Northern radical Republican jurists eager to punish the South for the murder of Lincoln? What *is* known is that their fatal decision sent shock waves across the newly reunited country, releasing an intense backlash that ruined careers and haunted trial participants for the rest of their lives.

During and after her trial, a few supporters imagined she was an innocent victim in John Wilkes Booth's lethal plot, and that her age and gender should have saved her from the gallows. Others believed that the primary witnesses whose testimony linked Mary to Booth's plans had lied on the stand, perjuring themselves to hide their own complicity in the assassination conspiracy and to save their own lives. These views dominated most histories written about Lincoln's assassination throughout the late nineteenth and twentieth centuries. It was not until long-lost interviews and confessions were uncovered by Lincoln assassination scholars, and a re-examination of court testimony was undertaken during the last few decades of the twentieth century, that a few historians began to take another look at the plot to assassinate Lincoln. Numerous articles and books published over the past two decades have added to the wealth of knowledge of the Booth conspiracy and the roles of his accomplices. Some of this new scholarship reveals that Mary Surratt was deeply involved, helping facilitate different parts of Booth's plan.[4]

Mary Surratt's role in the conspiracy was, as the original 1865 verdict suggested, quite damning. Surratt was no innocent bystander who, as some sympathizers would claim, was duped into complicity by her co-conspirator son, John, or the wily and handsome young actor John Wilkes Booth. Her mysterious and intriguing partnership with Booth helped seal Lincoln's fate that terrible night in April 1865. And her unwavering loyalty to Booth, her son, and the other accomplices guaranteed her execution that hot July day.

While the military commission that found Mary guilty never doubted its decision, five of the nine commissioners petitioned the President to show mercy because of her sex and age. At forty-two, Mary was viewed as an old woman, in spite of the fact that she was vibrant and healthy when she was arrested. Nearly twenty years older than her fellow conspirators, she bore a striking contrast to the young and brash men who carried out Booth's designs.

Should Mary have been executed? Historians and others may continue to argue this for generations more. But it was President Andrew Johnson, Lincoln's successor, who saw, perhaps most clearly, that Mary Surratt "kept the nest that hatched the egg."

CHAPTER ONE

"DEVOTED BODY AND SOUL TO THE CAUSE"

The boardinghouse at 541 H Street was dark and silent. It stood in stark contrast to its neighbors—in fact, to nearly the rest of the city. It was Palm Sunday, April 9, 1865, and Washington, D.C., was exploding with Union victory celebrations. The war was over. The Confederate forces, led by General Robert E. Lee, had officially surrendered earlier that day at the home of merchant Wilmer McLean near the village of Appomattox Court House in Virginia. One week earlier, Richmond, the capital of the Confederacy, had fallen to federal forces and lay in smoldering ruins from fires set by its own retreating Confederate army. Washington, the federal capital, had remained unscathed throughout the war, and now, this evening, the city was alive with jubilant bonfires set by exuberant partygoers.

It was a beautiful spring. Washington basked in the warm sun and brilliant greens of leafed-out trees and grassy parks, a stark contrast to the muddy and filthy army encampments scattered throughout the city and around the Capitol. The new season in the nation's capital reflected the new future for the country—no more war, a fresh beginning. The city was alive with soldiers, newly freed people, civilians, and a scattering of defeated rebels, all breathing in the clear spring air that seemingly had been denied them for years. The sense of relief and giddy energy electrified the city.

Disgusted by revelers dancing in the streets on a Catholic feast day, and distraught over the South's failure and defeat, Mary Surratt wept openly. For Mary and other Southern sympathizers, such victorious revelry only stoked the burning, bitter bile rising in their throats. Their hopes for a Southern victory had quickly and dramatically come to an end.

Tightly closing her drapes against the celebrations outside, not "one single ray of light" shone through Mary's house, reflective, she said, "of her feelings."[1] She "loved the South too much," one of her accusers later claimed; her optimism for a Southern victory, along with the professional and political aspirations of her rebel son John, had evaporated. Her dreams were replaced with despair, and now, perhaps, desperation.

John's professional future was not the only thing worrying Mary. She had no idea where he was or if he was safe. Though he frequently disappeared on undisclosed business for days at a time, this time she knew that he had gone to Canada, carrying secret messages and new Confederate orders from Richmond. But now that the war was over, what would become of him? Did he know that Lee had surrendered, and that the Confederacy was no longer in need of his services?

The last time Mary had seen her son was on April 3; John had just returned from Richmond in the company of Sarah Antoinette Slater, a mysterious young Frenchwoman and a fellow Confederate courier and spy. John remained but a few hours, leaving abruptly to spend the night in a hotel before departing on an early train for Montreal the next morning. While he had been in Richmond, a detective had stopped at the boardinghouse and spoken to one of the servants; John was under suspicion again for rebel activity, and the government was looking for him.[2]

Perhaps Mr. Booth knew where young Surratt was. Booth and John Surratt had become fast friends last November, after they had been introduced by a mutual acquaintance, Dr. Samuel Mudd of Bryantown, Maryland. Their friendship had flourished in Washington, D.C., where Booth spent a great deal of time and where John had moved since his mother had relocated the family from their tavern home in Surrattsville, Maryland, to the boardinghouse in the city. Booth had spent many hours at the H Street boardinghouse visiting John, Mary, and John's twenty-two-year-old sister, Anna, who had become quite infatuated with the dashing young actor. A like-minded Confederate sympathizer, Booth had much in common with the Surratts. Mary understood that he and her son were involved in some sort of undercover rebel activities. She may have had reservations about the riskiness of John's Confederate business, including his involvement in Booth's activities, but Booth's smooth-talking assurances may have calmed any fears she harbored. She considered him fine company for her son, from the "best society," she would later remark. Besides, after her love of family and faith, her passion for the South was "her meat and drink"; like Booth, she was "devoted, body and soul to the cause."[3]

The son of world-famous British actor Junius Brutus Booth, John Wilkes Booth followed in his father's footsteps. Booth made his debut on the American stage in the mid-1850s. A mediocre actor at first, he spent several years in Richmond refining his craft, eventually earning himself the theatrical accolades he craved. His time in Richmond also deepened the proslavery, pro-Southern attitudes that would feed his hatred of Lincoln and the Republican administration in Washington. During the Civil War, Booth's acting career prospered, allowing him to use his financial resources to aid the Confederate cause and to travel without suspicion in support of Confederate espionage.

Now one of the nation's best-known and most adored actors, Booth was handsome, successful, and intensely personable. All the residents of the Surratt boardinghouse enjoyed his company. His frequent visits there varied from casual social calls, which sent the girls and women in the house "brushing," "fixing," and swooning, to more intimate personal visits with Mary, John, or other boarders involved in clandestine rebel activities.[4]

John Wilkes Booth had become increasingly moody and frantic in the weeks and days leading up to that Palm Sunday in early April. His viciously pro-Southern stance only seemed to intensify as the war was winding down. Booth had dreamed of vanquishing Northern victories through clandestine operations of his own, but now, with the South collapsing, his opportunity to strike a blow against the North was disappearing. Convinced that the South's path to defeat could only be halted by a dramatic course of action, Booth became preoccupied with bringing the war to the steps of the White House.

Booth's daring plan was to kidnap the President and ransom his return in exchange for the release of Confederate prisoners of war. He had been carefully hatching this risky scheme since the fall of 1864, creating a network of supporters and assistants, and waiting for the perfect moment to execute the crime. By early spring, Booth had organized a disparate and motley crew of accomplices, assigning them each a distinct role to play. It would be the greatest dramatic production of Booth's career.

John Surratt was one of the earlier initiates into Booth's plans, and he in turn recruited George Atzerodt and David Herold, friends and associates Surratt knew to be trustworthy and sympathetic to the rebel cause. Booth enticed others, including Sam Arnold and Michael O'Laughlen, both unemployed boyhood chums, and Lewis Payne, a young Confederate soldier with a murky past. By the time Booth's plans were coming together that spring, there were probably a couple dozen people who knew of or were somehow involved in supporting Booth's scheme.

Ransoming Lincoln for the release of all Confederate prisoners would reinvigorate a shrinking and exhausted Confederate army, Booth believed. But by mid-March, Booth's kidnapping plans had met with repeated delays and costly overruns. After months of planning—buying horses, guns, and other supplies, and spending significant sums of money to feed and house his associates—he found himself running out of money. There could be no more delays.

Finally, on March 16, Booth's plans fell into place. The President had planned an excursion to the countryside for that day. John Surratt, a highly skilled horseman, would be the lead rider, in charge of chasing Lincoln's carriage and taking over its reins. The other men assumed their supporting

John Wilkes Booth, circa 1860–1865.

roles, taking positions at various places along the President's designated route to the country, and along the escape route out of Washington as well. But fate intervened: Lincoln changed his plans at the last moment and stayed in the city.

Booth and his accomplices imagined they had lost the only opportunity to execute their plan. Having exhausted his once-ample funds, Booth disbanded his group of accomplices, and they scattered to find other jobs and opportunities. John Surratt returned to his role as a rebel courier, satisfied that he was contributing something to the Confederacy. Arnold and O'Laughlen found employment in Baltimore, while Payne fled to New York City. Atzerodt and Herold returned to Washington.

Booth started drinking hard. But he would not abandon hope of avenging the South. He knew he had to do something, and soon. Booth's last stage performance—playing the lead role, the evil Duke Pescara, in *The Apostate*—fell on March 18 at Ford's Theatre. Abandoning his acting career, he told unsuspecting friends, would allow him to pursue lucrative business ventures. What they could not have expected or imagined was that by stepping down from the stage, Booth was freeing himself up to devote all of his attention to plotting another scheme to destabilize the federal government—this time, by murdering Lincoln and his top cabinet officers.

When Richmond fell in early April, Mary was unaware that her son John had already departed the rebel capital. John had the good fortune to have left before Confederate President Jefferson Davis and his staff had called for the city's evacuation as Union forces were rapidly approaching the city. John had been in Richmond to procure a new espionage commission from Davis's Secretary of War, Judah Benjamin. A seasoned courier and spy, Surratt had been given two hundred dollars in gold and ordered to Montreal to deliver dispatches to General Edwin Grey Lee, second cousin of famed General Robert E. Lee and a rebel officer and spy operative working in that city. Surratt left Richmond on the morning of April 1, unaware the city was about to be set afire by the retreating Confederate army and captured by advancing Union forces.

On the morning of the second, still unsure of where her son was and needing his assistance in conducting some business at her tavern and farm in Surrattsville, Maryland, Mary Surratt asked Louis Weichmann, a boarder, roommate, and former school chum of John's, to see Booth and his friend George Atzerodt, who were both staying at the National Hotel nearby. She needed to speak with them at the boardinghouse as soon as possible to discuss "private business."[5] Louis Weichmann had become very close to Mary and her daughter since the fall of 1864, when he moved into their H Street home. He was more than willing to accommodate his landlady.

Booth was not at his hotel, but Weichmann found Atzerodt standing in front of the nearby Pennsylvania Hotel with two bridled horses, one "blind of one eye."[6] George Andrew Atzerodt, a Confederate sympathizer who had business dealings with Mary's son and Booth, was a frequent visitor to the Surratt home. He lived in Port Tobacco, a small southern Maryland village on the Potomac River, and was a skilled smuggler. During the Civil War, trade and travel between the United States and Confederate States had been suspended. To enforce this ban, Union boats patrolled the Potomac and its Maryland tributaries, routing out illegal water traffic running contraband supplies, people, and secret messages to the Confederacy in Virginia. Outmaneuvering and slipping by Union patrols and river blockades became a great skill, for which some boat captains, like Atzerodt, were paid quite well.

Atzerodt agreed to speak with Mary, and he and Weichmann returned to H Street. Weichmann stayed outside with the two horses while Atzerodt went inside; what he and Mary spoke about is unknown. Nonetheless, this visit would mark a dramatic escalation in Mary's direct participation in the plot to assassinate President Abraham Lincoln.

When John Surratt arrived at his mother's boardinghouse during the early evening of the third, he was completely unaware of the fall of Richmond. Stunned by the news and disbelieving, he told Weichmann that the reports were wrong: he had just seen Confederate President Jefferson Davis and Secretary of War Judah Benjamin, and all seemed well. John hurriedly exchanged some of his gold for cash with John Holohan, another of the residents, before leaving for Montreal the following morning. Whether he saw Booth that night or not is unknown, but his commitment to the Confederacy apparently outweighed his obligation to Booth, and on the morning of the fourth, Surratt was on his way to Canada.

In spite of Richmond's fall and the escape of the Confederacy's cabinet and top rebel leaders, John felt it was his responsibility to carry out his assignment. Following Judah Benjamin's orders, John arrived in Montreal and waited for further instructions from rebel agents then living in Canada. If John had been assigned a role in Booth's new assassination scheme, then either he was unaware of Booth's time schedule, or he was not given a specific job in the final, mad, and murderous plan. Ultimately, his secret courier trip to Montreal would save his life.

During the week following Richmond's fall, Catholic Holy Week, the rapidly unfolding events in the Southern war zones riveted the nation's attention. General Ulysses S. Grant, the Union commander-in-chief, battled General Robert E. Lee in Virginia, finally forcing Lee's surrender. Union General William Tecumseh Sherman chased Confederate rebels in North Carolina, finally claiming victory in Durham. Though the war was now officially over, scattered skirmishes and open rebellion in some Southern sections kept Union armed forces occupied. Defiant Confederate regiments in Alabama, Louisiana, and along the Rio Grande in Texas would finally surrender in May, and rebel units would continue fighting in Oklahoma until the end of June.

On Tuesday, April 11, with John still away in Montreal and unavailable to help his mother, Mary asked Louis Weichmann to borrow Booth's buggy and to accompany her once again on a business errand to her former home village of Surrattsville the next day. Weichmann asked Booth for the favor, but found that Booth had sold his buggy. Instead, Booth gave Weichmann ten dollars to rent a coach for Mrs. Surratt.

The ride that day seemed uneventful—the trip to Surrattsville, about twelve miles from the city, took about two-and-a-half hours. Mary completed her business, and by early that evening she and Weichmann were back at the boardinghouse in Washington.

Two days later, Mary again asked Weichmann to accompany her on another business trip to Surrattsville. Weichmann, a clerk in the War Department, had the afternoon of Good Friday, April 14, off to celebrate General Robert E. Lee's surrender and the Union victory. Though clearly irritated by her repeated request and feeling a bit like a servant, Weichmann agreed to help Mrs. Surratt in return for her many kindnesses to him. He rented another buggy and took her into Southern Maryland late that afternoon. Within two hours of their return to

Washington early that evening, President Lincoln would be fatally shot in his presidential viewing box at Ford's Theatre while watching *Our American Cousin*. His murderer, John Wilkes Booth, would be racing to Surrattsville, the first stop on his planned escape route out of Maryland.

Later, Weichmann would observe, "That drive to Surrattsville, and the developments growing out of it, cost Mrs. Surratt her life. She dug a pit for others, but fell into it herself."[7]

Mary's boardinghouse was one of the first places detectives searched when they fanned across the city in pursuit of Lincoln's assassin. How did they know to go to her home? What had gone on there? How could a widow, mother, businesswoman, and devout Catholic be involved in such a heinous crime? Within three days Mary would be arrested; in less than three months she would be dead.

CHAPTER TWO

CREATING A LIFE, BUILDING THE NEST

B orn in 1823, Mary Elizabeth Jenkins was the second of three children of Archibald and Elizabeth Anne Jenkins, and their only daughter. Her older brother, John Zadoc, was born in 1822; her younger brother, James Archibald, in 1825. When Mary was two years old, her father died unexpectedly. Her young mother was left to raise and support her family alone on their modest plantation in Prince George's County, Maryland. Unlike many widows during that time, Elizabeth did not remarry. She became, instead, a very competent manager of her farm and slaves, expanding her holdings over the years and increasing her assets considerably.

Elizabeth Jenkins's success allowed her to provide private education for her children. In 1835, twelve-year-old Mary was enrolled in a Catholic girls' boarding school. Though Elizabeth had raised her children in the Episcopal church, her sister-in-law, Sarah Latham Webster, a Catholic, exerted some influence upon the decision to send Mary to the Academy for Young Ladies, a boarding school affiliated with St. Mary's Catholic Church in Alexandria, Virginia. Within two years, Mary had converted to Catholicism, rejecting the faith of her mother and setting her own independent course. When the school closed in

1839, Mary returned reluctantly to her mother's home near present-day Clinton in Prince George's County.[1]

Mary was sixteen years old when she met John Harrison Surratt, who was ten years her senior. John's family history is sketchy; few details of his early life are known. He was adopted and raised as an only child by Richard and Sarah Neale, a well-to-do couple who may have been relatives or close friends of his unknown parents. He grew up in Washington, D.C., on the large farm the Neales owned, called Pasture and Gleaning. During John's youth, Washington was a young and growing city dotted with numerous farms, mills, and merchant businesses that operated in tandem with the business of the national government. As John matured, the Neales divided their farm and gave portions of it to him to farm on his own.

The circumstances surrounding John and Mary's meeting remain unclear, but when they became involved John was already entangled in a relationship with a local woman, Caroline Sanderson, with whom he had fathered an illegitimate child named John Harrison in 1838. The relationship did not last, and though John never married Caroline, he faced a court order in 1840 forcing him to take financial responsibility for the baby.[2] Whether John Surratt maintained any relationship with his son and Caroline after the court judgment has not been recorded, and little is known of their fates.

In spite of his relationship with Caroline and the boy, John married Mary in August 1840 in Washington, D.C. The couple moved to a mill property that John had acquired near Oxon Hill, a small farming community south of Washington, D.C., along the Potomac River, and started their lives together. By 1844, Mary had given birth to three children: Isaac, Anna, and John Jr.[3] Within the year, the young family turned the mill over to another young couple, and the Surratts moved to a vacant house at Pasture and Gleaning, John's boyhood home. Richard Neale had died in 1843, leaving Sarah to run the farm alone. She soon became very ill, requiring almost constant care; John and Mary's arrival at the farm significantly eased her burdens. Just before she died in August 1845, Sarah transferred the last piece of the farm to John, allowing him to begin a new and promising career as a Southern planter.[4]

Mary became involved in fundraising for a new Catholic church, St. Ignatius in Oxon Hill, and by 1850, the church opened and welcomed the area's Catholic faithful. Led by Father Joseph Finotti, an Italian priest transferred from nearby Alexandria, the church thrived. Though Mary was an active participant in church life—she'd had all three children baptized in the Catholic church—John Surratt would have nothing to do with it and was said to have harbored deep resentment over his wife's commitment to Catholicism.[5]

Mary Surratt, circa 1850. Courtesy Surratt House Museum, Clinton, Maryland.

Anti-Catholic sentiment had raged in Maryland since it had been chartered as a colony to provide a safe haven for persecuted English Catholics. Embedded in European political conflicts and struggles with papal control, which led to the Protestant Reformation, anti-Catholic sentiment had deep roots. Protestant domination in early Maryland, however, offered no relief to Catholics settling in the new colony, and anti-Catholic sentiment continued well into the late nineteenth century. During the antebellum period, anti-Catholicism escalated with each new wave of Irish Catholic immigrants, combining religious bias with growing nativism and anti-immigration feelings.

John managed to increase his land and slaveholdings throughout the early years of his marriage, despite his bad habits and sometimes disreputable behavior. He was undependable and often failed to settle his debts. What's more, his excessive drinking and accompanying volatile behavior became more common, frightening Mary and the children.

During these times, women who lived with an alcoholic and abusive husband, as Mary did, received little support. Family members, neighbors, and the government often turned a blind eye to the problem. Relying on her faith to provide a temporary respite from a stormy marriage, Mary turned to her priest, Father Finotti, for spiritual and emotional comfort. But her increasing dependence upon Father Finotti became the fodder for gossip and idle talk that may have been partially based in truth.[6] In 1852, Finotti was unexpectedly and unceremoniously transferred to Massachusetts. Some suspected it was because of his relationship with Mary.[7] Meanwhile, her efforts to change her husband's behavior were met with rage and disdain.

In 1851, tragedy struck the Surratt household. Their home at Pasture and Gleaning was burned to the ground, and the Surratts barely escaped with their lives. A family slave suspected of the deed was never apprehended. His actions, if the allegations were true, illustrated the uneasy environment that defined life in this slaveholding community.

In the years following the Nat Turner slave rebellion in the summer of 1831, in which nearly two hundred whites and blacks were killed in Southampton County, Virginia, the nature of white/black relationships in the South changed dramatically. Southern slaveholders saw their worst nightmare made real: being murdered by their enslaved people while they slept. In Prince George's County, where the Surratts had settled, this nightmare permeated daily life. Periodic murders of white slave owners by their slaves, and the more-than-occasional setting of fires to homes, barns, and fields by angry and vengeful bondsmen, created a tense environment. In fact, the Surratt family physician, Dr. Bayne, who had attended the births of the Surratt children and had treated Sarah Neale in her dying days, lost three of his own children when they were poisoned with arsenic by a fourteen-year-old enslaved girl living in his household.[8]

In Southern Maryland counties, farmers depended heavily upon enslaved labor to plant, tend, harvest, and prepare for market the region's wealth of agricultural products. African Americans, both free and enslaved, constituted a majority of the total population. In Prince George's

County, for instance, a free labor system had not taken hold; 82 percent of the county's black population was enslaved, reflecting the white community's major financial investment in the institution of slavery. Indeed, its interest in the perpetuation of the slave system was far more significant, economically and psychologically, than in any other region of Maryland. The area's social, political, and economic character was more similar to heavily slave-dependent Virginia than to the rest of Maryland.[9]

By 1850, Southerners began threatening separation from their non-slaveholding and economically more powerful neighbors in the North. Frustrated by a perceived imbalance of power in Congress, as well as by increasing numbers of runaway slaves and increasingly vocal abolitionist activity calling for an end to slavery, Southern slaveholders felt that their way of life was in jeopardy. The flood of slaves escaping from their enslavers, particularly those living in border states like Maryland, Virginia, and Kentucky, had been escalating throughout the decades leading up to the 1850s.

To the thundering calls for disunion, Congress sought to enact a compromise to stave off what many believed would be an irreparable sectional conflict and, perhaps, civil war. As part of the famous Compromise of 1850, parity in representation in Congress between slave and non-slave states was temporarily suspended, as California was admitted as a free state and New Mexico was allowed to decide its own free or slaveholding status when it was ready to join the Union. To placate angry Southerners, Congress also passed a new Fugitive Slave Act, requiring all citizens in the North to assist in the capture and return of fugitive slaves living there.[10]

Highly punitive to the enslaved runaways and those who dared help or hide them, the new Fugitive Slave Act created an uproar in the Northern states, where it was viewed as an infringement upon personal liberty, local control, and state sovereignty. Heavy fines, jail time, or in the case of black people who assisted in the escape of slaves, sale into slavery, posed serious obstacles to freedom-seeking efforts. Runaway slaves, if caught, were no longer entitled to any legal protections in the

North, which led to many abuses. Roving slave catchers were known
to snatch free African Americans off streets in Northern cities and
towns, claiming they were former slaves, and carry them back to the
South for sale. Abolitionists actively encouraged resistance to this new
law, resulting in some dramatic and deadly confrontations with Southern masters and slave catchers.[11] Southerners, like the Surratts and their
white neighbors, felt outraged.

The Fugitive Slave Act did not slow the tide of enslaved people running away, nor did it stop those willing to help them. In fact, slave escapes escalated during the 1850s. As a result, John Surratt and other
men in his community formed posses to patrol the countryside, watching for possible runaways and unknown abolitionist emissaries who
they believed were luring away their slaves. Such community action
served to reinforce, physically and emotionally, the South's commitment to the slave system, fortifying a white Southern identity and social structure in defiance of what the community perceived to be a
more powerful and threatening Northern political and economic domi-
nance and free labor system.

When the Surratts' home was destroyed by fire, John was forced to
leave farming. He found work as a contractor for the Orange and
Alexandria Railroad, which was completing a segment of track from
Alexandria to Culpepper Courthouse, Virginia. Chartered in 1848, the
railroad company offered job opportunities to many Virginia and
Maryland men during the six years it took to complete the project.
With John now living and working out of state, Mary took the three
children and moved in with her cousin Thomas Jenkins and his young
family in Prince George's County. Why Mary moved in with this
cousin and not her mother or brothers, whose farms clustered in the
same area, remains unknown. Mary's marriage to John Surratt may
have caused family friction, or Thomas may have had room for the
young family, while the others did not.

Within the year, the railroad construction project was nearing completion, and John faced unemployment. But full-time farming was not his future, he'd determined. He had leased some of his farm properties, and was looking for more lucrative business opportunities. With the money he earned building the railroad and loans from friends, he decided to purchase almost two hundred acres at a major crossroads twelve miles south of Washington, D.C., in Prince George's County.[12]

Prince George's and its neighboring counties—Charles, St. Mary's, Calvert, and Anne Arundle—constitute what is commonly referred to as Southern Maryland. The region is bordered by the Chesapeake Bay to the east and the Potomac River to the west, and it boasts significant trade and travel routes to and from the nation's capital. The roads surrounding John Surratt's new property brought travelers and trade to and from Port Tobacco on the Potomac in Charles County to the south, from Piscataway Creek in Piscataway County to the west, and from Upper Marlboro and the Patuxent River to the east. John planned to build a tavern and inn to support his venture, capitalizing on the heavily traveled route to and from the city.

For Mary, John's plan had further advantages. The property was near her mother's plantation and the farms of her two brothers, bringing her back to the area of her childhood home and her network of family and friends. On the downside, building the tavern and inn would take months to complete, extending Mary's vagabond life longer than she had hoped.

For reasons unknown, when the tavern and inn were completed during the summer of 1853, Mary refused to move in. She may have resisted raising her children in an environment filled with strangers, drinking, and gambling. Her relationship with John may have deteriorated over the two years they had spent mostly separated, and perhaps life as a tavern keeper was not what Mary had hoped for her future. With Father Finotti gone, her support network had dissolved, leaving her to face her abusive and alcoholic husband alone. Meanwhile, her relationship with her cousin Thomas had seemingly deteriorated, so after two years of living with his family, she and the children moved into a small vacant dwelling back on the Pasture and Gleaning farm. In any event, her holdout wouldn't last. John was deeply in debt after purchasing the land and building the tavern, and in May 1853 he sold Pasture and Gleaning, forcing Mary and the children to leave that farm in December and move into the tavern.

The wood-framed, two-story tavern and inn contained four large common rooms, including a living room, barroom, dining room, and a large hallway. There were closets for storage on the first floor, five rooms and storage on the second floor, and two unfinished rooms under the eves in the attic space. A twenty-by-fourteen-foot kitchen was connected to the main part of the house in the back. The building supported three chimneys, hosting nine fireplaces. The walls were smoothly plastered and painted white. It was a substantial building, well constructed, with plenty of room for servicing frequent guests. A large stable and shed completed the property.[13]

The success of the tavern was immediate. After selling Pasture and Gleaning and other properties, John was able to settle most of his debts. He then purchased another piece of property in December 1853: a large four-story townhouse on H Street in Washington, D.C. The Surratts rented out the townhouse, and settled into life and business at their tavern and inn.[14]

Throughout the 1850s, Mary struggled with a heavy load of work in running the business with her husband. The Surratts hired a wheelwright and a blacksmith to service the many wagons, coaches, and horses that traveled through daily, expanding the crossroads into a small village. They farmed, too, growing food and raising livestock for sale or for use at the tavern. Milk, eggs, butter, meats, and vegetables, in addition to fish and oysters brought from the Chesapeake and the Potomac, provided tavern fare. Liquor, however, was probably the hostelry's lifeblood. Unfortunately, as one writer described it, John became the tavern's best customer.[15]

Raising their children in such a public place proved troubling to Mary. With John drinking heavily, more of the day-to-day running of

Mary Surratt's boardinghouse on H Street, Washington,
D.C., circa 1870–1880.

the tavern fell to her. In addition, their finances continued to fluctuate dramatically, and debts were piling up. Mary was frantic to get her children out of that environment and to provide them with the best education she could. Fortunately, increasingly brisk business brought temporary financial relief, and Mary was able to save enough tuition money to send the three children, now on the verge of adolescence, to Catholic boarding schools in Baltimore and Washington.

Education posed a dilemma for Southerners. In the North, public education had long been a staple of established cities and towns. But in the pre–Civil War South, publicly funded education was extremely rare. This was partly due to its less densely populated communities and rural agricultural neighborhoods, which precluded the establishment of towns and cities on the scale of those developed in the North. Fierce independence and elitism were also factors in the lack of interest in providing education to all citizens. Education for slaves was illegal, and schools for free black children were very rare. Poor whites fared little better. Southerners with means favored educating their children in private, whites-only academies, seminaries, and schools. Some wealthy white planters and businessmen sent their children to Northern private schools and academies, or hired private tutors to educate their children at home. The Surratts were fortunate to be able to send their children to Catholic boarding schools nearby.

In 1854, the Maryland legislature, recognizing the importance of the Surratts' businesses and their opportune crossroads location, chose the tavern to be the district's voting place. John was appointed the area's postmaster, and the Surratt Tavern became a new postal stop in an expanding United States postal system. The crossroads was renamed Surrattsville; John and Mary had created not only a new life, but also a new town.

John's drinking and excessive gambling continued to devour some of the profits the tavern was making. Gambling went hand in hand with drinking at taverns across nineteenth-century America, and particularly in the South, where it played a major role in male social rituals and customs.[16] Gaming and gambling included cards, dice, cockfighting, horse racing, and assorted other betting games, and involved large sums of money and assets. Slaves, real estate, and personal items like jewelry and horses were often gambled away. Nevertheless, John managed to keep himself out of debtor's prison.

Through borrowing and reinvesting the tavern's income, John expanded his business in Surrattsville. He sold more of his inherited property too, freeing him from mounting debts and allowing him to add and enlarge buildings on his tavern property. Within a few short years, the Surratts were curing their own tobacco, raising pigeons and hogs, managing a granary, storing corn, and supporting a carriage

Surratt Tavern in Surrattsville [Clinton], Maryland. From *Harper's Weekly*, 1867.

house for more sophisticated travelers, in addition to owning the blacksmith shop, wheelwright, stable, tavern and inn, and more than half a dozen slaves.[17]

By 1860, John was no longer just a heavy drinker; he had become an alcoholic and was drunk every day. Mary was frantic to keep her children insulated from drunken rages and foul behavior. Her problems compounded when her sons' boarding school, St. Thomas Manor in Bryantown, a few miles south of Surrattsville, unexpectedly closed. Mary turned to her network of priests and other Catholic faithful in the greater Washington and Baltimore region to find a place for eighteen-year-old Isaac, away from the tavern and his father. With their help, Isaac found a job in Baltimore. Mary's younger son, John Jr., still needed more schooling, but Mary could not afford tuition at the better private Catholic schools, like Boston College. Then her husband sold one hundred acres of their Surrattsville farm, giving Mary just enough to secure room, board, and tuition at a reduced rate for both John Jr. and Anna at nearby schools. John enrolled at St. Charles in Ellicott's Mills, and Anna remained at the Academy for Young Ladies in Alexandria.[18]

Throughout the 1850s, the Surratts had also slowly sold off some of their slaves to help relieve themselves of mounting debts. As a result, they had to hire more help for the tavern and farm and other businesses. By the end of the decade, Mary was probably bearing a substantial load of the day-to-day running of the tavern and inn. Mary would have become a familiar face to many travelers and an intimate community member for the men and women who lived in the county. As John's alcoholism and gambling defined his daily life, it was Mary who provided stability and consistency to the crossroads village. She would have also, more than likely, taken care of the postal business as well, sending, receiving, and distributing mail for her neighbors every day. In this position, she would form key business and social relationships that would influence her politics and economic decisions as sectional tensions were bringing the nation precariously close to civil war.

In November 1860, when Republican Abraham Lincoln was elected President, several Southern states threatened secession. During his campaign for the presidency, Lincoln argued that while the Constitution protected slavery in the states where it already existed, he would push Congress to outlaw the expansion of slavery into the new western territories opening up for settlement and statehood. He, like many Northerners, found slavery a "moral, social, and political evil." In his famous 1858 "House Divided" speech, Lincoln claimed, "A house divided against itself cannot stand," arguing that the "government cannot endure permanently half slave and half free. I do not expect the Union to be dissolved—I do not expect the house to fall—but I do expect it will cease to be divided. It will become all one thing, or all the other."[19] He believed, like many of his Republican supporters, that free labor was morally and economically superior to slavery.

Lincoln's election drove many Southerners to consider the unimaginable. Their response was swift and dramatic. In December, South Carolina voted to secede from the Union. Alabama, Mississippi, Florida, Georgia, Louisiana, and Texas soon followed. In early February 1861, delegates from those seven states met in Montgomery, Alabama, and the Confederate States of America was born. Jefferson Davis, a U.S. senator from Mississippi and President Franklin Pierce's former secretary of war, was inaugurated on February 17 as the secessionist President. Davis had initially opposed secession, but quickly changed his mind and led Mississippi to secede from the Union in late January 1861. Because of fierce political negotiations (or coercion, some would argue) by Abraham Lincoln and his staff, Maryland parted with its Southern neighbors and remained within the Union.[20]

After Lincoln's inauguration in March, the new President vowed to protect and hold federal property in seceded Southern states—at gunpoint, if necessary. When Lincoln tried to resupply Fort Sumter in Charleston Harbor in April, South Carolina promptly fired on the fort, forcing it to surrender to the Confederacy the following day. The Civil War had begun.

Virginia, Maryland's close neighbor both physically and psychologically, soon joined the Confederacy, and Richmond was named the new capital. Arkansas, Tennessee, and North Carolina followed suit for a total of eleven Confederate states. Marylanders in Prince George's County found themselves divided between loyalty to the Union and loyalty to their Southern slaveholding neighbors and their own slaveholding interests. Many, like Mary and her husband, found themselves swearing allegiance to the Union but secretly supporting the Confederacy.

Southern Maryland's close proximity to Richmond, the Confederate capital and a major trade center, allowed for a flourishing espionage, smuggling, and blockade-running network along Maryland's western and southern borders. Union boats patrolled the Potomac, impeding the illicit trade and transportation networks that were established between Maryland and its rebel neighbor, Virginia. Rebel spies and couriers relied heavily upon sympathetic Marylanders to help move illegal supplies, people, and messages to and from the Confederacy.

As the Civil War escalated during 1861, enslaved people in Southern Maryland began escaping in large numbers to the protection and safety

of Union army encampments around Washington, D.C. Frustrated
Marylanders like the Surratts went to these encampments and demanded the return of their enslaved property. In exchange for their
support of the Union, Maryland slaveholders were legally entitled to
keep their slaves, even after Lincoln signed the Emancipation Proclamation in January 1863, freeing all slaves in all the states that were in
open rebellion with the Union. Maryland and the other border slave
states that remained loyal to the Union were exempt from the provisions of the Proclamation.

Even before the Emancipation Proclamation, however, the demands of Maryland slaveholders for the return of their slaves often
fell on deaf ears. Some Union officers and soldiers stationed in the region were repulsed by the attitudes of local slaveholders, attitudes that
grew even stronger after they witnessed the terrible whipping, beating, and even killing of runaway slaves by slaveholders who had come
into the camps looking for them.[21] As time went on, more and more
soldiers and officers made it an unspoken policy to protect and hide
these runaways, creating even more tension with an already resentful
white population.

By mid-1861, Lincoln had ordered all United States mail service between the Union and the rebel states to be halted. An underground
courier system blossomed to accommodate not only personal mail between family, friends, and business associates, but also for spy networks in the Northern states and Canada. John Surratt's postmaster
position proved critical to the tavern and the family's future role as a
bustling communications hub for both legal and illegal business. Surrattsville's location near Washington, D.C., and its situation at an important crossroads that led to major trade, transportation, and
communication networks along and across the Potomac and Virginia,
proved an ideal spy lair. The tavern's sympathetic owners and neighbors helped secure its reputation as a safe haven among Confederate
spies, couriers, and smugglers.

But risk was inevitable. Many local people were being arrested and
hauled off to prison in Washington for spying and smuggling. Hun-

dreds of young Maryland men fled to Virginia and other Confederate states to join the rebel armed forces. Most Southern Maryland families had relatives, friends, or neighbors in the Confederate service. John Surratt, Sr., had to be very careful; he could lose his position if he were caught aiding and abetting a rebel spy. But most of his neighbors held strong pro-South feelings as well, and though they may not have all participated in clandestine and illegal activities, they were not about to turn him in to federal authorities.

While John's drinking and gambling continued unabated, Mary was managing the business and enjoying her role at the center of the local social, economic, and Catholic communities. In spite of wartime troubles, their rebel business was flourishing, enabling them to support a cause they believed in. Early Confederate battle victories in Virginia had emboldened Southern supporters, reaffirming Southern Marylanders' sense of righteousness and confidence in the Confederate cause. This self-assurance helped buoy an increasingly dangerous but growing underground smuggling and espionage network in the region. Though the tavern had more business than ever, John was spending and gambling even more, adding to his considerable debts. Unfortunately, Mary was most likely unaware of the extent of those debts.

Then fate took its turn. On August 25, 1862, fifty-one-year-old John Surratt, Sr., died unexpectedly, probably of a severe stroke. Anna was already home for the summer, but eighteen-year-old John Jr. had to be called home from St. Charles College outside of Baltimore. Isaac had just joined the Confederate army, and would not return home until well after the Civil War was over.

Suddenly, Mary was on her own. Years of estrangement from her mother and her brothers, exacerbated by her husband's behavior, left Mary to struggle independently. Widowed and facing large debts left by her dead husband, she would have to find a way to survive, not only for herself, but also for her daughter Anna and her youngest and favorite son, John. It would not be easy.

CHAPTER THREE

REBELS, SPIES, AND COURIERS

Bankruptcy now loomed large in Mary's world. She faced the very real possibility of losing her home and personal possessions, as impatient and opportunistic creditors vied for shares of her dead husband's heavily encumbered assets. Before he died, John Sr. had already been forced to sell some of the family's livestock, slaves, and portions of their farmland to satisfy outstanding loans and gambling losses. Mary was left with few liquid financial resources to pay off creditors. The war had depressed land prices in the area, and rising interest rates and inflation complicated her financial situation even further. With few legal protections, Mary was exposed to creditors eager to exploit the widow Surratt's vulnerable economic situation.

During the antebellum period, widowhood often resulted in great uncertainty and turmoil for dependent family members. In the absence of cash assets to cover creditors' demands, additional mortgages or the transfer of existing mortgages to surviving family members would occasionally be arranged so the family could keep their home and other property. But this was not always the case. Most married women were forbidden to own property, and often with the death of a husband the assets were transferred to the children directly or put in trust to be claimed when they reached the age of majority. Usually, the wife of the deceased man and the mother of his children was given either "dower rights"—that is, a one-third interest in the inherited assets during her lifetime (and not hers to freely give to anyone else)—or use of all the assets until the children came of age and claimed their inheritance. In these cases, the widow would become dependent upon her children for her living arrangements. While wives and daughters could inherit assets, most family wealth tended to follow the male children, with the eldest son typically receiving the largest share.

In order for a widow to maintain control of the family's property, the demands of the dead husband's creditors and the court probating the estate mandated speedy and orderly payment. This sometimes required the sale of all or portions of the estate's furniture, farm equipment, personal effects, slaves, homes, and land. Even agricultural and animal products, whether in the ground, harvested, live, or slaughtered, were potential assets for sale.

The wartime economy made Mary's limited options more complicated. Selling the properties in Surrattsville or Washington would have commanded a smaller sum than during better times; money was scarce and investors were uncertain of the future. Because of wartime credit problems, creditors were generally less tolerant, demanding immediate payments and readily threatening lawsuits. Saving her tavern and farm and paying off John Sr.'s debts required serious legal and financial help. Ben Gwynn, John Nothey, and other local men conducted some of the complicated legal transactions for Mary, but she was smart and capable, and seemingly managed to navigate the probating of her husband's estate successfully, without the loss of many of her possessions. Through new mortgages and consolidation of debt, Mary was able to keep her home and the Washington boardinghouse. These debt obligations and interest payments would burden her greatly, however.

Though Mary's mother, Elizabeth Jenkins, and her brothers, John Zadoc and James, lived nearby, they seemed to have offered little if any assistance to her. Strained relationships with her family, probably hardened over the years by John Surratt's behavior, may have created life-long ill will. Indeed, Elizabeth never visited nor sought to help Mary, even after her eventual arrest and during her trial. The Jenkinses' own financial situations may have also prevented them from offering her any monetary aid. Interestingly, Elizabeth Jenkins had herself survived the death of her husband as a young wife and mother, and had prospered as an independent widow. Perhaps she believed Mary could do the same.

Heavily encumbered with financial obligations, in addition to operating the tavern and inn, Mary found daily survival more difficult. She turned to her two younger children, John and Anna. Mary could neither afford their tuition nor operate the tavern and farm without their help. So John and Anna gave up plans for further education or out-of-town employment opportunities and stayed on to support their mother. Isaac, who was stationed with his Confederate unit in the Deep South, remained out of touch.

Fortunately for Mary, seventeen-year-old John Jr. was able to step into his father's shoes to fill the postmaster position. (Women were not allowed to hold this government post.) Appointed by the federal government on September 1, just one week after his father's death, young John Surratt needed only to swear a loyalty oath to the Union. The oath meant little, as his neighbors would equally demonstrate; it kept them out of Old Capitol Prison in Washington, where many disloyal citizens and rebel sympathizers were incarcerated, and ensured their freedom to continue rebel activity. Additionally, keeping the postmaster position in the family enabled the Surratts to maintain many of the illicit connections John Sr. had made in service to the Confederacy.

The Confederate Signal Corps and Secret Service, operating out of Richmond, had established a well-run spy and smuggling network throughout Southern Maryland. Rebel courier mail drops and way stations dotted the countryside; some temporarily, others lasting the entire war. The rebel network engaged the assistance of local smugglers, undercover agents, mail couriers, draft deserters, and others. In their service to the Confederacy, many of them passed along the road in

front of the Surratt Tavern, making it an essential way station to and
from Virginia.[1]

The Signal Corps and Secret Service was responsible for establish-
ing the clandestine mail system. Mail couriers were numerous, and
men and women like John Surratt, Thomas Jones and his brother-in-
law Thomas Harbin, and Sarah Slater operated quite successfully
throughout the region. Jones, for instance, operated the post office at
Allen's Fresh in Charles County, just south of Port Tobacco, while
Sarah Slater operated undetected as a courier. Postmasters in Southern
Maryland were natural recruits into the secret signal corps, as were
people who traveled about the countryside in the course of their legitimate daily business—among them, stagecoach drivers, salesmen, doctors, lawyers, and farmers going to and from the market.[2] Elbert G.
Emack, a suspected agent and an ardent gardener, traveled to Washington to pick up loads of manure, secretly hiding contraband materials for the Confederacy under his fragrant cargo.[3]

The illicit mail system was simple and effective. A coded letter to a
recipient in the Confederacy was addressed to the actual person it was
intended for, and after placing the letter in another envelope bearing
the name of the rebel "mail agent"—people like Thomas Jones and
John Surratt—it was sent through the regular U.S. mail system. Surratt
and Jones, upon receiving these letters at their mail drop, would throw
away the outside envelope and send the inside envelope along through
the underground courier system.

John Surratt, Jr., later revealed his role in the system, beginning in
the fall of 1862:

> I was not more than eighteen years of age, and was mostly en-
> gaged in sending information regarding movements of the
> United States Army stationed in Washington and elsewhere, and
> carrying dispatches to the Confederate boats on the Potomac. We
> had a regular established line from Washington to the Potomac,
> and I being the only unmarried man on the route, I had most of

the hard riding to do. . . . I devised various ways to carry the dispatches—sometimes in the heel of my boots, sometimes between the planks of the buggy. I confess that never in my life did I come across a more stupid set of detectives than those generally employed by the U.S. government. They seemed to have no idea whatever how to search men.[4]

The likelihood that any of this activity went on without Mary's knowledge—indeed, tacit approval—seems impossible. The drunken conversations, whispered meetings, and secret nods and hand signals at the tavern, and the letters addressed to her son (and perhaps herself) from unknown parties, would have been obvious indicators, never mind what she may have participated in directly.

While underground communications and transfers at the tavern provided brisk legal and extralegal business for Mary and her children, it also increased the Surratts' political and social status within the community. Many residents of Prince George's County strongly supported the "sesech" (secession) cause, and the tavern's ideal location between Washington, D.C., the Potomac River, and Virginia, and the pro-South loyalty of its proprietors, suited the needs of the community. But federal forces were not blind: they, too, could see the tavern's strategic location as an ideal communications drop and potential safe house for rebel spies.

The Surratts and their Confederate-leaning neighbors did not operate their clandestine operations with impunity. In fact, arrests for acts of disloyalty landed several Prince George's and Charles County neighbors in the Old Capitol Prison. Ben Gwynn, a friend and close neighbor, was one of the first to be arrested for smuggling contraband materials, including munitions, across the Potomac to Virginia.[5] But in spite of persistent federal efforts to shut down these clandestine operations, strong local rebel support and anti-federal sentiment kept the smuggling, illicit mail services, and operation of safe houses consistently reliable.

According to informants like Union supporter Thomas Robey, who lived near the Surratts, secessionist activity in Maryland began almost immediately after Virginia seceded from the Union and the first shots were fired on Fort Sumter in South Carolina in April 1861. Confederate spying and smuggling became commonplace. During a sweep of Southern Maryland during the summer and early fall of 1861, federal forces rounded up numerous suspected spies and rebel sympathizers. Maryland had not seceded from the Union, but strong secession feelings in Southern Maryland and on the Eastern Shore threatened Maryland's place in the Union. Maryland's then-Governor Thomas Hicks sought to control this growing pro-Confederate movement by supporting harsh federal treatment of suspected rebel supporters. Imprisonment in Washington's Old Capitol Prison and confiscation of rebel property was typical punishment for disloyalty. This treatment, however, further enraged proslavery and Confederate-leaning Marylanders.

Within months of that first federal seizure, however, many of those imprisoned at Old Capitol had been set free and their confiscated property returned to them. Swearing an oath of allegiance to the United States often secured the release of these Southern aiders and abettors, many of whom returned to their pre-incarceration activities. By mid-1862, for instance, the town of Bryantown, in neighboring Charles County, became a major depot for smuggling munitions and other supplies to Pope's Creek and Port Tobacco for shipment across the Potomac. Local residents coordinated and ferried people, guns, messages, and ammunition through the countryside for transport across the river to Virginia. Thomas Robey and his family, however, were notable among the few in their region who supported Lincoln and the Union. They maintained strong opposition to the Confederacy throughout the war in an increasingly hostile neighborhood.[6]

The Confederate Signal Corps and Secret Service also established a manual signal system along both banks of the Potomac River. Confederate homeowners on the Virginia side and rebel sympathizers on the

Maryland side coordinated a series of signals to pass secret messages back and forth to operatives in each region. Union gunboat patrols hampered this system only slightly; their habitual patterns and the lack of support from locals thwarted federal efforts to halt illicit communications. In addition, local ship captains, ferryboat operators, and resident fishermen knew the ins and outs of the river, its currents and tidal patterns, easily outmaneuvering Union patrols. Sneaking past and outrunning Union gunboats, known as blockade-running, proved to be a lucrative though dangerous line of work for many local watermen.

Fourteen months after assuming his father's post, John Jr.'s luck ran out. On November 17, 1863, federal authorities, long suspicious of illicit courier work conducted through the Surratts' tavern and post office, caught John in action. Lieutenant Lafayette Baker relieved John of his postal position on the grounds of "disloyalty."[7]

For unknown reasons, John was imprisoned for only a few days and then released. Mary must have been relieved that he eluded formal arrest for treason. A trial and courtroom defense would have required scarce financial resources, and put the family's property at risk of seizure by the federal authorities. Extended jail time would have meant the loss of John's help around the tavern and farm. But the loss of his postmaster position made him vulnerable to the Union draft—and worse.[8]

In July 1862, Lincoln called for three hundred thousand new recruits to the Northern army. Volunteers trickled in slowly, however: mounting casualties deterred many potential recruits. Under pressure to encourage and enforce enlistment, the War Department issued quotas that each state was expected to meet. They also added an enticement: hefty bounties of one hundred dollars for every able-bodied man willing to sign up for a three-year tour of duty.[9]

In August, when Maryland failed to meet its federal troop quota, Governor Augustus Bradford instituted a draft, forcing the enlistment of eligible young men throughout the state. Some counties offered additional enlistment bounties on top of the federal fee, but for proslavery men like John Surratt, Jr., these incentives meant nothing. In fact, recruitment continued at such a poor rate that federal troops stationed in Southern Maryland were soon enforcing the state's draft at gunpoint.[10]

By the fall of 1863, after numerous draft riots and attacks on enlistment officers throughout some Northern states, Lincoln began enforcing the draft system with martial law, imprisoning draft resistors and their supporters. Many young men scrambled to find a substitute who would enlist in their place. Substitutes had long been used to fill vacancies in the armed forces. Those with the financial resources to pay for a substitute offered private bounties to men willing to take their place for a price. This was part of a larger system of public and private bounties that provided financial incentives for those choosing to join up and risk their lives on the battlefield, while also enabling other young men to avoid armed service. By the end of the war, the North had spent nearly five hundred million dollars in bounties, in addition to the unknown number of private bounties.[11]

John's position as a federal postmaster had exempted him from the draft; with his arrest and the loss of his position, John would now be forced to serve in the Union army. To avoid mandatory service, he would have to pay for a substitute to take his place, or secure another federal job.

John's immediate replacement in the post office was Thomas Robey's son Andrew Robey. Having a Union supporter in the postmaster's position complicated John's ability to ensure safe passage of illegal mail to and from Richmond. Moreover, having a potential Union spy in the local postal business profoundly affected the region's rebel

courier system, dramatically changing the way John and other region-
ally based rebels would do business. Brazen and self-assured, John instead became a nearly full-time courier himself, bearing messages to
and from Richmond to various rebel contacts throughout the North, in
cities like Washington, Baltimore, Philadelphia, New York, Albany,
and eventually, in Montreal, Canada.

Beginning in 1864, the Confederate secret mail system was broadly and
rapidly expanded through the placement of Confederate agents in
Montreal, Toronto, Quebec, and many small border towns in Canada.
Established to further aid espionage activities, subterfuge, and terror
plots in the North, this Canadian arm of the Confederate Secret Service was quite successful—and a source of great irritation to the U.S.
government. Millions of dollars were deposited in Canadian banks to
fund illicit Confederate operations, supported and perpetrated by unknown numbers of rebel undercover agents. Among these agents was
Confederate General Edwin Lee, cousin of the celebrated General
Robert E. Lee. Within weeks of the establishment of the Canadian
Confederate headquarters, John Wilkes Booth himself would open a
back account in Montreal for channeling funds related to his kidnapping plot.[12]

A two-week turnaround trip from Richmond to Montreal and back
ensured rapid and continuous communications with top officials in the
Confederacy. Ciphered letters and miniature photographs, hidden in
shoes, buttons, clothing, and other items, made their way undetected to
and from Richmond. One of the main routes from Richmond to
Canada passed through Port Tobacco in Charles County and Surrattsville in Prince George's on its way north to Washington, Baltimore, Philadelphia, New York, and beyond.

John was in the right place at the right time.[13] Familiar with Southern Maryland and well connected to the local Confederate networks,
John segued smoothly into his new and expanded role. Little could he

or his mother have realized that his secret service experiences during 1863 and 1864 would provide him with just the right background and connections to aid in John Wilkes Booth's treacherous scheme.

John Surratt, Jr., was a "persistent Rebel" who sang "Secession songs very frequently," according to his old schoolmate Louis Weichmann. John and Weichmann had maintained a friendship since their days at St. Charles College. Weichmann had been successful in landing teaching appointments after he and John left school in July 1862, but John had had less luck. Louis tried to get his friend a position tutoring at Borromeo College, the Catholic seminary near Baltimore where he was working, but he failed. Over time, though, Weichmann observed that John's ambitions had changed quite dramatically—from dreams of the priesthood, teaching, or farming, to active talk of joining the "Rebel Service."[14]

During late 1862 and early 1863, John and Weichmann met occasionally in Washington. Weichmann was teaching there at St. Matthew's Institute, and John made occasional trips into the city to sell produce from the Surratt farm or to conduct legal and illegal courier business. In March 1863, when John was still serving as postmaster, Weichmann accepted his friend's invitation to spend the weekend at Surrattsville.

The two men left Washington together, but the going was very difficult; winter rains had left the road muddy and full of ruts, making the ride uncomfortably long. By the time they reached Surrattsville, Weichmann was doubly disappointed. The tavern and inn seemed shabby and run-down to him, not the bustling, vibrant places Surratt had described as a homesick boy at St. Charles.[15]

Nevertheless, Weichmann found Mary Surratt friendly and welcoming. A roaring fire warmed the damp chill that had settled into his bones during the uncomfortable trip. Anna, John's older sister, also lived at the tavern, and she impressed Weichmann with her intelligence and beauty. Mary was "genial and social" and "had the rare faculty of making a stranger feel at home at once in her company." She was, however, "devoted, body and soul, to the cause of the South." Weichmann would later claim, somewhat dramatically, that he had never met a woman "who so earnestly, and . . . so conscientiously, defended and justified the Southern cause as she."[16]

During his visit that weekend, Weichmann observed firsthand the rebel activities that so attracted his friend. As he later testified, John kept the bar where "rebel farmers of the neighborhood come to get their letters, to lounge, and to play cards." While there, Weichmann played cards with two "carpet bag"–toting Jewish men. At one point during the evening, Weichmann noticed that Mary Surratt took the bags from them. It was later learned that one of the men was "arrested crossing the Potomac with $50,000 upon him."[17]

On Saturday morning, a marching band from the Washington Navy Yard arrived at the tavern's crossroads to celebrate the election of local county Democratic officers. One of the revelers was David E. Herold, a friend of Surratt's and a clerk at the Navy Yard. Born and raised in the region, Herold was a frequent visitor to the Surratt Tavern. Herold shared a drink at the bar with the celebrating crowd before rejoining the band marching further down the road. Weichmann thought black-haired Herold to be a "seedy, frothy, monkey-faced boy."[18]

Louis Weichmann visited the Surratts again in September 1864, attending Sunday Catholic services with John in Piscataway, about five miles south of Surrattsville. There they met David Herold again, who was on a leisurely sporting expedition with a friend from Washington. Herold's passion for birding was legendary, though the possibility that he was also there to engage in rebel service cannot be ruled out.

By this time, suspicions about the Surratt family's activities were resurfacing, and federal officers were watching them ever more closely. Opportunities for John, who was now working as a personal courier, seemed limited. Army recruiting agents were continuing their pursuit of potential draftees, fueling Mary's worries about her son's fate.

John revealed to Weichmann that Mary was seriously considering leasing the tavern and moving the family to their soon-to-be-vacant townhouse on H Street in Washington—a property that John Sr. had purchased a decade before. Her plans, he told Weichmann, included taking in boarders—a "private boardinghouse," Weichmann recalled—and an invitation for Weichmann to move in.

Finding his friendship with John becoming more intimate, and enjoying the comfort and company of Mrs. Surratt and Anna, Weichmann felt "honored" and delighted at the opportunity. His current living quarters at Purnell's boardinghouse, on Nineteenth Street and Pennsylvania Avenue, were inadequate. They were also further away from his job at the War Department, where he'd been working since the start of the year. Weichmann's well-paying position as a clerk in the Commissary General of Prisoners in the War Department, a federal job that exempted him from the draft, would leave him with plenty of income to pay Mary Surratt's thirty-five-dollar-per-month room and board.[19]

Meanwhile, Mary searched for a suitable person to whom she could lease her property in Surrattsville. For economic, political, and perhaps even illicit reasons, Mary settled upon John Lloyd, a former Washington city police officer, bricklayer, and Confederate sympathizer. Lloyd had moved his family to Prince George's County in 1862 and apparently had some experience running a tavern. The choice of tenant seemed a natural, and the deal was secured. At Mary's request, Weichmann drew up the lease for the property; the rental fee of five hundred dollars per year covered both the farm and the tavern, relieving Mary of a substantial physical and financial burden and allowing her to escape the surveillance of troublesome federal detectives.

Leasing the tavern to John Lloyd ensured that the tavern remained a vital link along the Signal Corps and Secret Service routes through

Southern Maryland. If Lloyd was caught conducting rebel business, then Mary would not risk the loss of her property, only the loss of a paying tenant. Whether this move was part of a larger espionage plan on the part of Mary and her son is unknown, but certainly remains a possibility. The financial advantages to leasing the tavern and farm, moving to Washington, and taking in boarders may have made economic sense, but it would have required scarce financial resources to execute. Furnishing a ten-room house would have been quite costly. Taking into account additional reasons, such as expanding their espionage work, seems only natural to consider. In a letter dated September 21, 1864, John revealed to Weichmann that the family's plans to move to Washington would occur sooner rather than later, cryptically writing, "on account of certain events having turned up."[20]

The relocation to Washington did offer John better opportunities for employment, and a federal job in the city could secure his release, once again, from the Union draft. The possibility that the family's rebel spy activity could continue there in Washington in and through their home would have been luring as well. In fact, Surratt would later reveal that upon moving to Washington in late 1864, he "took a still more active part in the stirring events of that period. It was a fascinating life to me. It seemed as if I could not do too much [n]or run too great a risk."[21] Leaving behind the attention of federal detectives ferreting out spies in the countryside may have been ample inducement to move to Washington, but John's new career as a Confederate courier would flourish in the bustling city.

The gray brick H Street townhouse was large and comfortable. The street-level floor contained the kitchen and dining room, and a small hallway with interior stairs leading to the main living area on the second floor. A formal sitting room with a fireplace occupied the front of the second level, also accessed by wooden steps leading up from the street to a formal entrance. A large bedroom occupied the rest of the

John Surratt, Jr., circa 1865.

second floor, facing the rear of the building, overlooking a porch. The third floor consisted of a parlor and bedroom at the front, and a large bedroom in the rear. The attic, undersized and less comfortable under a low dormered roofline, was used less frequently but pressed into service when needed. It consisted of two bedrooms and a sitting area.

The house filled quickly with boarders, mostly relatives and acquaintances. Sometime in September, Anna moved in and began running the household. Though immature for her twenty-one years, as officers at her mother's trial would later testify, Anna was bright and intelligent and a capable housekeeper in her mother's absence. Though the tavern had been leased to Lloyd, Mary stayed behind for several weeks to tie up business in Surrattsville and help Lloyd settle in, and John traveled between the two residences until the fall harvest was complete.

By early October, Anna had her first boarder, a friend named Honora "Nora" Fitzpatrick.[22] Nora was a young, unmarried woman, the nineteen-year-old daughter of local bank collector James Fitzpatrick. Her background and reason for living in the boardinghouse instead of her father's home remain a mystery. Perhaps she was just a single woman eager for privacy and independence, or perhaps she was a rebel spy. Either way, Fitzpatrick would later provoke authorities' suspicions about her knowledge of Booth's plans, and would reveal damaging eyewitness testimony against Mrs. Surratt during the conspirators' trial.[23]

Nora Fitzpatrick's arrival was soon followed by that of Louis Weichmann, who moved into the boardinghouse on November 1. Nora and Anna shared a room, sometimes with Mrs. Surratt on the second floor, or sometimes in the attic. Weichmann and John Jr. shared the third-floor room in the rear of the building, when John was in the city.[24] John came and went, and according to Lloyd, still spent considerable time at the tavern in Surrattsville, much to Lloyd's chagrin. Over time, John's stays in the H Street house became less frequent as he traveled more often for the Confederacy, forcing Weichmann to share his room with temporary boarders, some of whom would be intimately involved with Booth's plots.

John T. Holohan and his wife, Eliza, and their two young children, Mary and Charles, moved into the two front rooms on the third floor. The Holohans came with a trusted recommendation: Eliza was the sister of Mary Surratt's friend, William Wallace Kirby, a Washington city court officer who lived nearby. John Holohan had been a stonecutter in Baltimore before the war but left that job to become a bounty broker, plying his trade in and around Washington.[25]

Another young addition to the household was Apollonia Dean, a nine-year-old girl from Alexandria who was enrolled at the Visitation School, a Catholic institution associated with nearby St. Patrick's Church. Mary's connection to St. Patrick's was probably the common thread between the two.

Detained by transitioning the business to John Lloyd and monitoring the harvesting of the season's crops on the farm, Mary was the last to move in. She finally made the move on December 1, bringing eighteen-year-old Olivia Jenkins, her brother John Zadoc's daughter, with her. Courier activities kept John busy in Southern Maryland, but the fall harvest delayed John's move as well. In mid-November he wrote to Weichmann, indicating that while "taking care of securing the crops" was hindering his move to the city, he was more than ready to leave Surrattsville. Perhaps a hint of what was to come, Surratt bade farewell to "ye God forsaken country. Old Abe, the good old soul—may the Devil take pity on him!"[26]

Young Lou Weichmann happily settled into the Surratt household. With the arrival of more permanent boarders like the Holohans, the

Surratt house was alive with activity. An occasional temporary boarder lodged at the house—some known to the Surratts, others unknown. Mary advertised rooms for rent in the *Washington Star,* once in late November and twice in December. By the end of December, the house was full, and any later vacancies were taken through word of mouth or by conspirators involved with John Jr. and Booth.[27]

The H Street boardinghouse teemed with life, and according to Weichmann, was a peaceful and pleasant place to live. But the peacefulness would be "short lived," he would later recall. A "fiend with a heart as black as hell" would soon appear, bringing death and ruin to their world.[28]

CHAPTER FOUR

KEEPER OF THE NEST

"[Mary Surratt] kept the nest that hatched the egg."
—PRESIDENT ANDREW JOHNSON

O n a crisp and clear evening, two days before Christmas 1864, Lou Weichmann and John Surratt were strolling down Seventh Street, shopping for the approaching holiday. As they passed Odd Fellow's Hall, they ran into Surratt's old neighbor from Charles County, thirty-one-year-old Dr. Samuel A. Mudd. Mudd, a country physician and modest plantation owner, had known the Surratts since the 1850s. With him was the strikingly handsome and friendly John Wilkes Booth. Mudd introduced Booth as a new acquaintance who was interested in purchasing his farm near Bryantown, about ten miles from the Surratts' tavern in neighboring Prince George's County. Booth was impeccably dressed, Weichmann noticed, a "man of the world and a gentleman," while Mudd appeared not as well attired. Oddly, Weichmann recalled, Mudd referred to Booth as "Mr. Boone."

In fact, Mudd's farm was not for sale. And the meeting on Seventh Street only appeared to be by chance; the real reason Booth and Mudd were together in Washington was to meet with John Surratt. Their "chance meeting" on the street with Weichmann, as testified to and later admitted by Mudd, would be one of the key pieces of evidence that would help send Mudd to prison for his role in the assassination. But it would also begin the Surratt family's intimate relationship with Booth.[1]

Mudd and Booth had already met at least twice, near the doctor's home in Charles County. In November, Booth traveled to Bryantown to visit with Dr. William Queen, a known Confederate sympathizer and rebel operative in that area. Arriving on Friday, November 11, Booth stayed through the weekend with Dr. Queen and his family, attending Sunday services with them at St. Mary's Church, about six miles south of Bryantown. There, Booth was introduced to Dr. Mudd. Another staunch Confederate sympathizer, Mudd was also a rebel courier, aiding the flow of secret documents and messages through the Southern Maryland countryside.[2]

Mudd was usually a regular attendee at his own parish church, St. Peters in Prince George's County. Mudd's purpose in being so far from his own home on that particular Sunday, and the nature of his discussions with Booth, remains unclear, although Confederate espionage and courier work seems likely.

After leaving Southern Maryland that weekend, Booth settled into a room at the National Hotel in Washington. From his base of operations at the hotel, Booth orchestrated his complicated plans to kidnap the President, easily traveling back and forth to Southern Maryland, Philadelphia, New York, and Canada to meet with like-minded Southern sympathizers and financial supporters.

In December, Booth was back in Charles County. Still pretending to be looking for property to purchase in the area, he was reinforcing and fortifying relationships among local rebels and securing support for his still-vague kidnapping plans. Booth stopped by the Queens' home again on Saturday, December 17, spending the night with the family and attending church once again the following morning. After mass, Booth met with Dr. Mudd at the Bryantown Tavern, where Mudd introduced him to a Confederate Secret Service agent, Thomas Harbin.

Harbin, a thirty-year-old local farmer turned spy, oversaw an extensive undercover rebel operation that included Prince George's, Charles, and St. Mary's counties—Maryland terrain abutting the Potomac River and crucial to smuggling and spy networks in Virginia and elsewhere. At one point, Harbin also served as Bryantown's postmaster, much as John Surratt had done in Surrattsville.[3]

Booth was becoming more convinced of the feasibility of his plan to abduct the President. As he moved forward with his plot, his web of accomplices grew. Harbin had moved his base of operations to Virginia and could be useful in supplying information, supplies, and support through trusted local sympathizers and active operatives. Harbin offered an excellent link between Southern Maryland and Richmond, where Booth hoped to hide Lincoln while waiting for his ransom demands to be met.

After Booth's meeting with Harbin, he traveled back to Samuel Mudd's home and spent the night there with Mudd's young family. The following morning, on December 19, Mudd helped Booth purchase a one-eyed bay horse from a neighbor, George Gardiner. Riding the horse back to Washington the next day, Booth boarded it at a stable near the National Hotel, where he checked in for the remainder of the approaching Christmas holiday.

Booth was a smart man; he knew that he had to organize a larger cadre of fellow conspirators to ensure the success of his daring plan to smuggle the kidnapped President through the Maryland countryside, across the Potomac, and into Virginia. He needed significant financial resources to secure various assets, such as fresh horses, guns, and safe hideouts along different routes out of Washington and into Southern Maryland, to accommodate any possible contingency.

Harbin and Mudd both knew that the Surratt Tavern was one of a few safe stations along the vital "underground" route from Virginia to Washington, D.C. Securing John Surratt's help, and the safety of the Surratt Tavern, could prove to be critical parts of the secret support network Booth would need. John's ties to the Surrattsville community and the tavern could provide one of several way stations Booth would need on a furious and dangerous journey out of Washington once the kidnapping took place. Either Mudd or Harbin could have suggested Surratt to Booth, but in any case, it was Mudd who arranged the introduction.[4]

On the evening of December 22, Booth and Mudd were on their way to Mary Surratt's boardinghouse on H Street to see John. But the "chance meeting" on the street offered a better opportunity for Booth to advance his plans. Once the congenial introductions were made, Booth, or "Boone," as Weichmann believed, invited them for a drink and conversation in his room at the National.

Weichmann later recalled that it became apparent the three men had important and secret business to discuss. After ordering drinks and cigars for everyone, Booth escorted Mudd to the adjacent hallway for a private conversation; they called Surratt out to join them a few minutes later, leaving Weichmann alone. Soon, Mudd reentered the room, apologizing for his rudeness; he claimed Booth was interested in purchasing his farm, but "does not want to give me enough for it."[5] Booth and Surratt soon followed Mudd back from the hallway, resuming their confidential conversation around a small table in the center of the room, several feet away from Weichmann's chair. Weichmann later testified that he could not hear their words, but observed Booth intently drawing lines on an envelope he had taken from his breast pocket.

Within the half hour, the men finished their discussion and Mudd invited them all to the Pennsylvania House on C Street, just across from the National, where he was staying with his cousin Jeremiah. Mudd and Weichmann chatted in the bustling bar, while Booth and Surratt settled in near the crackling fireplace, renewing their private conversation and having a "jolly time together."[6] Mudd entertained Weichmann with deceptive confessions of his great loyalty to the Union. He probably felt it better to display allegiance rather than his true feelings as a Confederate sympathizer. Perhaps he assumed this was the safest bet, given that Weichmann was attired in the blue regimental uniform occasionally required for his job in the War Department.

At about ten-thirty, Booth bade farewell to his newfound friends. Mudd said goodnight shortly thereafter, and John Jr. and Weichmann returned to the boardinghouse on H Street. As they were strolling home, Weichmann learned that "Boone" was in fact John Wilkes Booth, the celebrated actor. He also learned that John was going to act as agent for Booth in his purchase of a farm in Southern Maryland. It was all a ruse to disguise Booth's main purpose to engage John in his scheme, but Weichmann remained an outsider, even at this early date when plans were just then taking shape. Months later, Mary Surratt would tell Weichmann that "Dr. Mudd and the people of Charles County are getting tired of Booth and are pushing him off on John."[7] In fact, John had quite happily signed onto Booth's grand scheme to kidnap President Lincoln, and Mary knew it.

Over the next few months, Booth became a regular visitor to the H Street boardinghouse, spending hours in conversation with John Jr. and Mary, or passing frivolous time entertaining the other residents of the house. They shared, along with Mudd and many others from Southern Maryland, a disdain for the Union and a passion for maintaining slavery.

Almost immediately, John began his own recruitment efforts. As a rebel courier, he knew many of the blockade-runners, spies, and other dispatch riders throughout Southern Maryland and Washington who could be instrumental in Booth's kidnapping scheme. Within a few short weeks, Booth and Surratt had rounded up an unlikely group of young men, including Booth's boyhood friends Samuel Arnold and Michael O'Laughlen, Confederate soldier Lewis Payne, scouts and blockade-runners David Herold and George Atzerodt, and Confederate agent Dr. Samuel Mudd.

With the Christmas and New Year holidays over, Booth began visiting the Surratt house more frequently. Mary Surratt met Booth sometime in early January, and the two quickly developed a close bond. Their confidential friendship stimulated intrigue and fascination among some of Surratt's boarders. A rebel sympathizer herself who readily provided shelter and support to spies and couriers in need of sanctuary, Mary shared Booth's dislike of Lincoln, the Republican Party, Northern bolitionists, and the demise of slavery in Washington and Maryland. Mary had grown up in Southern Maryland and knew its terrain and inhabitants well; she had learned through her husband, and now her son, who could be trusted, who could be called upon in secret, and who had the financial or physical resources that would be needed, and provided without question, to Booth in the coming days.

Weichmann and Eliza Holohan both remarked that Booth spent most of his time with Mary during his frequent, sometimes daily, visits.[8] John was often not at home, and Mary, it would seem, became his surrogate.

"Their interviews were always apart from other persons," Weichmann revealed later in court. "Sometimes, when engaged in general conversation, Booth would say, 'John, can you go upstairs and spare me a word?' They would then go upstairs and engage in private conversation, which would last two or three hours. The same thing would sometimes occur with Mrs. Surratt."[9]

Mary appears to have been an attentive listener and wise counsel on the numerous occasions Booth sought her private company. An intelligent older woman and a seasoned Confederate supporter, Mary provided emotional, intellectual, and logistical support, in addition to a safe and comfortable home. She was the perfect camouflage, and so convenient to Booth's plans—the respectable company of a widowed boardinghouse keeper, where private conversations could be kept and Southern sympathies would be nourished and embraced.

Mary's political beliefs were not out of step with those of her neighbors. Washington was haven to thousands of Confederate sympathizers. Despite the federal government's best efforts to root out spies, secret agents, couriers, and potential wartime threats, the strong Southern feelings and pro-Confederate loyalties of many of Washington's citizens proved formidable and nearly impenetrable. Familial and social connections, often entwined with financial and political networks, offered consistent and dependable protection for espionage activities. Straddling two slave states, Maryland and Virginia, Washington was deeply embedded in the culture of slavery and its attendant Southern social and political customs. Despite its role as the seat of a Northern-dominated federal government resisting the expansion of slavery, Washington remained a society rooted in the economies of slave labor and the slave trade.

Anna Surratt, Mary's twenty-two-year-old daughter, was developing a serious flirtation with Booth. And this, some have argued, infuriated Lou Weichmann. Booth "created a fluster among [the house's] female inmates," Weichmann later complained. Anna and her roommate, Honora Fitzpatrick, were so smitten by Booth's attention that they purchased photographs of him, displaying them proudly in the house. After all, they were close acquaintances of one of the nation's most dashing and famous entertainment superstars.[10] "He was so handsome, so fascinating, so winning in his ways," Weichmann grumbled.[11] Anna had apparently rebuffed Weichmann's own attempts at romantic attention. Even young John found the young women silly when Booth came calling. In a letter to his young cousin Belle Seaman, John revealed that Booth's arrival would send the women of the house scurrying, primping, and pinching. Writing to Belle one evening in early February, while the women lounged around the parlor, John mockingly described his sister, Anna, dreaming of Booth. "But hark," he wrote, "the door bell rings, and J. W. Booth is announced. And listen to the scamperings of the [women]. Such brushing and fixing."[12]

But was Anna the only woman in the household with a romantic interest in Booth? Was Mary also infatuated with him, and could this have contributed to her deep involvement with his plans to kidnap and later assassinate Lincoln? The possibility remains, but there is no evidence to suggest this was so. More than likely, Mary was intensely attracted to Booth's charisma and his commitment to avenging Southern defeat.

Once she was settled into the boardinghouse, Mary pushed John to get a legitimate job. Just after Christmas, he landed a job with the Adams Express Company. The company's business had been booming throughout the war, and over the New Year, business was particularly heavy shipping soldiers' boxes and possessions.

Sometime around January 10, John asked for a two-week leave. His boss, Charles Dunn, refused him; it was arrogant and inappropriate for a new employee, barely two weeks on the job, to ask for a leave of absence. John pleaded; his mother needed him to drive her to Prince George's County on "urgent business." According to Dunn's later testimony, John claimed that Mrs. Surratt needed "protection." Protection from what is not clear. Then Mary herself made an appearance at the Express office and pleaded her son's case to Dunn. Once again, Dunn refused John the leave of absence. John quit that day, never bothering to collect his two weeks worth of pay.[13] John later told Weichmann he decided to take "French leave," that is, leaving without saying good-bye or without permission.[14]

John left immediately for Southern Maryland. He did not take his mother to Prince George's County, but went directly to Port Tobacco. Apparently, Mary did not have urgent business that needed her immediate personal attention, nor did she need her son's "protection" after all. John's own urgent business in Port Tobacco, according to later testimony, was part of the strategic planning for Booth's scheme. Booth's plans had become quite elaborate, involving a couple dozen men who would aid in the capture and conveyance of Lincoln through the Maryland countryside and across the river to Virginia. John's obligation to Booth apparently trumped his need for a secure job.

In Port Tobacco, John met up with Thomas Harbin, and Harbin's brother-in-law and notorious rebel, Thomas Jones. His mission was to secure river transportation in advance of the President's kidnapping; three boats were needed. Surratt and Harbin secured one of them from Richard Smoot, a local farmer and blockade-runner who, in partnership with James A. Brawner, owned a large, sturdy, flat-bottomed boat for illegal smuggling across the Potomac. John needed immediate possession of the boat so its availability would be assured at a moment's notice. Smoot hesitated, arguing that his blockade-running business was quite profitable and that he did not want to interrupt it. Surratt impressed upon him that the boat's urgent acquisition was in "consequence of an event of unprecedented magnitude in the history of the country, which would startle and astound the entire world." Smoot had heard rumors about an abduction plan, so he assumed this was what Surratt was planning.[15] Indeed, even at this early date, there was a relatively widespread impression among rebel sympathizers that kidnapping plans were in the works.

Smoot sold the boat for two hundred and fifty dollars, half placed in trust with a sympathetic local judge, the rest paid upon use of the boat. At Surratt's direction, Smoot turned the boat over to George Andrew Atzerodt, a German immigrant and coach maker living in Port Tobacco who was also heavily involved in blockade-running. When Smoot delivered the boat, Atzerodt "casually remarked that a desperate game was to be played." A desperate game indeed.

Atzerodt moved the boat to Goose Creek, and a short time later, to Nanjemoy Creek, southwest of Port Tobacco, where George Bateman, another smuggler and runner, took control of it.[16] Atzerodt could easily be bought: for the promise of a small, unspecified fortune, he agreed to take Surratt and his men across the river when the abduction took place. He was under the impression that the action would take place momentarily, and gave up all his other business activities. Ed Martin, a Confederate agent who happened to be waiting for Atzerodt to smuggle him across the river when Surratt showed up, later testified that Atzerodt reneged on his promise to take him to Virginia after Surratt left. Atzerodt told Martin that he had more important and lucrative business to attend to, having "been engaged that day in 'buying boats'; that they were going to have relays of horses on the roads between Port Tobacco and Washington." Martin believed Atzerodt was involved in a proposed escape of Confederate officers from prison, and that Atzerodt was going to row them across to Virginia. "I am going to get well paid for it," he assured Martin.[17]

By early January, Booth's plot and John Surratt's role in it had matured to the point where specific arrangements were secured, money was being paid, and the circle of accomplices was growing wider. Atzerodt made arrangements to have fresh horses available at T.B., a small village crossroads in Prince George's County about halfway between Washington and the Potomac River. More horses were positioned in Virginia, part of the larger relay system secured by Atzerodt and the others for their race out of Washington to Richmond with the captured President.[18]

With John Surratt's guidance, Booth's recruitment of accomplices continued through January. After securing the assistance of Atzerodt, John introduced Booth to his friend David E. Herold. Surratt and Herold had known each other for years; Herold was an avid bird hunter, and his frequent visits to Southern Maryland for sport made him an ideal guide to the area. Herold lived near the Washington Navy Yard with his mother and sisters, and was employed by the pharmacy at the Yard. Not only could Herold provide expert direction through the countryside for Booth's flight to Virginia with the kidnapped President, Herold's knowledge and access to pharmaceuticals like chloroform, a relatively new drug, could come in handy if Booth needed to sedate the President.[19]

Months before he'd met Samuel Mudd and John Surratt, Booth had been honing his scheme to kidnap the President. In the summer of 1864, Lincoln's nomination once again as the Republican Party's choice for the presidency infuriated Booth. Booth saw Lincoln's potential reelection as a death knell for both the Confederacy and the institution of slavery. In early August, Booth met with two boyhood friends in Baltimore, Sam Arnold and Michael O'Laughlen, to discuss his new, still-undeveloped plans. Arnold and O'Laughlen did not know each other before the meeting. Both eagerly signed on to Booth's scheme.[20]

By the fall, Booth's plans to abduct the President and hold him hostage in exchange for Confederate prisoners of war had taken on elements of a psychotic obsession. Friends and family had noticed a marked difference in Booth's personality and his near mania on avenging the South. His obsession was perhaps necessary. Successfully executing such a bold plan required mapping out and coordinating scores of details. This would take money, a trustworthy network of people, and material support, including guns, horses, boats, and shelter. Passion, hatred, and later, fame, motivated Booth, but greed would help motivate some of his accomplices. Promises of significant remuneration for their services helped persuade supporters who may otherwise not have bought into Booth's plot. They would be heroes, Booth convinced them, and wealthy too.

Booth's last recruit was Lewis Thornton Powell, alias Lewis Payne, a former Confederate soldier who'd been wounded and captured at Gettysburg in the summer of 1863. Following a period of recovery in the hospital at Gettysburg, Powell escaped and fled to Virginia, where he signed up with the notorious Colonel John S. Moseby's 43rd Virginia Cavalry Battalion. Moseby's Rangers, as they were called, were an amazingly successful rebel unit specializing in guerrilla raids on

Union supply lines in northern Virginia near Washington. In January 1865, after serving with Moseby for more than a year, Powell surrendered himself to Union forces encamped in Fairfax, Virginia. Claiming civilian refugee status and using a new alias, Lewis Payne, Powell fraudulently obtained a pass into Maryland after swearing an oath of allegiance to the Union. Making his way to Baltimore, Powell, now Payne, moved into the Branson boardinghouse on Eutaw Street.

Maggie Branson, daughter of the proprietor, was a nurse who had taken a liking to Payne while he was a patient in the Gettysburg hospital. Branson was a Confederate sympathizer who confined her nursing care to the Confederate wounded, raising the suspicions of hospital officials. She disappeared around the same time several wounded Confederate prisoners escaped. Payne may have been one of them.[21]

The Branson boardinghouse served as a rebel safe house, where Maggie and her sister Mary vied for Payne's affections. Payne's history remains somewhat murky; at the time of the trial it would be the source of considerable speculation. He was the son of a Baptist minister, born in Alabama, but later moved with his family to Live Oak, Florida, where the family farmed a little and Reverend George Powell preached and drank heavily. Payne's two older brothers fought and died for the Confederacy, a shock that Payne may have never recovered from.[22]

On January 21, John Surratt and Louis Weichmann took the train to Baltimore and checked into the Maltby House. Though traveling together, the men had separate business to conduct in the city and spent most of their time there apart. John boasted of having three hundred dollars and a private appointment with an unidentified gentleman in Baltimore, but kept the details from Weichmann. Weichmann was meeting with Father Paul Dubriel, the president of St. Mary's Seminary in Baltimore, to discuss his plans to begin theological training in the fall.

Weichmann had long hoped for admission to theological school to study for the ministry. After two years of waiting, Weichmann had finally received a coveted recommendation and permission from Bishop John McGill, head of the Roman Catholic diocese in Richmond, to pursue his theological studies. Weichmann needed an additional recommendation and permission from Father Dubriel before making arrangements to begin his course of studies.[23]

On the following day, Weichmann and Surratt went their separate ways, both returning in time for afternoon dinner. It is likely that Surratt met with Payne at Branson's boardinghouse, giving him money for his support.[24] How Booth met Payne and brought him into the conspiracy is unclear, but Payne's attachment from this date forward is unmistakable. The introduction may have come through David Preston Parr, a Confederate secret agent who owned a china business in Baltimore.[25] Parr had met Payne through the Bransons, and, recognizing the potential of this strong Confederate soldier, he sought to introduce him to Surratt. Whether Parr knew John Surratt and Booth were looking for recruits for their kidnapping scheme or he thought Surratt might find some useful position for Payne in the Confederate Secret Service or Signal Corps is not clear. Payne would later claim Parr employed him in the china shop, an imaginary job used as a front for inquiring authorities. Booth paid for Payne's living expenses directly or through John Surratt with funds passed on by the Confederate Secret Service office in Richmond.

Over the next few months, the intertwining of Mary's own life and actions with Booth's plans intensified. Her strong pro-South beliefs and her intense pride in her son guided her deeper and deeper into Booth's web.

Mary must have been partially, if not completely, knowledgeable of her son's activity at this time; her bold effort to lie for him at the Adams Express Company shows complicity at an early date. In fact, on

January 3, John Surratt transferred his share of the family inheritance to his mother, including portions of both properties, livestock and farm equipment, furniture and other personal items, and a few mortgages owed to the Surratt family. To have decided at this moment to transfer his assets to his mother for what appears to be safekeeping must have been a direct result of John's newly established relationship with Booth and Booth's plans. Protecting the family's assets from seizure should John be caught was a priority, given Mary's tenuous financial state.

Despite the comings and goings at her boardinghouse, Mary seemingly had few personal friends in Washington, and didn't appear to make many social calls outside the boardinghouse either. Weichmann later testified that a Catholic priest and longtime friend, Father Bernardin F. Wiggett, visited occasionally. And Weichmann did accompany Mary to church on some Sundays. But the only other times Mary seems to have left the house were the few trips back to her tavern in Surrattsville.

Eliza Holohan's brother, William Wallace "Walter" Kirby, was a court officer in Washington's criminal court and lived nearby in the neighborhood.[26] He was a frequent caller at the H Street boardinghouse, visiting with his sister and brother-in-law, nieces, and the rest of the household. He seemed to have taken a sincere interest in Mary's well-being. Mary would later claim he was related to her, although the familial connection is not clear.

Some of the people who visited or boarded at the house were later identified as rebel couriers and spies, or co-conspirators. Augustus Spencer Howell, blockade-runner, spy, and courier, visited the home, boarding there several times over the months leading up to the assassination. The French-born courier and spy Sarah Antoinette Slater (a.k.a. Kate Thompson and Olivia Floyd), who sometimes traveled with John Jr., also stayed at H Street. Both Howell and Slater would later be arrested for their activities, although their relatively brief incarcerations produced little consequence to themselves or their business.[27]

George Atzerodt was the first of the conspirators, after Booth, to come to Mary's H Street home. Within a few days of the Baltimore trip, Weichmann recalled arriving home after work around four-thirty in the afternoon to find Atzerodt waiting for John and Mary Surratt. Mary was away, visiting with her sick mother in Prince George's County at the time, but John arrived soon thereafter. Atzerodt was allowed to board in the back room of the attic floor.[28]

According to Brooke Stabler, the manager at Howard's Stables on G Street, located directly behind Mary Surratt's house, Booth, John Surratt, and Atzerodt came frequently to the stables together, sometimes several times a day. Stabler believed that the two horses boarded there belonged to John Jr., their board paid by Booth. One of the horses was the one-eyed bay horse Booth had purchased back in November from George Gardiner, Dr. Mudd's neighbor in Charles County. In late February, John instructed Stabler to allow Atzerodt to "have my horse whenever he wishes to ride, also my leggings and gloves."[29]

Sarah Antoinette Slater boarded with Mrs. Surratt in February and March. The first time, she arrived accompanied by an unidentified young man, probably one of several rebel escorts she required while traveling back and forth from Richmond. Weichmann retrieved her trunk from her carriage and brought it into the house. He found her mysterious and intriguing. She wore a "ladies mask," that is, a veil, concealing her face down to her chin. Mary told Weichmann that Slater was an associate of Howell's, clearly indicating what kind of business she was involved in.

Slater was a French national living in North Carolina. A dark-eyed beauty, Slater's charm, intelligence, and daring placed her in an important position within the Confederate Secret Service. As a French citizen, Slater could ask for sanctuary at the French Consulate if she were ever caught smuggling contraband.[30]

One of Slater's most important assignments involved bearing secret dispatches between Richmond and the "St. Albans raiders" in Canada.[31] The raiders were a group of Confederate rebels who had escaped Union imprisonment. In October 1864, they crossed the Canadian border into Vermont, and held the townspeople of St. Albans hostage while they robbed four of the local banks of over two hundred thousand dollars. Fleeing back across the border with their plunder, the raiders were chased by Canadian authorities, who captured a few and recovered a little less than half the money. The quick release of the raiders infuriated the U.S. government, but Canada was a neutral country; they refused extradition back to the U.S. Even the stolen money confiscated by Canadian officials was returned to the raiders, who, much to the chagrin of the Vermont banks, continued plotting and planning raids on border cities and towns.[32]

Slater eventually became involved in Booth's plot, though her role was never fully revealed, even after intense interrogation by the police. George Atzerodt later testified that Slater, known to him as Kate Thompson, traveled between Richmond and New York City with John Surratt, where John used a secret signal system Slater and her widowed sister employed. Somewhere, in front of a hotel on Broadway, Surratt would pass a "small switch with a waxed end and a piece of red ribbon on the butt, handed horizontally through the fingers." Atzerodt also claimed that Slater "went with Booth a good deal. She stopped at the National Hotel." She knew Booth's kidnapping plans too, he claimed.[33]

Augustus Howell, a smarmy and arrogant blockade-runner who may have known the Surratts prior to the war, also stayed at the H Street boardinghouse. A former resident of Prince George's County, Howell had joined the First Maryland Artillery, a Confederate regiment, at the start of the war. After leaving the rebel army in 1862, he settled in King George's County in Virginia to facilitate his new profession: contraband smuggling and blockade-running. This brought him by the Surratt Tavern frequently and, in early 1865, to the boardinghouse in Washington too.[34]

On February 20, when Howell was staying at the H Street house, he met Louis Weichmann. Over the three days Howell boarded at the house, he taught Weichmann a cipher code for the alphabet, supposedly one used for conveying secret messages from and to Richmond. Weichmann said he had great fun with it, showing it off to his office mates at the War

Department. He ciphered a Longfellow poem to stump a Mr. Cruickshank, who "was in the habit of making puns and enigmas himself; and I told him I would give him an enigma which he could not make out."[35]

Howell and Slater appear to have been a dispatch and blockade-running team. Howell seems to have been the go-between, introducing Slater to the Surratts and to other agents, like James H. Fowle, who later testified about the rebel work of John Surratt and George Atzerodt.[36] At the end of Howell's stay at the Surratts' in late February, Weichmann saw Howell leave with Sarah Slater, who waited in a carriage outside the boardinghouse for Howell to gather his things and join her. Where they went immediately is not clear, though they did make their way back to Richmond together.[37] Fowle claimed that Atzerodt rowed them all across the Potomac River himself at least once.[38]

Atzerodt visited the H Street house "fifteen to twenty times" in the weeks leading up to the assassination. His first introduction to Weichmann and the boardinghouse residents came late in February, when Howell was staying there. John made the introductions all around, but "the young ladies, they did not understand [Atzerodt's] name." Anna, Nora, and Eliza thought they were being funny and clever, and "named him 'Port Tobacco.'" In spite of Atzerodt's frequent visits to the house, Mrs. Surratt did not care for him.[39] Atzerodt was a heavy drinker, and upon finding liquor in his room, Mary asked that he leave.[40] But his eviction did not prevent him from visiting the house and conferring with Mary or John in private.

Sometime during February, Lewis Payne arrived at the boardinghouse, inquiring after John Surratt. After he learned John was not there, Payne asked to see Mary. Introducing himself as James Wood, Payne requested lodging. It was late and Mary was a little irritated; she had already cleared supper from the dining room table and was ready to relax for the evening. Payne was served dinner in Weichmann's room, where he slept for the night. He left the next day.

The comings and goings of John Jr., and the visits and meetings with Atzerodt, Herold, Payne, and Booth, concerned Weichmann enough to question Mary about it. Weichmann later testified that he approached Mary one day, inquiring why "John brought such men as Herold and Atzerodt into the house, and associated with them."

"Oh, John wants to make use of them for his dirty work," she replied. When pressed by Weichmann as to what kind of "dirty work" she meant, Mary responded cleverly, probably suspicious of his prying questions: "John wanted them to clean his horses," she claimed.

Boarding at Howard's Stables on G Street, Booth's horses and carriage were available to all the conspirators. In fact, even Mary thought the horses belonged to her son, and so did some of the other conspirators. That suited Booth, of course, and their frequent use by all the men served to confuse investigators in the early days of tracking and arresting Booth's fellow accomplices. Brooke Stabler believed the young men were a bunch of "young gamblers and sports," an impression Mary encouraged.[41]

With the addition of Payne, Booth's inner circle of conspirators was complete. There would be other collaborators with varying roles in the abduction scheme—dozens, in fact, who knew of or were intimately involved in planning, securing, and facilitating Booth's capture of the President and escape through Southern Maryland and into Virginia. Many remain unidentified, but even the few who were discovered were almost never brought to trial. Payne, Atzerodt, Herold, Arnold, O'Laughlen, and John and Mary Surratt would remain Booth's intimate core of conspirators, while a few others would become vitally important last-minute accomplices during Booth's desperate run from the authorities in the days following his assassination of President Lincoln. Some would lose their freedom for helping Booth; the rest would pay with their lives.

By the middle of February, choosing the perfect date for the kidnapping consumed Booth's time. He began telling everyone that he was giving up acting. Those on the inside knew he was abandoning the stage for a desperate cause, but the rest of the world thought he was going into oil speculation, anticipating a huge financial payoff. With many contacts, either personal or through his co-conspirators, Booth began to document Lincoln's daily activities and habits. Based on those schedules, Booth's planning for the best time to swoop in and capture the President took on a feverish pitch.

During the week approaching Lincoln's second inauguration on March 4, Weichmann heard Mary claim that "something was going to happen to Old Abe which would prevent him from taking his seat, and that Gen. Lee would make a movement that would startle the whole world." Weichmann was never sure exactly what she meant. He had been reading aloud an Associated Press dispatch from Louisville, Kentucky, in Washington's *Morning Chronicle*, alleging "the rebels are expecting very soon to startle the whole country and astonish the whole world."[42] Mary responded with assurance that this indeed was true.

What was Mary referring to? And what did the portentous news dispatch mean? There are three possibilities. First, Mary's personal conviction, based on blind faith and hope, that Robert E. Lee would make a massive military strike at Washington and drive Lincoln out of the White House. Second, that she was actually referring to General Edwin Grey Lee, Confederate commissioner and secret agent in Montreal, with whom Jefferson Davis had entrusted plans to organize escapes of Confederate soldiers from Union prisons in the North. Edwin Lee became part of the extensive network supporting Booth, John Surratt, and many others. Third, and most probable, there were two disconnected events Mary conflated in her comment to Weichmann: Lincoln would literally not be inaugurated into office because she knew Booth would kidnap him first, and, in addition, Lee had separate and independent plans to change the course of the war through a change in military tactics. Lee's ability to turn the war around was a hopeful but futile dream shared by many Southerners. Nevertheless, Mary's comments and the report in the papers seemed, in hindsight, a warning sign of impending and desperate action to save the Confederacy when its future was bleaker than ever.

On the day of the inauguration, Booth obtained a pass to the grandstand in front of the stage where Lincoln was sworn in for his second term as President. Booth, Payne, Atzerodt, Surratt, and Herold all attended the inauguration, putting them within striking distance of the President as he took the oath of office. Whether they had planned for an attack that day is unknown. But during a drunken tirade weeks later, Booth told fellow actor and friend Samuel K. Chester, "what a splendid chance I had to kill the president on the 4th of March."[43]

For all of Booth's planning and preparation, and in spite of Lincoln's relative lack of armed protection—a weakness that encouraged the boldness of the kidnapping scheme—the opportune time to capture the President never seemed to materialize. Booth, Surratt, and their fellow conspirators remained stymied by unscheduled changes to Lincoln's daily calendar.

During February and early March, Payne, O'Laughlen, and Arnold seemed to be adrift in Baltimore, while Herold and Atzerodt hung around Washington, making forays into the Maryland countryside for hunting and blockade-running, respectively. John Surratt kept up his own courier work back and forth to Richmond, while his mother continued running her boardinghouse, providing shelter to rebel spies and couriers in addition to her more permanent guests. All were waiting for Booth to schedule the right time to execute his grand plan.

Finally, Booth arranged for a conspirators' meeting at Ford's Theatre to study the theater layout and the presidential box, and to visualize the possibilities of a capture there. Booth was well known to John Ford, the theater's owner, having performed there numerous times. He called in a favor and engaged the two theater boxes generally reserved for President Lincoln when he came to the theater for a show. Booth invited Payne and John Surratt to see *The Tragedy of Jane Shore* on the fifteenth of March.

Payne almost didn't make it to the important meeting. On March 12, he was arrested and thrown into a Baltimore jail for beating up a black maid at the Branson's boardinghouse. Payne lost his temper when the young servant woman refused to clean his room, calling him names to boot. Her perceived insolence set Payne off on a tirade: he "struck her . . . threw her on the ground and stamped on her body, struck her on the forehead, and said he would kill her."[44] The young woman filed a complaint with federal marshals—her understanding was that her accusations would get more attention from federal authorities than from the local police—and they arrested him. Using his original alias of Lewis Payne, the civilian refugee from Virginia, he managed to get himself released the following day by swearing another oath of allegiance to the Union and promising to stay north of Philadelphia. David Parr promptly sent him to Washington on orders from Booth, a serious and blatant violation of his release. Payne would have to be very careful not to attract any attention in Washington.

Payne checked into Mary's H Street house, where he introduced himself as Lewis Payne, a Baptist preacher. Anna, Eliza, and Nora, however, kept calling him by the name "Wood." Weichmann did not recognize him, at first, as the same man who had stayed one night back in February under the alias James Wood. Payne told them that he had been arrested in Baltimore, had taken an oath of allegiance, and was "now going to be a good and loyal citizen."[45] Mary allowed him to stay in the attic room.

Weichmann was concerned: Payne did not look, or act, like a preacher. Wearing a beautiful new gray suit, Payne also had fine linen shirts and a light linen coat in his bag. Perhaps most importantly, Weichmann wondered, why would the man called Wood be using the name Payne?

On March 14, John returned to the boardinghouse and to his shared room with Weichmann. Payne came to the room and asked John for a private moment; Weichmann obliged them. Weichmann was becoming deeply troubled over the secrecy and the shady characters with whom

John was involved. The following day, Weichmann discovered a false mustache on the table in his room. Feeling mischievous, he hid it in his toiletries case. Later, Payne came searching the room, but Weichmann said nothing. The disguise only added to Weichmann's increasing suspicions about his friend John and his associates. Eliza Holohan was also suspicious of Payne. She told Anna that she "did not think he would convert many souls; he did not look as if he would."[46] Mary, however, thought he "was a great looking Baptist preacher."[47]

Weichmann's curiosity got the best of him. Later that afternoon, he went up to Payne's attic room, only to discover John and Payne sitting on the bed "playing with bowie knives . . . two revolvers and four sets of new spurs."[48] He went to Mrs. Surratt, expressing his concern over what he saw. Mary told him "not to think anything of it . . . John was in the habit of riding out into the country, and that he had to have these things for protection."[49]

Weichmann wanted to join the two men for the evening performance of *Jane Shore;* to view a play from the presidential box was a real treat. John flaunted his precious ten-dollar tickets, but when Weichmann tried to grab the tickets, Surratt taunted him and told him he was not invited for "private reasons."[50] Adding insult to injury, John invited Nora Fitzpatrick and young Apollonia Dean instead of Weichmann. The girls, however, were a subtle cover for the conspirators, who were eager to examine the very spot where Booth hoped to execute his kidnapping.

As John and Payne were preparing to leave with Nora and Apollonia, Payne put on Weichmann's blue regimental jacket. Payne was at great risk of being seen and arrested for violating the terms of his release from jail in Baltimore. The mustache, Weichmann smugly recalled, would have improved the disguise.[51]

After the performance at Ford's, the girls went home. Meanwhile, all seven co-conspirators—Surratt, Payne, Arnold, O'Laughlen, Atzerodt, Herold, and Booth—met and settled into a private dining room reserved by Booth at Gautier's for a night of eating, drinking, cigars, cards, and intense discussion about the kidnapping plans. Booth explained that the next time Lincoln attended a performance at Ford's, they would spring into action. Booth had already gathered handcuffs, rope, guns, pistols, ammunition, horses, and a carriage. The rest of the plot required readiness and a swift, organized ambush.

After hours of reviewing and rehashing strategy, changing everyone's role in the plan several times, and vigorous drinking, Samuel Arnold became belligerent, opposing the scheme and claiming "it could not be done or accomplished" safely. O'Laughlen joined in, the two of them arguing that the whole plan was too risky. "If ever, which was an impossibility, to get him out of the Box and to the [Eastern Branch] Bridge we would be stopped by [a] Sentinel," Arnold reasoned. "Shoot the Sentinel," Booth retorted. Arnold had not signed up for murder, maintaining that he "wanted a Shadow of a chance . . . and I intended to have it, that he [Booth] could be the leader but not my executioner." Booth threatened Arnold if he backed out now; Arnold challenged him to shoot him then and there. Cooler heads prevailed, but Arnold allegedly demanded that the kidnapping be done "this week," or he would no longer participate.[52]

Tension was building, forcing Booth to become more desperate. He had only a couple of days before Arnold's ultimatum was up, at which time he would lose one, if not two, of his co-conspirators.

On the sixteenth, Booth learned through a friend in the theater business that Lincoln was scheduled to attend a benefit performance of *Still Waters Run Deep* on the afternoon of the seventeenth at the Campbell Hospital near the Soldiers Home, a favorite Lincoln retreat on the outskirts of Washington. The opportunity Booth had been hoping for had suddenly, and without warning, appeared.

Booth's original kidnapping plot had involved grabbing the President while he was traveling back to the city from one of his frequent trips to the Soldiers Home. Now this plan could be reactivated: they would intercept the President's carriage, overpower the driver and any escorts, and John Surratt would take the reins. Booth, Payne, Atzerodt, Arnold, and O'Laughlen would ride alongside the carriage as it raced into Southern Maryland along the planned route to Surrattsville, where they would change carriages, retrieve fresh horses, make their way to the Potomac, and cross into Virginia.

During the early afternoon of the seventeenth, Booth called the conspirators together outside Mary's boardinghouse, where they received their instructions. Herold was ordered to take the spare carriage loaded with shotguns, carbines, a pistol, dagger, a sword, several feet of rope, and a monkey wrench (used to fix carriage axels) to a rendezvous point along the road to Surrattsville. Herold set out, as instructed, and the rest rode off together. When they reached Seventh Street, the road to the Soldiers Home, they split up and took their prearranged positions along the road. There they waited for a couple of hours—but the President did not go to Campbell Hospital that afternoon, and the scheme failed.[53]

When Weichmann returned home from work that afternoon, Payne and John were not there. At dinner, Weichmann found Mary weeping. "John has gone away, John has gone away," she cried. Anna Surratt told Weichmann, "If anything were to happen to my brother John through his acquaintance with Booth, I would kill him."[54]

At about six o'clock, John Surratt suddenly burst into Weichmann's room. "He had a revolver in his hand," Weichmann later testified,

> . . . one of Sharpe's revolvers, a four-barreled revolver, a small one, you could carry it in your vest pocket. He appeared to be very much excited. . . . He [said], 'I will shoot any one that comes into this room; my prospect is gone, my hopes are blighted; I want something to do; can you get me a clerkship?' In about ten minutes after . . . Payne came into the room. He was very much

excited, and I noticed he had a pistol. About fifteen minutes afterward, Booth came into the room, and Booth was so excited that he walked around the room three or four times very frantically, and did not notice me. He had a whip in his hand. . . . The three men went upstairs into the back room, in the third story, and must have remained there about thirty minutes, when they left the house together.[55]

Weichmann had no idea where they were going, but he was forced to face some uncomfortable facts. The Surratts' friendship with Booth and the others concealed "some hidden purpose," the object of which Weichmann was now convinced was illegal.[56] He could not have foreseen, however, that the object was murder.

CHAPTER FIVE

THE ASSASSIN'S ACCOMPLICE

News of the failed capture had not yet reached David Herold. He was still waiting on the road to Surrattsville with his load of guns and provisions. As night came on, he decided to head toward the Surratt Tavern on the off chance that his co-conspirators had taken a different route past him. Along the way he ran into a friend, Walter Griffin, who accompanied him to the tavern, where they settled in for a few hours of card playing and drinking.

At ten o'clock, Herold's accomplices still had not shown up, so he decided to head further down the road to the village of T.B., and to stay the night there at the local tavern and inn. He asked the tavern keeper if he could bring his guns and ammunition inside. The tavern keeper agreed, keeping the larger guns behind the bar, while Herold took the rest to his room. Herold asked to be awakened if John Surratt arrived looking for him.

In the meantime, John had returned to his mother's boardinghouse; Payne, Arnold, and O'Laughlen went back to Baltimore. Atzerodt stayed behind, joining John the next morning for a ride into the Maryland countryside. Their mission was to locate Herold and bring him back to Washington. They unexpectedly ran into him retracing his route on the road from T.B.; he was hoping to run into his co-conspirators or hear news of what had happened. Herold had tried to convince the tavern keeper at T.B. to keep all the weapons until they were called for, but was refused. But John knew just where they could secret the contraband: they would ride to the Surratt Tavern, where John was confident that Lloyd, a loyal Southerner, would allow them to hide their goods.

When the three men arrived in Surrattsville, they ran into George Atzerodt's brother, John C. Atzerodt, who was, ironically, a government detective. Atzerodt and his brother sat down for a drink together, while Surratt and Herold waited nervously. They could not risk being exposed. Once the detective left, Surratt and the others approached Lloyd and told him they wanted to hide the guns. Lloyd was nervous: the men had come with "two carbines with ammunition . . . a rope from sixteen to twenty feet in length, and a monkey wrench." Not knowing where to hide it all, Lloyd hesitated, but John knew the house inside out. He told Lloyd that there was a secret place in an unfinished room on the second floor in the rear of the building, above the tavern kitchen, where the contraband could be stored safely. The men put the items in a gap behind the wall and rested them on the floor joists above the dining room where they would be seen by no one. Surratt promised Lloyd that the items only needed to be secreted for a few days and that he would then come back for them. Surratt, Herold, and Atzerodt then rode back to Washington.[1]

The night of the failed abduction, Booth purportedly went to New York. In actuality, he must have stayed in Washington, as he was scheduled to perform in *The Apostate* at Ford's Theatre on the next day, the eighteenth. Appearing as the evil Duke Pescara, this would be Booth's last performance. He gave tickets to Surratt, Weichmann, Herold, Atzerodt, and John Holohan. After the play they shared oysters and drinks, then parted ways. Booth went off to New York, joining Payne and David Parr, who had gone there a few days before on unknown rebel business. Booth, it seems, was not giving up on his plans.

Louis Weichmann was becoming more and more apprehensive. Unable to keep his suspicions to himself any longer, he revealed some of the strange incidents and odd characters coming and going from the Surratt house to his supervisor at the War Department, Major Daniel Gleason. Gleason did not take Weichmann seriously at first, but he and other office employees suggested Weichmann keep an eye on things. Later, after the assassination, Gleason would remember his conversation with Weichmann and put the pieces together. By then, of course, it would be too late.

Even before he spoke to Gleason, Weichmann had already written his former professor, Father J. B. Menu at St. Charles College, cryptically revealing his suspicions that John and Mary Surratt were involved in something very illegal. Menu wrote back asking for more details, cautioning Weichmann to proceed with great care. But Weichmann never saw his letter: it had been intercepted by someone. The letter was later found among Booth's possessions after he was gunned down for assassinating Lincoln. It was thought to be unimportant, and its existence was never made public. Oddly, Menu would later steadfastly defend John Surratt at Surratt's trial in 1867, shunning Weichmann as a traitor and liar.[2] It would have helped Weichmann defend himself against accusations that he was part of Booth's circle of conspirators if he knew his vindication had been among the items in Booth's trunk.

On March 23, Eliza Holohan arrived at Weichmann's office with a telegram she had accepted for him at the boardinghouse. The telegram, which spelled his name incorrectly as "Wickmann," was sent from John Wilkes Booth in New York. "Tell John to telegraph number and street at once," Booth wrote. When Weichmann returned home from work that day, he gave the telegram to John and asked him the meaning of it. "Don't be so damn inquisitive," John told him.[3]

Booth was setting up a trail of evidence against Weichmann. He probably had Menu's letter to Weichmann by now and knew that Weichmann could destroy his plans by revealing his suspicions to others. Over the next few days, Booth and John Surratt would concoct a few more incriminating pieces of evidence, placing Weichmann in the middle of the conspiracy as insurance against any future attempts to betray them.

The mysterious telegram referred to the Herndon House, a board-inghouse operated by Mary Murray, where Payne was scheduled to stay upon his return to Washington. Surratt had already checked the place out, and had sent his sometimes girlfriend, Anna Ward, to inquire about the availability of rooms. Weichmann had in fact been with John when he double-checked the reservation. Sometime around the twenty-third, Surratt and Weichmann went to the Herndon House, where John asked if he could speak with Mrs. Murray privately. She seemed confused, forcing John to remark within earshot of Weichmann, "Perhaps Miss Anna Ward has spoken to you about this room? Did she not speak to you about engaging a room for a delicate gentleman, who was to have his meals sent up to his room?" Oh yes, Murray then remembered, the room would be available on the twenty-seventh.[4] Clearly Booth was not abandoning his scheme; rather, something new was afoot.

Booth arrived back in Washington very early on the twenty-fifth, and checked into the National Hotel; he may have been escorting Sarah Slater from New York. Slater was carrying letters for Confederate Sec-retary of State Judah Benjamin in Richmond from General Edwin Lee in Montreal. John Surratt picked Slater up at the train station that morning and drove her to the boardinghouse. Mary had been watching for them, and as soon as they pulled up in front of the house, she came out and climbed into the carriage. They were headed to Surrattsville, where Slater was to meet Augustus Howell, who would escort her to Richmond. Why Mary went along is unclear.

When John, Mary, and Sarah Slater arrived at the tavern, they learned that Howell had been arrested. Federal detectives had picked him up there the night before on suspicion of rebel activities. Slater still needed an escort—it was too dangerous for her to ride alone all the way to Richmond—so John Surratt decided to take her instead. A Sur-rattsville neighbor, David Barry, happened to be at the tavern when they arrived; he agreed to take them to Port Tobacco in the rented car-riage, and then return the team of horses and buggy back to Brooke Stabler at Howard's Stables the following day.[5]

Mary took the public stagecoach back to Washington. When she got home she asked Weichmann to go over to Howard's and tell Stabler that the horses and buggy would not be returned until sometime the next day. On the morning of the twenty-sixth, as Weichmann was preparing to go to church, Mary asked him to stop by the National Hotel first, and to tell Booth she needed to speak with him privately. Weichmann was beginning to feel like an errand boy. Nevertheless, he did as requested. On his way down Sixth Street, he ran into George Atzerodt, who was also on his way to see Booth. Arriving at the National together, the two men parted ways after Weichmann delivered Mary's message.

When Booth arrived at the boardinghouse later that day, Mary told him that Howell had been arrested, and, as a consequence, John had taken Sarah Slater to Richmond and probably would not be back for a week or more. Their private conversation near the kitchen stairway intrigued Weichmann. He had decided to take the advice of his supervisor, Daniel Gleason, and to pay closer attention to activities in the house.

For Booth, this news complicated matters. Booth was in the middle of reorganizing his plot and would need John Surratt back in town.[6] Additionally, if the feds were watching the Surratt Tavern, then their escape route was becoming more risky. Time was running out.

On Sunday morning, April 2, Mary asked Weichmann to go to the National Hotel and tell Booth that she needed to see him. If Booth was unavailable, she said, Weichmann should find Atzerodt instead and tell him to come to the house as soon as possible. Mary had gone to Surrattsville the day before for unknown reasons, returning that evening after supper in the company of her brother, John Zadoc Jenkins. Weichmann later assumed that whatever Mary had done on Saturday in Surrattsville was somehow connected to her request to see Booth or Atzerodt the next day.

Booth was not at the National, so Weichmann proceeded to the Pennsylvania House, where he knew Atzerodt to be staying. He found Atzerodt standing in front of the hotel with two horses: Booth's one-eyed mare and another, smaller horse. Weichmann and Atzerodt rode to Mary's house together; Atzerodt went inside while Weichmann waited outside with the horses. When Atzerodt reemerged, he and Weichmann rode off to church together, never discussing the private conversation Atzerodt had with Mary.

Later that afternoon, Mary asked Weichmann to go back to the Pennsylvania House and ask Atzerodt if her brother, John Zadoc, could use one of the horses to ride back to Surrattsville. Once again the dutiful boarder, accompanied by John Zadoc, returned to the Pennsylvania House and delivered the request. Atzerodt told Weichmann that he would need to get Payne's permission before allowing John Zadoc the use of one of the horses. Weichmann thought this odd—he had been under the assumption that the horses belonged to John Surratt—but Atzerodt refused to explain why Payne should have a say in the matter. Nevertheless, they all went to the Herndon House, where Payne was still boarding, to make the request. The journey proved a waste of time: Payne would not give his consent.

When Weichmann returned to deliver the news to Mary, she was furious. She told Weichmann that she thought it "very unkind of Mr. Atzerodt; that she had been his friend, and had loaned him her last five dollars out of her pocket." Jenkins was forced to spend another night at H Street and to walk back to Surrattsville the next day, a trip of about four hours on foot.[7]

Payne's refusal to allow the horse to be used by Jenkins is curious. Booth and John Surratt were usually in control of the horses, but now Payne was in charge of them. To refuse Mrs. Surratt's request seemed impolite and risky, considering she was John's mother and a Booth confidante. With John out of town, however, and Booth's plans in transition, Payne's role as a co-conspirator was clearly becoming more important.

After John had accompanied Sarah Slater to Richmond the week before, he had remained there to meet with Confederate Secretary of

War Judah Benjamin. Benjamin had given Surratt two hundred dollars in gold to conduct a courier mission to General Edwin Lee in Montreal. John may have sent a message to his mother before he left Richmond on April 1, informing her of his pending arrival home, a fact that she would have relayed to Booth.

As John was secretly weaving his way home through illicit travel networks across the Potomac to Washington, however, General Ulysses S. Grant and his Union army were taking the city of Richmond. How John got past them undetected and unaware of their advance on the Southern capital seems remarkable. He had been gone but a few hours when the city exploded into a roaring furnace of desperate fires, set by a hastily retreating Confederate government. Civilians were left to fend for themselves; some fled with the army, others stayed behind to fight the fires and try to save their homes. But much of the city burned out of control. Confederate bureaucrats and soldiers tried to take as many official records and secret documents as possible, but with Grant bearing down quickly on the city, the decision to burn whatever could not be safely taken was made hastily, tragically destroying thousands of colonial, antebellum, and Civil War records. Though the Union army tried desperately to squelch the fires, the city would smolder for weeks.

When John arrived at his mother's boardinghouse on the evening of the third, he was stunned to learn that Richmond had fallen. It was not possible, he argued with Weichmann. He had just been in Richmond and the government was still operating, he told Weichmann, and he had seen "Benjamin and Davis and they told me it would not be evacuated!"[8] His mother was distraught; it would only be a matter of time before the South would capitulate and the war would end in failure for the Confederacy.

In their shared room, John showed Weichmann "nine or eleven" twenty-dollar gold pieces he had been paid in Richmond for his work. Surratt needed to convert some of the gold into cash immediately, but Weichmann could not help him. Instead, Surratt approached John Holohan, who obligingly gave him sixty dollars in return for two gold pieces, telling Surratt "you are good enough to me for [the rest of] the money."[9]

John had pressing matters to attend to and could not stay long in Washington. His new assignment in Montreal seemed more vital, now that Richmond had fallen, and he needed to get there as quickly as possible. Besides, government detectives were on the lookout for him—federal officers had inquired of one of Mary's servants about John's whereabouts just days before. He could not risk being arrested now at his mother's house.

Surratt checked into the Metropolitan Hotel with Sarah Slater, who was also planning to go to Montreal. The following morning, on the fourth, they both took the early train to New York for the first part of their journey to Montreal.[10]

Throughout the following week, victory celebrations continued, even though the Confederacy had not officially surrendered. Now that Richmond was under federal occupation, the Confederate government without a home and its members fleeing all over the South, the excitement and anticipation palpitated throughout Washington. However, Mary and Southern sympathizers like her were becoming increasingly distraught over the prospects of a Southern defeat. And Booth was becoming desperate.

While the original conspiracy to kidnap Lincoln may have had the blessings of Confederate President Jefferson Davis and his staff, the plan to murder Lincoln seems to have been an independent decision made by Booth in the last days of the Civil War. However, the President of the Confederacy must have been fully aware of another scheme in the making that had targeted Lincoln's life.

In the days after the evacuation of Richmond, a group of rebel soldiers working in the Confederate Torpedo Bureau joined with Colonel John S. Moseby's Rangers in Fauquier County, Virginia. Their plan involved secretly slipping into Washington and planting explosives in a hidden tunnel beneath the White House, killing Lincoln as he met with his cabinet. But on April 10, a Union cavalry regiment tracking Moseby's men fired upon the group at Burke Station, Virginia, a few miles from Washington. They captured the team's explosives expert, Thomas Harney, and threw him and his accomplices into Old Capitol Prison, effectively destroying their plans to blow up the White House.[11]

Booth knew of the bombing scheme, but was seemingly under the impression that the plan was the work of a New York Confederate espionage network with which he was in communication. Whether this was correct, or whether the New York contingent was formulating its own independent attack on the White House, Booth was determined to strike his own blow before the others met with success.[12] George Atzerodt testified later that Booth told him about "a party in N. York who would get the Pres. certain. They were going to mine the end of Kirk House, next to the War Dept . . . [and he] said if he did not get [Lincoln] quick the N.Y. crowd would."[13] Booth would have his opportunity within a few short days.

On April 10, Mary approached Weichmann again, asking him if he would take her to Surrattsville the next day so she could conduct some urgent business. John H. Nothey, a neighbor in Prince George's County, owed her $479 plus thirteen years' interest for land he had purchased in 1852 from John Sr. At no time during those thirteen years had Mary or her dead husband tried, through the courts anyway, to collect on this debt. Now Mary was suddenly determined to collect it.[14]

The next morning she sent Weichmann to inquire whether Booth would let her use his buggy and horses. Booth told Weichmann that he had sold his buggy and one of the horses. Weichmann was puzzled: "I thought they were John Surratt's horses." Booth told him, no, they were his, and he then gave Weichmann ten dollars to rent a carriage for Mrs. Surratt. Weichmann procured the team and took the day off from his job to drive Mrs. Surratt to the tavern.

Coincidently, George H. Calvert, a wealthy landowner who lived near Washington and whose father had loaned the Surratts money in 1852, was now pressuring Mary to pay off the outstanding debt. Calvert had successfully sued John Surratt, Sr., at least twice before Surratt's death in 1862, and each time the courts had found in Calvert's favor, ordering the Surratts to pay. However, Calvert had received little if any payment, and was once again demanding settlement. Calvert had become aware of debts owed to the Surratts, according to Mary, and was forcing her to collect on those debts to pay him. Oddly, Calvert did not notify Mary of his demand for settlement until at least a day, and possibly three, after her trip to Surrattsville that Tuesday.

A light rainfall accompanied Mary and Lou Weichmann as they left Washington at around nine o'clock that morning. About four miles outside the city, in a small, newly developing Washington suburb called Uniontown, they passed another carriage heading into the city. In it was Mary's tavern tenant, John Lloyd, and his sister-in-law, Emma Offutt, Offutt's little boy, and a neighbor, Walter Griffin.[15] The carriages halted several yards apart, and Lloyd jumped out and hurried over to speak with Mrs. Surratt. Mary spoke to him in such a low tone that he could not hear her. "Her language was indistinct," Lloyd later testified, "as if she wanted to draw my attention to something, so that no one else would understand."[16] Weichmann was seated next to Mary, but her voice was so low that he could not hear her either.[17] Lloyd did not understand what she was talking about until she "came out plainer, and asked me about the 'shooting irons.' I had myself forgotten about their being there. I told her they were hid away far back, and that I was afraid the house might be searched." She continued to be vague about what she wanted, however, and Lloyd was getting nervous. "Finally she came out bolder with it, and said they would be wanted soon. I told her that I had an idea of having them buried; that I was very uneasy about having them there."[18] The tavern was being watched closely, and Lloyd had heard it was going to be searched by federal authorities. He did not want the weapons to be found there.

Mary abruptly changed the subject. The tone of her voice shifted so that it was now loud enough for Weichmann and Emma Offutt to hear. She expressed concern over the arrest of Augustus Howell at the tavern, and said she was going to argue for his release.[19] Lloyd asked her about her son John; he had heard rumors that "soldiers were after John to arrest him for going to Richmond." Mary laughed at Lloyd, cleverly chiding him that if John could go "to Richmond and back again in six days, he must be a very smart man indeed."[20]

When Mary and Weichmann arrived at the tavern, John Nothey was not there as expected. Mary sent a messenger to find Nothey and to tell him to come see her at Bennett Gwynn's house. Gwynn and his family were fierce rebel sympathizers; several had joined the rebel army early in the war. Gwynn was an original witness to the mortgage transaction between Nothey and John Surratt, Sr., in 1852. His expertise as a land agent would be important to Mary as she tried to collect her outstanding debt from Nothey.

Mary and Weichmann had dinner with Gwynn and then returned to the Surratt Tavern, where they found Nothey waiting for them. Weichmann later testified that Mary, Gwynn, and Nothey went into the parlor and transacted their business, and within a short time, Mary emerged, climbed back into the carriage with Weichmann, and returned to Washington.[21]

Lloyd, in the meantime, was still confused as to what exactly he should do with the weapons. On his return from Washington, he ran into Atzerodt in Uniontown. When he asked Atzerodt what he should do with the guns, George said, "Bury them."[22]

The continuing delay in executing Booth's kidnapping plan created problems along the conspirators' relay network from Washington through the Maryland countryside to the Potomac. False starts, lack of communication, and the impending cessation of hostilities between the warring states had discouraged some participants. Some believed the kidnapping would never happen and had made other plans. Payments for services were delayed; many had expected the kidnapping to take place during February or March. Now it was April, and still nothing.

Richard Smoot, the Charles County farmer who had sold his boat to John Surratt on credit, was one of the players who'd become impatient. Smoot had sold the boat back in January and had expected payment by now, but had received nothing. Half the fee remained in trust with Judge Stone in Port Tobacco, and the rest was presumably still held by John Surratt. Smoot had given up lucrative smuggling opportunities when he turned his boat over to Surratt and Atzerodt; he thought it would be used very quickly. When he confronted Atzerodt about the status of the plan and his money, Atzerodt kept putting him off, talking "evasively as to specific dates." He assured Smoot that the boat would be used soon and that he would get his money. Nearly three months later, the farmer had been put off long enough.

Finally, Smoot tracked down Atzerodt in Port Tobacco. It was early April, and Smoot wanted his money, now. Atzerodt assured him that the scheme was still in play and that he should expect payment for his boat soon. Not persuaded, Smoot sought out John Lloyd at the Surratt Tavern, demanding to know where he could find John Surratt. Lloyd directed him to Mary at her boardinghouse in Washington. Smoot later revealed:

> I went to the capital and called upon Mrs. Surratt at her home the Wednesday morning before the assassination. I was met at the door by Miss Annie Surratt, with whom I had a slight acquaintance, and she conducted me into the presence of her mother who was seated in the parlor. I asked the old lady where I could see her son John. For a moment her face was a study. She really made me uneasy with her penetrating look of inquiry. She evidently was not satisfied with my appearance, for after a brief silence she informed me that she was unable to tell me of the exact whereabouts of her son, or when or where I could see him. I saw that I was under suspicion, and so told her the object of my visit. In an instant her whole demeanor

changed. Her face brightened and she extended me a most cordial greeting. She eagerly inquired if the boat was in place and easily accessible, as it might be called into requisition that night.[23]

Smoot told her that he no longer had possession of the boat. Blockade-runner George Bateman had taken it and hidden it somewhere near Nanjemoy Creek, near the Potomac River southwest of Port Tobacco. Suddenly, Mary became "anxious"; fearing that Smoot had been followed, she told him to leave her house and the city at once. Before he left, Mary showed him a letter John had written from Canada to a "Miss Mitchell," presumably another local rebel contact, indicating John would be back in Washington on Friday. Mary asked Smoot to come back then, at which time he would see "John and the boys."[24]

In spite of a collapsing Confederacy, Surratt continued conveying secret messages and documents from Richmond to various contacts in Washington, Maryland, New York, and Montreal. Surratt, after all, was a valuable and devoted Confederate courier and spy, and this was perhaps his first obligation or duty. His relationship with Booth at times took second place to his role as a rebel messenger. Waiting for Booth to take action required lengthy intervals of idleness, time Surratt used well to provide service to Richmond. Since the day in December when Booth and Surratt had been introduced on Seventh Street in Washington, the two had combined resources and vital connections among their fellow Confederate spies and sympathizers to create a dependable and supportive network to help carry out Booth's abduction plans. But John still needed to earn an income, and working for Davis and Benjamin and the Confederate Secret Service proved lucrative while also fulfilling his desire to play a profitable role in thwarting Northern interests and advancing the rebel cause.

John Surratt remained deeply loyal to Booth but may have been unaware of Booth's final decision to assassinate the President on April 14. John's unexpected secret courier mission to Montreal in early April had removed him from daily contact with Booth, and in fact was on a spy mission in Elmira, New York, on the day of the assassination. If he had been assigned a role in the broader assassination scheme, he was either unaware of Booth's time schedule or, because he was unavailable, was not given a specific job in the final murderous plan. Ironically, his trip to Canada saved his life but served to send his mother to the gallows.

On April 14, Booth met with Atzerodt and Herold to finalize his plans. His intention was to assassinate not only President Lincoln, but also Secretary of State William Henry Seward, General Ulysses S. Grant, and Vice President Andrew Johnson. Booth believed this would ensure that there would be no immediate presidential succession, leaving the federal government leaderless and in disarray. He told Atzerodt and Herold that John Surratt was in the city. As far as Herold and Atzerodt knew, Surratt was ready to assist Booth in attacking Lincoln in the President's box at the theater. The plan was to kill General Grant—he and his wife, Julia, had been invited to join the Lincolns at the theater that evening—at the same time.

Booth may have deliberately set up Surratt, knowing that he was out of town and would not be participating in the final drama of the war. Perhaps he told Atzerodt and Herold this lie so they would believe that a key co-conspirator was still on board and that the plot would proceed as planned. In fact, neither the two men nor any of the other co-conspirators actually saw Surratt in Washington after April 3.[25] On the other hand, Surratt may have been planning to return to Washington from Canada on the fourteenth, but never arrived. Nevertheless, Atzerodt and Herold believed Surratt was in town, and Booth's comment, placing John in the city on the day of the assassination, would resurface during the police interrogations of Atzerodt and Herold following their arrests, and would directly link John to Booth's plot.

On the morning of the fourteenth, Mary and Lou Weichmann attended Good Friday services at St. Patrick's Church. After mass, Weichmann went to work, only to discover that Secretary of War Edwin Stanton had declared that all War Department employees who wished to observe Good Friday would be "relieved from duty for the day."[26] Weichmann happily took up the offer. After attending additional services at St. Matthew's Church, Weichmann went back to the boardinghouse to spend the rest of the day reading and lounging about.

Sometime around two o'clock, Mary asked Weichmann if he would take her to Surrattsville. She had urgent business once again, she said. In a letter dated April 12, George Calvert was again demanding his money.

Mrs. M.E. Surratt:

Dear Madam—During a late visit to the lower portion of the county, I ascertained of the willingness of Mr. Nothey to settle with you, and desire to call your attention to the fact, urging the settlement of the claim of my late father's estate. However unpleasant, I must insist upon closing up this matter, as it is imperative, in an early settlement of the estate, which is necessary.

You will, therefore, please inform me, at your earliest convenience, as to how and when you will be able to pay the balance remaining due on the land purchased by your late husband. . . .

Geo. H. Calvert, Jr.[27]

She must go back to Surrattsville, she told Weichmann. He agreed to accompany her, taking six dollars from her to rent a horse and buggy for the journey. Just as Weichmann was about to leave the house, Booth arrived. He entered the parlor to speak privately with Mary. When Weichmann returned with the transportation, Booth was still there, but on his way out.

It was nearly three o'clock and Mary was now ready to leave. While getting into the carriage, she suddenly stopped. "Wait, Mr. Weichmann, I must get those things of Booth's." She ran back into the house and quickly reappeared with a small package, about six inches in diameter, wrapped in newspaper. She placed it carefully on the floor of the buggy, telling Weichmann that it was "glass, and [I am] afraid of it getting wet."[28]

Booth must have spoken to Mary earlier in the day and learned of her pending trip to Surrattsville. Or perhaps he specifically asked her to make the journey for him, and she used her business with Nothey as a cover to travel there again. Booth needed someone to alert Lloyd that the items stored at the tavern would be needed that night, and Mary was the perfect choice to deliver not only the message, but the last-minute supplies needed for his escape out of Maryland. He had already asked Atzerodt to go tell Lloyd to get the guns out of their hiding place, but Atzerodt, now leery and uncomfortable with Booth's murder plot, had spent the afternoon riding around the city instead of doing what he was told.[29] Atzerodt had been chosen to murder Vice President Johnson as part of Booth's revised scheme—a role he did not want. Booth probably sensed he could not totally trust Atzerodt, and so he turned to Mary, a trusted co-conspirator and sympathizer, instead.

Mary was cheerful on the trip to Surrattsville, Weichmann later noted, "taking the reins in her own hands several times and urging on the steed." Just three or four miles outside of the city, they came upon some pickets relaxing beside the road. Mary called out to a farmer nearby and asked him when the sentinels were scheduled to leave their post. By eight o'clock, he said—news she "was glad to know. . . ."[30] This was important information, as Booth and his accomplices would need a clear road as they fled the city later that night.

When Mary and Weichmann arrived at the tavern, Nothey was not there. Mary asked her traveling companion to write a note for her:

Mr. John Nothey,

Dear Sir:

I have this day received a letter from Mr. Calvert intimating that either you or your friends have represented to him that I am not willing to settle with you for the land.

You know that I am ready and have been waiting for these last two
years; and now, if you do not come within the next ten days, I will set-
tle with Mr. Calvert and bring suit against you immediately.

Mr. Calvert will give you a deed on receiving payment.[31]

Mary gave the letter to Ben Gwynn, who was passing by the tavern, asking him to deliver it to Nothey and read it to him. Nothey lived just three miles from the tavern; why Mary did not travel the additional distance to deliver the message herself seems odd. Nothey was unaware she was coming to town that Friday, and she did not request to see him again at the tavern. In fact, she gave him another ten days to settle with her. If a letter was all that was necessary to complete her business, as it seems, why go all the way to Surrattsville when, at the cost of a "three-cent postage stamp, an envelope, and a sheet of writing paper," the letter could have been mailed from Washington?[32]

After sending the letter off with Gwynn, Mary brought the wrapped package into the inn and showed it to John Lloyd's sister-in-law, Emma Offutt, placing it on the sofa in the parlor. Emma later testified that Mary "said she was requested to leave it there." Mary then asked where Lloyd was. It was about five-thirty and getting late, and she needed to speak with him privately. Emma told her that he had been to court in Marlboro and had not yet returned.[33]

Mary lingered. Shortly, Lloyd pulled up to the tavern, driving around to the kitchen in back with fresh fish and oysters. As he was unloading the seafood, Mary grabbed the package she had placed on the sofa and walked through the house and out into the yard to speak with Lloyd, alone. Emma stood nearby, but was unable to hear their conversation.

"Talk about the devil and his imps will appear," Mary called to him.

"I was not aware that I was a devil before," Lloyd shot back. Lloyd had been drinking heavily, and his drunken state no doubt aggravated Mary.

"Well, Mr. Lloyd, I want you to have those shooting irons ready; there will be parties here tonight who will call for them." She handed him the package she had brought from Booth, and ordered him to also "get two bottles of whiskey ready," reminding him again to be sure that all those items would be ready when "called for that night."[34]

Lloyd's drunkenness was widely noted. The tavern bartender, Joseph Nott, and Emma Offutt, as well as many others testified that Lloyd had been drinking quite heavily for several weeks. Patrons at the bar also agreed that Lloyd was "pretty tight that night."[35] After court had adjourned in Marlboro earlier that day, Lloyd played cards and drank for a couple of hours with his friends James Lusby and Richard Sweeney before heading back to Surrattsville. Lusby and Sweeney testified that their friend was "very drunk," and "considerably under the influence of liquor, and he drank on the road," too. However, Sweeney also said that Lloyd was sober enough to drive his horse and buggy well, keeping to the road and not deviating from it.[36]

After delivering her message, Mary returned to the front of the tavern and climbed into the buggy, where Weichmann was waiting for her. Weichmann was just getting the horse to move, when, within a few feet of the tavern, the buggy's front spring bolt snapped and became detached from the axle. Weichmann halted immediately. Mary hurried back into the tavern and asked Lloyd to help fix it. Lloyd, in spite of his intoxication, successfully reattached the spring with a piece of cord, and Mary and Weichmann were finally back on the road to Washington.

Lloyd returned to the inn, where he began to feel sick. Emma helped him off with his jacket and he lay down on the sofa. It was not long, however, before he went back into the bar and started drinking. Before going to bed at eight o'clock that evening, he prepared two bottles of whiskey and retrieved one of the guns and other items from their hiding place beneath the floor joists in the second floor storage room. He took them to his room, "so as to have them convenient for any parties that might call that night." Then he unwrapped the package Mary had given him: in it was a pair of French field glasses. He promptly fell asleep, awaking at just about midnight when two men arrived at the tavern, demanding the items Mary had told him to have ready.[37] Unwittingly, Lloyd had become another participant in Booth's deadly web.

On the hurried ride back that evening, Mary told Weichmann she was anxious to get home before nine; she was meeting a "gentleman" at the house at that time. Weichmann asked if it was Booth, but Mary made no response either way.

Washington was alight again with celebrations. The hoisting of the American flag over Fort Sumter in Charleston Harbor on Good Friday launched victory celebrations that lit up cities all over the country. Bonfires, parties, and general carousing marked the day's great significance in the nation's capital. Hundreds of Washington Arsenal employees and soldiers were preparing a festive march down Pennsylvania Avenue that evening, complete with a marching band. They were planning to serenade various government dignitaries, including Secretary of War Edwin Stanton.

The sun had set by the time Mary and Weichmann came upon the city in all its animation. Its bright aura of celebration prompted Mary to remark, "I am afraid all this rejoicing will be turned into mourning, and all this glory into sadness."[38] Weichmann later swore she also remarked that "after sunshine there was always a storm, and that the people were too proud and licentious, and that God would punish them."[39] As they entered the city, they heard music and caught a glimpse of the parade of Arsenal employees marching up Seventh Street to Pennsylvania Avenue.

Weichmann dropped Mary off at about eight-thirty, returning the horse and buggy to the stable around the corner before making his way back to the house, where he joined Mary for a late supper. While eating together in the dining room on the ground floor, they heard footsteps quickly climbing the front steps to the second floor main entrance. Weichmann assumed it was the unnamed man Mary was expecting at nine o'clock, and asked her if she would like him to answer the door.

"No," she wearily replied, climbing the stairs to the main hallway above. Weichmann heard the front door open and footsteps move into the parlor directly above him. The visitor stayed but a few minutes, Weichmann later testified, leaving as he came, down the front steps and into the night. Booth had possibly made his third and final visit that day.[40]

Eliza Holohan had been waiting for Mary to return from Surrattsville to attend Good Friday church services. About a quarter past nine, Mary agreed to go to church, even though services had been going on for nearly two hours already. Mary "took her bonnet and shawl and put them on," Eliza noted, and the two women proceeded down the street. They had only walked a short distance, passing two neighboring houses, when they decided to return home. The women paused at the top of the stairs for several minutes before going back inside, Eliza noting that a slight warm drizzle had made for a "heavy, disagreeable night."[41]

Richard Smoot returned to Mary's boardinghouse to see John at about nine-thirty that evening. When he arrived there, he noticed a woman standing on the porch, her face hidden by a "huge sunbonnet." As he started to ascend the stairs, the woman quickly moved inside the open door, abruptly turning around asking "who is it?" After identifying himself, Smoot inquired if John had returned. Mary said no, but she was sure that the boat would be used that night, and that he would get his money "in a day or two." Mary was in a "state of feverish excitement," Smoot claimed. She rushed him out of the doorway, telling him to "leave the city and not be seen at her house again."

Smoot became alarmed; he felt that something significant was in motion and he did not want to be caught in the middle of it. Trying to get out of the city at that late hour was a problem, as the last public coach over the Long Bridge and into Southern Maryland left at ten o'clock. Racing to get to the bridge, he arrived too late. Determined to get out of the city, he decided to walk to Alexandria and spend the night in a hotel, and catch the morning stage to Southern Maryland.[42]

Weichmann came upstairs and joined Mary, Anna, Eliza, and Nora, who were already settled into the parlor. Mary appeared to be agitated and irritable. When asked what was wrong, Mary said she "was very nervous and did not feel well." She then asked Weichmann which way the Arsenal "torchlight procession" was marching. To the White House, he replied, to "serenade the President." Weichmann later claimed he was unaware that the President would be at Ford's Theatre that night.

Then, unexpectedly, Mary asked Weichmann to pray for her intentions. In Catholicism, fellow practitioners are sometimes called upon to pray for each other's "intentions"—that is, to pray for what one had done or is planning to do, pray that it is the correct path and not for one's own glorification but for the glory of God. Weichmann asked her what her intentions were, but she would not say, only asking him again to pray for her. Weichmann found it difficult to fulfill her appeal because she remained so elusive. Later he would reflect upon this request and wonder if her "intentions" involved her role in Booth's plans.[43]

Weichmann, Anna, Olivia, and Nora were teasing each other, laughing, and "having a good deal of fun" in the parlor. Mary became increasingly tense, made worse by the playful bantering between Weichmann and the girls. Finally, she scolded them and sent them fleeing to their rooms for the night.

A few short blocks away, the President, Mrs. Lincoln, and their guests were enjoying *Our American Cousin* at Ford's Theatre. General Grant and his wife, Julia, had declined the Lincolns' invitation at the last moment, deciding, instead, to travel to Burlington, New Jersey, to celebrate the end of the war with their children. In their place, the Lincolns invited a young couple, Miss Clara Harris and her fiancé, Major Henry Rathbone.

The foursome had arrived late to the theater, but had settled in comfortably and were laughing at the play, when, suddenly, a crazed John Wilkes Booth burst into their private box and shot President Lincoln in the head at point-blank range. In the scuffle that ensued, Booth stabbed Major Rathbone, deeply cutting his arm. Leaping onto the edge of the box, Booth raised his dagger and yelled to the audience below, "Sic semper tyrannis!" (Ever thus to the tyrants!) before jumping to the stage. In the midst of his dramatic leap to the lighted floor, Booth caught one of his spurs on the festive red-white-and-blue swags adorning the President's box, upsetting his balance. When he landed on the stage floor, he twisted his leg and broke it. In his wild state, however, the injury failed to slow him down. Facing a stunned crowd that was too confused to act quickly, Booth's escape from the theater was surprisingly swift and unimpeded.

Booth jumped on his waiting horse and raced to the drawbridge over the Eastern Branch of the Potomac, on the road out of the city, where he met his accomplice David Herold. They conned the guard—who had orders to prevent any crossings after nine o'clock at night—into letting them pass, and off they rode to Surrattsville.[44]

Across the city, Lewis Payne was knocking on the door of William H. Seward's home. Seward, who had recently been severely injured in a carriage accident, was recuperating at home. William Bell, Seward's servant, answered the door. Pretending to be a messenger from Seward's physician, Dr. Verdi, Payne told Bell that he was there to deliver medicine to Seward on Verdi's orders. Bell was insistent that he could not see Seward, but Payne pushed his way upstairs. Frederick, Seward's son, intervened outside of his father's bedroom door. Payne attacked him brutally, beating him nearly to death with the butt of the pistol.

The commotion aroused other members of the household. Payne rushed into Seward's room, where daughter Fanny and army private Foster Robinson were caring for Seward. Payne lunged at Robinson, slashing and stabbing him in and around his head, leaving him immobilized. Payne looked past Fanny and focused on his primary victim, Secretary of State Seward. Payne tore at Seward's flesh with a knife, leaving gaping and near-fatal wounds about Seward's head and neck. As other members of the household came rushing to Seward's room,

Payne fled, attacking Augustus Seward, another son, and Emrick Hansell, a State Department employee, on his way out of the house. The confusion and serious wounds Payne inflicted on nearly everyone in the house enabled him to quickly and easily get away. He left confident that he had successfully carried out his violent part in Booth's murderous plot.[45]

Between two-thirty and three o'clock in the morning, Weichmann took a trip to the outhouse in the backyard. Upon returning to his room, he was startled by the ringing of the front doorbell. Jumping into his pants and leaving his shirt wide open, he stumbled to the door.

"Who is there?" he called out.

Detective James McDevitt from the Metropolitan Police answered loudly, "Detectives, come to search the house for John Wilkes Booth and John Surratt."[46]

"They are not here," Weichmann replied.

"Let us in anyhow," McDevitt ordered.

Weichmann rushed to Mary's room. "Here, Mrs. Surratt, are detectives who have come to search the house."

"For God's sake! Let them come in. I expected the house to be searched," she answered mysteriously from the other side of her door.

McDevitt entered the house, accompanied by four colleagues: Lieutenant Skippon and detectives John Clarvoe, David Bigley, and John F. Kelley. Weichmann, still in his stocking feet, led them into the parlor, but the men immediately spread out through the house, searching for Booth and Surratt.

Several officers accompanied Weichmann to his room. They looked in his closet, under the bed, and in the hall. Weichmann demanded to know why they were looking for Booth and John.

"Do you pretend to tell me you do not know what happened last night?" one of them asked.

Weichmann said he had no idea what they were talking about.

Detective Clarvoe seemed shocked that Weichmann had not heard the news.

"I will tell you," Clarvoe said to Weichmann, drawing a bloody necktie from his pocket. "Do you see that blood? That is Abraham Lincoln's blood. John Wilkes Booth has murdered Abraham Lincoln and John Surratt has assassinated the Secretary of State."[47] At that moment, the police were unaware that Seward had survived the attack and that the assassin was Payne, not Surratt.

Weichmann was stunned. Clarvoe asked Weichmann if he had been in the house all night. No, he said, he had been in Surrattsville with Mrs. Surratt and had arrived home at about eight-thirty that evening. Suddenly, it was all becoming clear to him.

"Great God," a visibly shaken Weichmann exclaimed. "I see it all! I see it all now!"[48] The many visits and secret meetings, the weapons, strange men coming in and out of the house, fake mustaches, and all the other seemingly innocuous details now confirmed far more than his worst suspicions. Booth had been planning to murder the President!

The officers then moved to search the Holohans' rooms. Clarvoe and McDevitt explained why they were there, showing John Holohan the bloody tie as proof of their words. Holohan, too, was shocked. The officers found nothing in those two rooms and moved on to the fourth floor attic rooms, where Anna and her cousin Olivia were sleeping. Holohan tagged along behind the officers as they searched more of the house, still disbelieving this was all happening.[49]

Weichmann followed the detectives down to the second floor, where they began to interrogate Mrs. Surratt. Standing in the doorway to her room, Mary had quickly and privately changed her clothing while the officers were searching the rest of the house, a detail Clarvoe noted and later testified to. While Clarvoe spoke briefly to Detective McDevitt, Weichmann approached Mary.

"What do you think, Mrs. Surratt?" he asked her. "President Lincoln has been murdered by John Wilkes Booth, and the Secretary of State has been assassinated!" Weichmann left out her son's name to spare her feelings at that moment, or so he later said.

Mary appeared to be shocked by the news.

Detective Clarvoe turned his attention back to Mary.

"Mrs. Surratt, I want to ask you a couple of questions; and be particular how you answer them, for there is a great deal that depends on them. When did you last see John Wilkes Booth?"

She had seen him at two o'clock that day, she told them.

"When did you see your son John last, and where is he?" Clarvoe demanded.

She told the officer that she had not seen her son for two weeks; she suspected he was in Canada, having received a letter from him on the fourteenth, postmarked in Montreal on the twelfth. When asked to produce the letter, Mary claimed she could not find it.

Mary was becoming defensive and irritated. She demanded to know what was going on, and she reminded the officers that there were "a great many mothers who had no idea where their sons were."[50]

Having received a packet of letters from John's on-and-off girlfriend, Anna Ward, a little over twelve hours before, it seems incredible that Mary, the mother so devoted to her son and so concerned about his whereabouts and well-being, would misplace his most recent correspondence. What was she hiding?

Unable to find Booth, John Surratt, or any other suspicious characters at the H Street house, the police left. Anna, by now nearly hysterical, screamed out, "Oh, Ma! Just think of it, that man [John Wilkes Booth] having been here in this house before the assassination! I am afraid it will bring suspicion upon us!"

"Anna, come what will," Mary coolly responded, "I am resigned. I think J. Wilkes Booth was only an instrument in the hands of the Almighty to punish this proud and licentious people."[51]

Weichmann could not sleep the rest of the night. What had Booth done? What had they all done? Was his friend John really a murderer? He lay awake, replaying the last few months' events—the secret conversations and meetings, the strange and unsavory characters visiting and staying at the house, John's frequent absences from the city, the unaccounted-for gold pieces, and, most disconcerting, Booth's frequent presence at the Surratt house.

Weichmann became convinced, in those early dawn hours, that John Surratt could not have committed the attack on Seward. After all, he had seen the letter from John to his mother the day before—even if he hadn't read it. It was strange, Weichmann thought, that Mary was unable to produce it and provide proof that her son could not have participated in the violent events of the day.

By five o'clock in the morning, restless, afraid, confused, and anxious, Weichmann dressed and hurried around the corner to Howard's Stables on G Street. There, he discussed his suspicions with Brooke Stabler. By then, Weichmann had become convinced that Atzerodt was Seward's attacker, not Surratt. An odd and rough sort of character, Atzerodt fit Weichmann's image of a brutal assassin.

On his way back to the boardinghouse, Weichmann ran into John Holohan. Holohan confided that he, too, was suspicious of what had been happening in the house over the past few months. The two agreed to find McDevitt at the police department and reveal their suspicions.

Weichmann and Holohan returned to the boardinghouse and took their breakfast, catching up on the latest assassination details in the early edition newspapers. Weichmann was greatly relieved to learn that Seward's assailant was a much larger man than John Surratt. But this fact did not disentangle John from this fatal event. John's intimacy with Lincoln's assassin still raised serious questions in Weichmann's mind. What did John know about Booth's plans?

As the rest of the household joined them, breakfast that morning was tense and somber. Weichmann told Mary and the others that he was going directly to police headquarters to tell them all he knew, although he was not yet clear about what exactly he did know. There likely would be a more thorough investigation of the house and its residents, Weichmann told Mrs. Surratt and the other guests.

Anna told Weichmann to stop talking. As far as she was concerned, Lincoln was "no worse than . . . the meanest nigger in the army."

Weichmann later claimed he told her, "She would soon find out differently."[52]

CHAPTER SIX

A SHREWD WITNESS

Early eyewitness testimony and various pieces of evidence gathered since the night of the assassination clearly linked Booth and his associates to the Surratt residence on H Street. Uncoordinated investigations between the two centers of law enforcement, the Union army and the Washington Metropolitan Police department, prevented early organization of data and hampered effective coordination and analysis of evidence. But both agencies simultaneously recognized a definite pattern linking the events of April 14 with John Surratt, Jr. And both already had files on Surratt, who had long been the subject of local and federal scrutiny because of his rebel courier activities.[1]

Secretary of War Edwin Stanton was in charge of monitoring and coordinating all aspects of the investigation into Lincoln's murder and Seward's attack. The frantic pursuit of Booth and his accomplices by different agencies conducting the searches plagued Stanton's efforts from the beginning, a problem that would later generate great criticism against him.

Disorganization and competition between the district police and the army caused significant delays on several fronts, resulting in a waste of precious time and potential loss of evidence. The house at H Street was not searched thoroughly the early morning hours on April 15 after the

assassination; the officers raiding the house were looking for Booth
and John Surratt, not material evidence. By the seventeenth, however,
the importance of the boardinghouse to Booth and his associates was
becoming more obvious, but the delay gave Mary almost three full
days to hide or destroy evidence and anticipate more intensive questioning by the authorities.

The great volume of evidence related to Booth's plot, gleaned from
early interrogations, casual comments, and secret tips from informants,
would lead authorities to quickly arrest five of the eight people who
would be tried within a month for conspiring with Booth to kill Lincoln and other members of his cabinet. Some of this initial information
would become important evidence against Mary; the rest would seal
the fates of the others.

Some evidence was uncovered through hard, professional detective
work, and some simply through dumb luck and good timing—two
blessings Mary did not have. Misfortune and bad timing, in combina-
tion with deception and obfuscation, would shadow her for the rest of
her short life.

An early eyewitness statement taken by federal authorities in Washington is one example of the luck authorities would encounter during
the earliest stages of their investigation. Susan Ann Mahoney Jackson,
a newly hired live-in servant at the Surratt house, gave erroneous testimony to Provost Marshall Henry H. Wells, commander of an army in-
vestigative unit charged with probing the assassination and tracking
down Booth. Out of fear, confusion, or a misunderstanding, Jackson
mistakenly claimed that three mysterious men had come to the house
after the assassination. She said they had spoken to Mrs. Surratt, whispered about John Jr. being at the theater with Booth, and then disappeared in a buggy after one of the men had changed his clothes.
Unfortunately for Mary Surratt, Jackson was mistaken.

Jackson had been living and working in the house about two weeks
when the assassination occurred. At that time, she was unfamiliar with
most of the characters involved in the plot and did not understand the

meanings of conversations she heard that day. In this instance, however, Jackson's incorrect statement guided the government to suspect not only John Surratt, but his mother as well. Therefore, the government's chance raid on the H Street home netted them far more than they could have imagined or hoped for in their quest to uncover Booth's plot and seize the guilty parties.

The three men Susan Jackson had heard at the Surratt house after the assassination were Weichmann, Holohan, and Metro Police officer James McDevitt, who had come to the house late Saturday morning after Weichmann had made a confession and given his own testimony to the Washington, D.C., police. Weichmann had given a long statement to the authorities outlining Booth's activities, as he understood them, over the past few months. In it, he identified several of Booth's accomplices: David Herold, George Atzerodt, Lewis Payne, Dr. Samuel Mudd, and John Surratt. At the time he was not willing to accept the idea that Mary, too, was an accomplice. His affidavits and interviews reveal that he did recognize that her welcoming Booth into their home was unfortunate and had disrupted their normally pleasant home life. But it would be some time before Weichmann began to connect the series of events that would ultimately expose Mary as one of Booth's important fellow conspirators.

Susan Jackson should have recognized Weichmann and Holohan when they came to the house, but the chaos of the investigation and the intensity of emotions surrounding the interrogations may have completely confused her memory. She may have met John Jr. once and the accomplices briefly, if at all. If what the authorities were telling her about John and his friends was true, then she must have been quite concerned about whom to trust. Everyone in that house, then, could be an accomplice, for all she knew. Colonel Wells was completely unaware of Weichmann's own statements to the local police, which would have shed a different light on Mary's statements and perhaps shifted his priorities away from the Surratt household, if only temporarily. A delay of even a day might have saved Mary's life.

When Weichmann, Holohan, and McDevitt left the boardinghouse, they started swiftly for Surrattsville. McDevitt hoped to interrogate John Lloyd and others in Surrattsville, Bryantown, and surroundings in order to uncover the whereabouts of Booth, Herold, and their supporters. Weichmann's and Holohan's testimonies jump-started the quick arrests of some of the accomplices, particularly Atzerodt. Later in the week—after being diverted and lied to by Lloyd—Weichmann, Holohan, and McDevitt headed for Baltimore, then New York and Canada, in pursuit of John Surratt.

On Monday the seventeenth, Colonel H. H. Wells, based on Jackson's testimony and other evidence pointing to John Surratt as Booth's main accomplice, commanded a detail of armed guards and officers to the boardinghouse with orders to arrest Mrs. Surratt and anyone else who was in the house with her. This was no fishing expedition; several of Wells's men surrounded the house to prevent any possible escape attempts.

Shortly before eleven o'clock in the evening, with guards in place, Eli Devore and five officers climbed the front stairs and knocked on the door.

From behind a closed curtain hanging in an open window by the door, the officers heard Mary cautiously inquire, "Is that you, Mr. Kirby?"

"No, Madam," Devore responded. "I want this door opened."[2]

Another officer noted Kirby's name.

Mary opened the door to the officers, who, upon entering the dimly lit hall, inquired if she was Mrs. Surratt. Calmly identifying herself as the widow of John H. Surratt, Sr., and the mother of John H. Surratt, Jr., Mary appeared neither surprised nor concerned that officers had come to her home so late at night.

Major H. W. Smith noted Mary's exceedingly calm countenance; it was as if she had been expecting them. She showed them into the parlor where Anna, Nora, and Olivia were sitting. Smith inquired as to who the young women were, and Mary introduced them. Other officers moved about the rooms, searching for anyone else who might be in the house. Smith turned to the women and told them that he was there to bring them to General Christopher C. Augur's office for interrogation. Augur was the Union commander of the Department of Washington at the time. As the officers rounded up the rest of the boardinghouse residents, Major Smith observed that not everyone shared Mary's cool demeanor. Anna Surratt was particularly surprised and upset by the late-night intrusion and the armed guards searching the house.

There were few people left in the house by that night: the Holohans had quickly moved out the day before, leaving the women and two African-American servants, Susan Mahoney Jackson and her fiancé, behind. When Smith announced, again, that he was there to arrest them all, Anna became visibly emotional, sobbing, "Oh, Mother! Think of being taken down there for such a crime!"

Mary scolded Anna for her lack of control, then wrapped her arms around her daughter's neck. Her inaudible whispers into Anna's ear ended the young woman's emotional outburst.[3] This surprised Smith, who also noted that Mary never asked why they were all being arrested.[4]

Major Smith called for a carriage to take the women to Augur's headquarters for questioning. Smith suggested to Mary that, given the damp and drizzling night, they might need additional clothing for the ride. As Mary moved to retrieve shawls and hats, Smith stopped her, reminding her that the house was "under suspicion" and that he must accompany her wherever she went in the house. While Smith followed Mary into the bedrooms, Detective John Clarvoe guarded the other three women in the parlor to "see that no papers were destroyed and that no communication passed between the ladies." In the meantime, two additional detectives, Richard Morgan and a man named Samson, arrived to assist Smith.

While the women sat in the parlor, the officers carefully searched every room in the house, taking time to record details and collect possible evidence. Believing that the residents may have been in league with Booth, the guards looked at everything with suspicion.

Captain W. M. Wermerskirch searched Mary's room, finding a bullet mold and percussion caps, which are used to ignite gunpowder in the barrel of a gun to fire off the ball. These were odd items for the mistress of a boardinghouse to have in her room, Wermerskirch thought. Miscellaneous papers, letters, lithographs, and *cartes-de-visite* of mostly Confederate generals were found about the house, singly and in albums. One *carte-de-visite* bore the Confederate flag, along with the inscription, "Thus will it ever be with Tyrants, Virginia the Mighty, *Sic Semper Tyrannis*," the same Latin words that Booth had called out as he jumped from the presidential box at Ford's Theatre.

Raising everyone's suspicions, however, was another item that had been almost completely overlooked. A framed picture called *Morning, Noon, and Night,* popular at the time and given to Anna by Louis Weichmann for her birthday, sat upon the mantle in Mary's room. At first it was left unnoticed and untouched by the officers, but one young policeman, Lieutenant John W. Dempsey, inadvertently noticed that a piece had been torn off the back. Looking closer, he realized there was something secreted inside. It was a photograph of John Wilkes Booth.

As Anna, Nora, and Olivia waited for the carriage to arrive, Mary turned to Smith and asked him if she could kneel and pray. Smith saw no problem with her request, and Mary knelt to the floor. Just then, the sound of footsteps ascending the front steps caught the attention of Smith and the other officers. Wermerskirch and Morgan crept up behind the door with their pistols drawn. Smith, with his hand on his own belted gun, waited in the hall. He fully anticipated meeting the "Mr. Kirby" Mary was expecting when the officers had first arrived.[5] Morgan and Wermerskirch opened the door upon the first knock, exposing Smith to the unknown guest. That "peculiar knock," the *Baltimore Clipper* eagerly reported later in the week, would be the beginning of the unraveling of Booth's plot and Mary's fatal path to the gallows.

A tall, muscular, grimy man with a pickax resting on his shoulder stood in the entryway. He seemed surprised when greeted at the door by Smith, pistol in hand.

"I guess I am mistaken," the man said, as the door unexpectedly shut behind him, trapping him in the hallway between Smith, Morgan, and Wermerskirch.

"Whom do you want to see?" Morgan asked, tightening his grip on his revolver.

"Mrs. Surratt."

"Then you are right; walk in."

The unknown man was dressed in a dark grey coat, dark pants, and a cap fashioned from the sleeve of a shirt. He was "full of mud, up to his knees, nearly," Wermerskirch noted. What the officers were unaware of was that the man was Lewis Payne. Authorities were still under the assumption that John Surratt had been Seward's attacker, and were unaware of the additional accomplices and their roles in the assassination plot.[6]

After brutally stabbing and beating Seward and Seward's two sons, Payne had fled into the night on his own; Herold had abandoned him to fend for himself. During that night, Payne skulked around the city, trying to find a way out. All the bridges and roads were shut down because of curfew and then, later, all exits from the city were blocked in an attempt to prevent the escape of Lincoln's assassin. In his wanderings, Payne found an abandoned coat, a suitable replacement for his conspicuous, blood-spattered one. He had lost his treasured expensive beaver hat during his attack, so he cut the sleeve from his undershirt and wrapped it tight around his head. For the next two days, he hid in Glenwood Cemetery, about a mile and a half northwest of the Surratt boardinghouse.

During the late-night hours of April 17, the cold, hungry, and desperate Payne made the fateful decision to seek help from Mary Surratt.

Unwilling to spend another night in the damp cemetery, he grabbed a pickax from the grave diggers' shed and made his way to the H Street residence he was so familiar with and where he had found shelter before. In an example of astonishing poor timing, Payne found himself confronted at Mary's door by federal authorities who had just begun their search of Mary's house and were questioning all its residents.[7]

Recognizing the incriminating position he had just put himself and Mary in, Payne claimed to be a common laborer hired to dig a ditch for Surratt the following morning. Richard Morgan later testified that Payne's odd conduct and appearance raised further suspicions. Morgan continued his interrogation of Payne in the hallway:

> I asked him when [did Mrs. Surratt send for him]. He said, "In the morning." I asked him where he last worked. He said, "Sometimes on I Street." I asked him where he boarded. He said he had no boarding house; he was a poor man who got his living with the pick. I put my hand on his pick-ax while taking to him. Said I, "Have you any money?" "Not a cent," he replied . . . I asked him why he came at this time of night to go to work. He said he simply called to find out what time he should go to work in the morning. I asked him if he had any previous acquaintance with Mrs. Surratt. He said, "No."[8]

Morgan asked where Payne was from and how old he was. Payne admitted he was about twenty, but lied about his identity. He claimed to be Lewis Payne from Virginia, showing Morgan his signed oath of allegiance. When Morgan told Payne he would have to go to General Augur's office for further questioning by Colonel Wells, Payne flinched.

Payne's story, poorly concocted and unconvincing, only deepened doubts about Mary. Smith, who had returned Mrs. Surratt to the parlor and had joined Morgan in his questioning of Payne, asked Mary to come to the hallway.

"Do you know this man, and did you hire him to come and dig a gutter for you?"

Standing within three feet of Payne, Mary swore she did not know him. Raising her right hand in an overly theatrical fashion, she said, "Before God, sir, I do not know this man, and have never seen him, and I did not hire him to dig a gutter for me."

Payne was promptly arrested.

Upon arriving at the general's headquarters a little after midnight, Mary was taken in for questioning immediately. Payne arrived there shortly afterward. Anna, Nora, and Olivia were seated with Payne to await their interviews with Augur's staff.

Colonel Henry Wells began questioning Mary. Her answers show a defiant and arrogant woman, obviously trying to protect herself, her son and daughter, Booth, and the other conspirators as well. Who would have expected that it would be a woman who would refuse to inform on the other conspirators? She'd had three days since the night of the assassination, when officers first came to her door to question her, to prepare herself for this questioning. No doubt she had decided that deception and obfuscation would be the best defense, and would perhaps buy her time. Her testimony under hostile interrogation reveals a woman initially in control.

At the start of her examination, Mary seemed confident and prepared. Admitting freely that Booth had become a frequent visitor to the H Street home, she remarked that "sometimes he called twice a day." She was not surprised her son had become friends with Booth, proudly noting that she considered her son "a country-bred young gentleman . . . capable of forming acquaintances in the best society," a testament to the status Booth could claim as a famous actor. She also admitted, rather indiscriminately, that Booth "called frequently when my son was not there."[9]

When asked why she thought her son and Booth had become friends, especially in light of the assassination, she claimed she did not know what the attraction was, and that she was as shocked by Booth's attack as anyone. She claimed that Booth never discussed politics, but in light of contrary testimony given during the conspirators' trial, this seems highly unlikely. Everyone who knew Booth knew his strong pro-South and anti-Lincoln stance. He hid these feelings from no one. In the initial interrogations, Mary also moderated her own pro-Confederate views, telling her examiners she believed the "South acted too hastily."

The interrogators were anxious to discover where John Surratt was. At that time, they were still working under the assumption that John had been in the city on the fourteenth and had participated in the assassination scheme through the attack on Seward. As Mary was being interrogated, Payne was about to be identified by Seward's servant, William Bell, as Seward's attacker. At that moment, however, Mary may have been unsure herself: she had not seen John since April 3, and though she had received a letter from him dated April 12 and supposedly sent from Montreal, she could not be sure of his whereabouts since then.

The letter had been lost, Mary told the interrogators. It may have flown out the window when she tossed it aside in expression of her grief at her son's indefinite absence. John had not paid the fifty-dollar draft exemption fee to keep him out of the Union army, and Mary was worried that would get him into trouble, she claimed. Weichmann later testified that the letter had been delivered by John's sometimes girlfriend, Anna Ward, and that Mrs. Surratt had read the letter to guests at the noon dinner table on the fourteenth, editing what she revealed as she read the letter aloud. Perhaps she had destroyed the letter deliberately because it contained secret correspondence, messages, or directions for her to follow. Anna Ward had left several letters with Mary that night, but in their search of the house, investigators found none of Mary's correspondence. Years later, a family rented the H Street house and became bothered by a squeaky floorboard located in the closet of one of the rooms. A carpenter called in to repair the board discovered it covered a stash of letters. According to oral tradition, the mother of the family, after looking at the letters, burned them, remarking that there had already been too much misfortune and misery in that house. Whether this story is real or another one of the many conspiracy myths surrounding this intriguing tale may never be known.[10]

Mary revealed to the investigators that on the evening of April 3, the last time she had seen John, he had two gold pieces in his pocket, which he was hoping, he told her, to exchange for "greenbacks," or currency. John Holohan, the boarder, exchanged the gold for him, after which John Surratt left for Canada.

"No man on the round earth believes he went to Canada," the interrogator told her.

"I believe it," Mary retorted.

The examiners already knew John Surratt had more than two gold pieces. Holohan had told them that Surratt had approached him about exchanging two hundred dollars in gold—ten pieces in all—but that Holohan could only exchange two.

Why would John need so much cash? To travel to Canada, or to return to the South, "as he did, and as he had been and back before," they suggested to Mary. The interrogator pursued this line relentlessly, but Mary denied her son ever went "South."

"He has never been away long enough to go South and back," she claimed.

They knew she was lying.

"How long does it take to go across the river?" the detective asked her, trying a different tactic to get her to admit that John made trips back and forth to Virginia.

"I don't know the width of the river," Mary carefully replied.

"How wide do you suppose it is?"

"It varies, I suppose, but I never crossed it except at Alexandria."

"Do you know how wide the Potomac is at Fairfax?" The detective wasn't getting anywhere with his line of questioning.

"I do not know. I was never there." Mary was probably telling the truth.

"It would take a great while to go there," the detective told her.

The interrogators were hoping to trap Mary in a lie, and they were slowly forcing her into a corner.

"You certainly could go to Fredericksburg and back in four days, to Richmond and back in a week," they informed her, "and your son had been passing a great many times for a great while longer than that."

Mary wavered. "I don't think he has," she replied.

"Oh, yes he has. Have I made any error in my record so far as his movements are concerned?"

"No, Sir; that is all correct." A little admission, but Mary would give little more.

They asked her about Atzerodt. She admitted to knowing him as "Port Tobacco"; that he had been allowed to stay at her boardinghouse briefly until she discovered alcohol in his room and threw him out. She was evasive about how often she had seen Atzerodt at her house afterward. She also denied that John remained friendly with him, saying that they were not "associates." Anna Surratt, interrogated eleven days later, would reveal a more intimate friendship, locking Mary in another lie.[11] Atzerodt's own admissions would seal her fate.

The examiners next questioned Mary about David Herold.

"What was the name of the other young man?" they asked.

Mary was confused and assumed they were questioning her about Payne, who had so foolishly come to her home that night, casting serious suspicions on the Surratt household.

"I think his name was Wood."

She should have stopped there, but perhaps realizing her mistake, continued: "There were some two or three, one was light complected who staid about a week."

"What was his name?"

"Indeed I don't remember it." She was falling into another trap.

"There was a young gentleman who used to meet your son, whose mother lives over the Navy Yard Bridge. David or Daniel Herold?" they asked, prodding her.

"No such man visited my house, I assure you."

Producing a photograph of Herold, the investigators prodded her again, but she denied knowing the man pictured. Another lie.

"He is a very intimate friend of your son's," they chided her.

"Well, Sir: I assure you he is not a visitor to our house, on the honor of a lady," she snapped back. Another lie. Mary had seen Herold at her home in Washington as well as the tavern in Surrattsville.

Wells changed his line of questioning back to the three men Susan Jackson had mistakenly identified as coming to the house on Saturday morning and meeting privately with Mrs. Surratt.

"I will be happy to have you give me the names of the three men who came to you on Saturday and had a private conversation with you."

Mary seemed puzzled. "Last Saturday?"

"Yes, Madame."

"No three gentlemen came to my house, I assure you."

"How many did come?"

Mary was still puzzled. "You mean the men who came in and searched the house?"

"No, you know who I mean," Wells insisted.

"I pledge you my word of honor that only one gentleman came there except Mr. Kirby. Father [illegible], I think was in there to the best of my knowledge; and I don't know if Mr. Kirby was there on Saturday."

Mary, still on guard, was clearly trying to figure out whom Wells was asking about without falling for a trick or revealing any other information.

"I mean the three men," Wells asked again, "who came to your house and you had a private conversation with them, and supposed you were alone, but you were not?"

"Last Saturday?"

"Perhaps Friday. Now . . . I want you to tell me."

"Upon my word, that I do not know," Mary asserted, clearly getting frustrated. "Upon the honor of a lady, I do not remember anybody except Mr. Wicket [Weichmann]."[12]

Still believing Jackson's testimony was accurate, Wells kept pushing Mary for an explanation. Mary, on the other hand, was truly confused but increasingly wary and concerned about what Wells was trying to get her to admit to. She had things to hide, and was no doubt fearful of revealing anything, especially since she was unclear as to what Wells already knew. She had to be careful of any entrapment.

Wells became exasperated. He was getting nowhere. After asking Mary again and again about the three men, he may have started to realize that there might have been some sort of misunderstanding. But he still thought Mary was hiding something. Softening his approach, Wells took a different tact.

"I don't know but I have misunderstood you. Do you say to me that no two or three or four men ever came to your house the last three or four days on Friday, Saturday, or Sunday?"

The comings and goings at the boardinghouse over the past three days must have been racing through Mary's mind. Then she remembered.

"On Sunday I think three or four men came there while I was at church. I assure you on the honor of a lady that I would not tell you an untruth."

Wells was getting more frustrated and tired. He had barely slept the past three nights, and now, in these early morning hours, he must have felt he was on the verge of some important discovery. His prime witness, however, was cleverly avoiding the truth, a truth that Wells was wholly ignorant of because it was based on the misunderstanding of a frightened and confused servant girl.

"I assure you, on the honor of a gentleman, I shall get this information from you. . . . I know they were there!" Wells exclaimed, losing his temper. Then he decided to reveal a little more of what he knew. "I mean men who called at your house and wanted to change their clothes?"

Mary seemed to understand more clearly, now, what Wells was getting at.

"Mr. Wickman [Weichmann] and Mr. Holohan and one of the detectives came there; that might have been Sunday morning—they came in a carriage—that was, I think, on Sunday morning. Mr. Wickman went to his room and changed his clothes . . . they went up to Mr. Wickman's room."

Mary had finally identified the men Wells was looking for, but they both still misunderstood the purpose of Weichmann's visit to the house that Saturday, not Sunday, morning.

Wells thought they were finally getting somewhere. "What did you say to them?"

"Nothing except to say good morning or something of the kind."

"Will you tell me, in the presence of Almighty God, who first mentioned the name of Mr. Booth to that party?"

Wells was reenergized; he was getting somewhere, or so he seemed to have thought.

"I don't remember," Mary replied obstinately. Now understanding that they were perhaps talking of the same group of men, what would Mary have to gain keeping her conversation with Weichmann and Holohan secret?

"Indeed you do; I pledge you my word you do, and you will admit it, and I should be very glad if you would do it at once!" Wells was working himself up again.

"If I could, I would do so."

Wells paused. "Reflect a moment, and I will send for a glass of water for you." Another officer brought a glass of water for Mary. Everyone settled down a bit.

"Now, will you be kind enough to state who first made the remark in relation to Booth?"

Mary certainly knew what Wells was getting at. Weichmann, Holohan, and McDevitt had come to the house Saturday morning after Weichmann and Holohan had been questioned by the police. Weichmann had asked Mary for a photograph of John, which she had provided willingly. After all, it showed that John Surratt could not have been Seward's attacker on the night of Lincoln's assassination. John bore no resemblance to the then-unidentified man, who was described by members of Seward's household as tall, dark, and muscular. By Saturday morning, Booth was the prime suspect as Lincoln's murderer and everyone in the house knew it. So it seems inconceivable that Booth's name would not have been mentioned by Weichmann or Holohan in their conversation with Mary. She also knew by then that John was a suspect as well. But she denied it.

"I don't remember that his name was mentioned."

Wells pushed, hard. Mary backed down.

"Well, I don't remember that Booth's name was mentioned. I think to the best of my knowledge the conversation that took place was this. These gentlemen came in and asked how I felt." Weichmann and Holohan were likely concerned for Mary's well-being given the news that John was considered one of the assailants and a Booth associate. "I told them I felt as well as I could expect to feel," she acknowledged. "Then something was said in relation to my son."

Wells was pleased. "That is getting near it . . . I want to know if you believe what was said about your son being in the theatre with Booth."

"There was nothing said about his being in the theatre with Booth."

"No, what I ask of you is, whether you think your son was there with Booth?"

"No, Sir, I do not believe he was there, if it was the last word I had to speak."

Wells did not believe her, and reworded his question. "I want to know what answer you made when the remark was made there?"

Mary must have begun to suspect Weichmann and Holohan as informants. Both had left with a detective on the morning after the assassination and had not returned to the H Street house since. Where had they been? Her thoughts must have been racing. How can she protect her son, the others, and herself, not knowing what information Wells may have collected from Weichmann and others?

"If it was made," she carefully admitted, "I pledge you my word of honor I did not hear it, because before I finished answering, Mr. Wickman stepped in and said, 'I am ready now.' They were waiting for Mr. Wickman: they bid me good morning and walked out. If I remember it, I assure you, if I heard it, I would tell you."

Would she have? The men must have asked Mary something about John and Booth, because her next response seems puzzling.

"I was too much hurt; you can imagine a mother's feelings to hear such a thing from the face of one she did not expect."

From whose "face"? Weichmann testified that he had asked for a photo of John to give to authorities. He must have told Mary why they needed it—but for some reason she would not reveal the exact conversation. Hearing that her son was a suspect and sought by the authorities for the near-fatal assault on Seward and his son undoubtedly upset Mary. She must have felt an uneasy fear and betrayal.

She told Wells that William Kirby had been there at the time, and that Wells would have to talk with Kirby.

The interrogation turned to other avenues. A letter signed "Kate" was shown to Mary, who claimed her bad eyesight prevented her from clearly reading it. She denied any knowledge of the letter or the mysterious Kate.[13] If she knew that the letter was from Sarah Slater, using her sometimes alias "Kate Thompson," she did not reveal it. However, she did recognize and acknowledge a photograph of Booth. Interestingly, she could see this photograph easily, but would later claim poor eyesight prevented her from sewing or reading letters, and recognizing people, near and far, at any time of the day.

Then interrogators circled back around to Payne, who was now being interrogated in another part of the headquarters.

"Did you meet this young man arrested this evening within two or three days and make arrangement with him to come to your home this evening?"

"No, Sir," Mary asserted, "the ruffian that was in my door when I came away? He was a tremendous hard fellow with a skull cap on, and my daughter commenced crying, and said these gentlemen came to save our lives. I hope they arrested him."

Mary was still unaware that Payne had been arrested, and further implicated herself by denying she knew him.

"He tells me that he met you in the street and you engaged him to come to your home."

"Oh! Oh! It is not so, Sir; for I believe he would have murdered us everyone, I assure you."

Payne could have killed them, of course, but that was not his intention.

"He had some kind of weapon," she offered in defense.

"When did you first see him?"

"Just as the carriage drew up, he rang the door bell, and my daughter said, 'Oh! There is a murderer!'"

"Did you ever engage a man to come and clean your yard?"

"No, Sir; I engage a black man, I never have a white man."[14]

The interrogation was over. It was three o'clock in the morning, and Wells and his men had gained little in the way of real information that would help them find John Surratt or discover new details about Booth's elaborate plans. They did get a good sense of Mary's personality, however: a mother fiercely proud and protective of her son. Anxious to get anything out of her, Wells had unknowingly forced Mary into a corner from which she would never fully extricate herself. To her credit, Mary had tried to outmaneuver Wells with her evasive responses and denials. But the answers she provided and her disavowal of so much that Wells knew to be true moved her from a low-level suspect (of which there would be hundreds over the following weeks) to a prime suspect under arrest for complicity in Lincoln's assassination.

The other women's interrogations were initially brief and of little value. Nora Fitzpatrick would later testify that as they sat in the anteroom waiting for their questioning and then their release, Anna became nearly hysterical. Someone, perhaps a guard, suggested that Payne, there in the room with them, was Anna's brother. Exhaustion and fear was taking its toll on her fragile state. Nora testified that Anna had snapped, saying that "that ugly man was not her brother and that whoever said that was no gentleman."

In the meantime, Payne's odd behavior, his striking and incongruous appearance, and his peculiarly timed arrival at the Surratt household, which authorities instinctively knew was no accident or mistake, increased suspicions about him. Searching Payne's pockets, the officers found mostly personal-care products: hair pomade, a comb and hairbrush, and two toothbrushes. His clothing, on closer inspection, was of fine cashmere. Odd, they thought, for a poor laborer to have such items. More important, Payne could not account for the bloodstains on his shirt, nor the name "J. Wilkes Booth" in his fine leather boots.

Combining these pieces of evidence with Payne's size, smooth hands, and clean-shaven face—all so similar to the description of Seward's assailant—must have so excited Wells and his staff. They felt sure they had actually caught Seward's attacker. An armed escort rushed to the Seward home to rouse William Bell out of bed. Bell, the Seward's house servant who had opened the door to Payne, raced back to headquarters to identify this suspect.

Payne, positioned purposely in a dark, crowded room, could hardly disguise himself when Bell slowly entered and the gaslights turned up. Bell froze. He immediately recognized the assailant and began to tremble. Payne smiled. Yes, Payne had tried to assassinate Secretary of State William Seward and had nearly succeeded, Bell told them. Wells had his man.

The women stayed at Wells's office the entire night. Early the next morning, they were transferred to Carroll Annex in Washington's Old Capitol Prison. There prison officials read the charges against them, asking them a few personal questions and filling out administrative forms attendant to their indefinite imprisonment. Officers led them to their separate rooms on the second floor, leaving them alone in their terror. The women would suffer terribly over the next few weeks.

By April 20, authorities had rounded up six of the conspirators who would go on trial the next month. Sam Arnold, caught because of correspondence found in Booth's trunk, led to the surrender of Michael O'Laughlen, who turned himself in when he learned the Provost Marshall General of Baltimore discovered that he and Arnold were best friends and Booth associates. Theater owner John Ford fingered Ed Spangler as one of Booth's assistants; Spangler was promptly arrested at Ford's Theatre a few days after the assassination. George Atzerodt was arrested on April 19 while hiding in a cousin's home just north of Washington. Arnold and Atzerodt quickly made confessions, helping authorities expand their search.

Within a week of Mary Surratt's arrest, military detectives arrested Dr. Samuel Mudd, imprisoning him at Old Capitol. By the end of the month, the conspirators would be transferred to the Arsenal Prison to await their trial.[15]

Haughty, defiant, and self-assured, Mary had had three days from the time of Lincoln's murder to the day of her own arrest to craft a confession of her own. Years of illicit activities and clandestine relationships had taught her the finer points of obfuscation and diversionary tactics. She was partially successful at arguing her innocence and that of her son, but her arrogance, obstinacy, and misdirected faith in gendered social conventions only made her look more suspicious. Now that Lincoln was dead and the government was frantically looking for Booth and getting little cooperation from possible witnesses, Mary must have felt capable of weathering this storm. But she would soon be proved wrong. Deadly wrong.

CHAPTER SEVEN

THE "MATERFAMILIAS"
OF THE CRIMINALS

At first, Mary may not have recognized how serious the situation was for herself and for Anna. But incarceration at the Old Capitol's Carroll Annex would quickly change that. The Annex was a segregated section of the main prison, where female criminals and notorious Confederate spies were housed during the war. Nora Fitzpatrick was jailed there on the same night that Mary and Anna were brought in, and all three women suffered dreadfully.

Each cell accommodated two women; fortunately, Mary and Anna were soon allowed to room together. This was a great comfort to the weak and frightened Anna, who, at twenty-two, appeared unusually immature, nervous, and high-strung. Over time, the stress, coupled with overwhelming fear and anxiety, would nudge her closer to a nervous breakdown. Indeed the strain of separation from her mother later on during the trial would weaken Anna to the point where she would nearly lose her mind. Nora was three years younger than Anna and considerably less fragile; she seemed to cope with her circumstances more successfully.

The Old Capitol Prison had originally been a large boardinghouse, purchased by the federal government at the start of the Civil War to house criminals and political prisoners. The Carroll Annex was added in 1862 to house female criminals, as well as the growing numbers of male and female Confederate spies and sympathizers, and Union deserters. Designed to hold one thousand inmates, the Annex was twice the size of the Old Capitol, which accommodated five hundred prisoners. At the height of the war, however, the prison held more than twenty-seven hundred prisoners, creating an unbearably crowded and unsafe environment.

Conditions at the Annex were only marginally better than for men housed at the Old Capitol. Unlike the women's two-bed rooms, the men lived in large halls that slept twenty to twenty-five. But regardless of which part of the prison they lived in, male and female prisoners endured incredibly unsanitary conditions. The rooms were plagued by filth and squalor, rats, roaches, bed bugs, and fleas. Death and disease were commonplace. No inmate was spared the dehumanizing and degrading experience.[1]

While Mary and Anna breathed stale prison air, young John Surratt was being protected by Confederate collaborators and sympathetic Catholic priests in the rolling hills outside of Montreal. John had apparently been on a spy mission in Elmira, New York, when the President was shot; he barely managed to escape to Canada. Afterward, he remained hidden, successfully thwarting U.S. government efforts to apprehend him. John was fully aware that his mother and sister were under suspicion and being held in prison, but their suffering did not provoke him to surrender.

As the days passed, the public devoured daily accounts leaked to reporters about Booth's madcap scheme. News stories about Payne's fortuitous capture and the arrests at the Surratt boardinghouse spread quickly. The fact that a middle-aged woman had clearly played a significant role in the assassination plot added an especially lurid and melodramatic spin. The media frenzy that resulted not only helped sell newspapers, but exposed the conflict between notions of proper nineteenth-century feminine decorum and the realities of female depravity. Stereotypes of improper female behavior encouraged the public impression that Mary was somehow predisposed toward illegal and criminal activity. As just one example, the *Chicago Tribune* reported that upon searching the Surratt home, "much evidence was found, showing it to have been a regular treason brewing nest. Letters were found containing expressions of diabolical hate toward the President. . . . The house was found in a very disordered condition, the beds all unmade, the clothes piled on chairs, and everything in confusion, showing very plainly that the inmates had other business on hand than the usual business of housekeeping." Mary was described as "shabbily dressed." Trial and conviction by the press had begun.[2]

While the authorities in Washington tried to piece together what they believed to be an extensive and elaborate assassination plan sanctioned by the highest levels of the Confederate government, confusion reigned in Southern Maryland as federal marshals and Union soldiers tracked Booth and Herold.

Early attempts to hunt down and capture Booth were hampered by rebel supporters and accomplices who were sympathetic to Booth's cause or somehow connected to his plot. One of them was Dr. Samuel Mudd. Within hours of the assassination, Dr. Mudd was treating Booth's broken leg, and providing both Booth and Herold with food and shelter. Nearby and unaware of how close Booth was to them, investigators began setting up temporary headquarters in Bryantown, less than five miles from Mudd's home. The detectives fanned out into the countryside looking for Booth, interviewing and interrogating possible accomplices and witnesses. But Mudd kept his cool and his secret guests hidden. It would be days before the authorities would question Mudd, and by then, Booth would be gone.

Knowing the local manhunt would discover them if they stayed at Mudd's, Booth and Herold left the doctor's home to seek aid from Samuel Cox, a Confederate agent and sympathizer known to Herold.

Guided by Ozwell Swann, an innocent local black farmer, Booth and Herold safely reached Cox's plantation, ten miles south of Bryantown, during the early morning hours of the sixteenth. With federal detectives so close, Cox was fearful the men would be discovered at his home, so he passed them off to rebel agent Thomas Jones. Cox hoped Jones could help Booth and Herold cross the Potomac to Virginia. It would be five long days, however, before Jones could successfully get the two men across the river.

As the manhunt for Booth and his accomplices expanded, the nation plunged into a period of intense public mourning coupled with growing rage. While Southern Marylanders were sheltering Booth, communities throughout the North were seeking out possible traitors and collaborators, adding to the swelling ranks of suspects. Loyal and disloyal citizens alike bore the brunt of a vengeful public anxious for retribution. One newspaper reporter noted in the aftermath of the assassination, "There were tears in the eyes of all good citizens; but on their lips were the cries and vows of vengeance."[3]

Following its own leads, the federal government was tracking suspected co-conspirators, spy rings, and illicit rebel activities in cities like New York, Boston, Chicago, and Philadelphia. But some citizens took the law into their own hands and meted out their own forms of perceived justice on suspected rebel sympathizers. In Fall River, Massachusetts, Leonard Wood, a "Venomous Copperhead . . . and notorious . . . secesh sympathizer and liquor dealer" was heard proclaiming that the assassination of Lincoln was the "best news he had heard for forty years." Set upon by an "indignant crowd," he was chased and "booted" through the streets. Fearful authorities arrested him and placed him in jail for protection as much as for legal reasons. After ransacking his shop, the mob turned on other known Southern sympathizers in the town.[4] Another Massachusetts man, George Stone, from Swampscott, shared Wood's sentiments, announcing that Lincoln's death was the best news he had heard in four years. Stone was tarred and feathered.[5] All over the Northern states, such expressions of "satisfaction" with Lincoln's murder met quick and often violent responses.[6] Many innocent victims and flagrant sympathizers were prudently placed in jail for their own protection, where some languished until they denounced their views and took oaths of loyalty. Others were required to fly the American flag at half-mast in honor of the slain President.

Immediately after the assassination, preparations began for President Lincoln's elaborate and very public funeral. The event was scheduled for Wednesday, April 19. The day before, thousands had waited in line to view Lincoln's body as it lay in his grand coffin in the East Room of the White House. Sobs and gasps broke the somber silence throughout the day. On the nineteenth, six hundred specially invited guests, including the new President Andrew Johnson, the cabinet and Supreme Court, members of Congress, diplomats, family and friends, General Grant and various officers and soldiers, crowded the East Room and adjacent rooms for President Lincoln's funeral rites. Tens of thousands of men, women, and children waited solemnly outside. The city itself, draped in black crepe, stood in stark contrast to the beautiful, warm, and sunny day, bright with shades of spring grass and newly blossoming flowers and trees.

At noon, as the services began at the White House, communities across the country simultaneously conducted their own memorial service for their dead President. It would be more than fifty years later before radio, and then later, television broadcasts, reached and connected citizens across the nation and abroad. But on this very solemn day, millions of Americans shared their grief collectively in churches, synagogues, and meetinghouses at the same time as those mourning in Washington.

After the service, Lincoln's coffin was brought out to a waiting funeral carriage. Pulled by six white horses, the hearse moved down Pennsylvania Avenue. Lincoln's favorite horse, the horse he had named "U.S.," followed the carriage, riderless. Thousands of citizens and soldiers, including the sick, wounded, and disabled, joined in the procession through Washington to the rhythm of a slow, muted drum beat. Bystanders wept openly as the funeral car rode past them.

Lincoln's body was removed to the Capitol rotunda, where he lay in state for public viewing the next day. Thousands more moved through the building to view the dead President and pay their last respects.

On Friday morning, Lincoln began his long ride home to Springfield, Illinois. As one historian noted, this portion of the funeral procession "was the mightiest outpouring of national grief the world had yet seen."[7] Millions of Americans would wait by the sides of railroad lines from Washington to Albany, New York, to Chicago and Springfield, Illinois, and all the small towns, villages, and hamlets in between. Hundreds of thousands participated in specially planned funeral processions through the cities of Baltimore, Philadelphia, New York, and Chicago. It would take twenty days for Lincoln's body to reach Illinois. On May 3, his funeral car finally arrived in Springfield. A national salute was held at six o'clock that evening; the nation's official mourning for its murdered President was finally coming to a close.[8]

Mary and Anna had only been incarcerated for two days when Lincoln's funeral took place. Few tears were probably shed by the women; they and most of the inmates were Confederate sympathizers. In addition to rebel spies, couriers, and smugglers detained in the Annex, there were women charged with both petty and serious offenses, such as assault and murder. But many of the prisoners were Southern supporters who disobeyed or flagrantly resisted federal wartime rules and regulations. In the aftermath of the assassination, federal detectives and Metropolitan Police arrested hundreds of men and women alike on the slightest suspicion of association with Booth's plot, but even more were jailed for insubordination and refusing to swear an oath of loyalty to the Union. One woman was jailed for refusing to drape her home in black mourning fabric in honor of the dead President.

One of the inmates was a well-to-do rebel sympathizer, thirty-four-year-old Virginia Lomax, who had been arrested on general suspicion of being involved in the conspiracy to assassinate Lincoln. Lomax, a probable Confederate spy, later published an account of her experiences in the prison, writing indignantly about the women's treatment there.[9] For a middle-class woman of some means, the living conditions were deplorable and unacceptable. Lomax complained often. Sometimes the complaints worked, and conditions improved. More often they fell on deaf ears.

The dangerous conditions and outright neglect forced the women to rely on one another. Those prisoners who had the financial resources—or brave friends or relatives—could arrange to have additional food or other items brought from home for comfort. But there was no guarantee the items would reach the intended inmate. The women tried to use their influence as a group to improve conditions, but were rarely successful. Nevertheless, Lomax and others like her found kindred spirits among their cell-mates. They created a supportive network borne of necessity, reinforcing their sense of injustice, self-righteousness, and unwavering disdain for the Union.

Virginia Lomax's new roommate was Nora Fitzpatrick. Nora had been released from jail shortly after being transferred to the Annex. But once authorities had uncovered enough information to realize that the Surratt boardinghouse was perhaps the central meeting place for the conspirators, the police decided that Nora knew more than she was revealing, and arrested her again.[10] They hoped that more jail time would loosen her tongue.

The dismal cells tested the mental and physical health of the women. Lomax's and Nora's room had two barred windows facing the prison yard where prisoners took their daily exercise. Under each window stood a number of barrels for various uses, such as food, personal waste, and storage. Soot, dirt, spiderwebs, bugs, grease, and grime coated the floors, walls, and ceilings. Lomax's cell had been papered over, but the damp air had loosened the wallcovering and it hung in torn pieces off the walls. Each room had a fireplace. An iron bed, pillow, straw mattress, sheets, and a brown blanket were assigned each prisoner. While the sheets were clean, Lomax noted, her mattress and pillowcase were stained with blood, and her blanket was infested with bugs. A small table and chair completed the furniture in the room. Dishes and eating utensils brought in with each meal were rarely washed.[11]

Food was no better. Dinner, served around eight in the evening, consisted of pots of a mysterious coffeelike substance, molasses, milk, two pieces of bread, and a pat of butter. The dishes, forks, knives, and spoons were often broken and sticky with repeated use. Flies and ants swarmed the sugar. Small bits of candles were given to the prisoners for light, but Lomax complained that prison authorities refused to provide enough of them to last many hours.

Breakfast and lunch consisted of little more, though occasional soups with meat and potatoes offered slightly more substantial fare. Lomax remarked later that the meat was usually of unknown origin and the potatoes raw. She was fortunate that Nora's father had sent a basket of food, but that did not last long. Their refusal to eat the prison fare, and having to share their meager cakes with mice and roaches, quickly reduced their stash.[12]

Extensive reinterrogations of suspects and jailed witnesses took place between April 25 and 29. Nora, who had already been grilled several times by the authorities, was questioned again. This time, however, she revealed more information that directly linked Mary Surratt to the plot. Perhaps spending a couple of weeks in a damp, filthy, vermin-infested prison cell had convinced her to be more forthcoming and less protective of people to whom she owed no loyalty.[13]

Nora repeated information similar to that she had disclosed in earlier interviews, but this time she led the detectives closer to the core of the conspiracy. When asked how often Booth came to the Surratt boarding-house, Nora replied, again, that he came frequently. More questions about visitors and occasional boarders at the house followed. Then, one of the detectives asked her if Booth and some of these visitors ever meet privately, "apart from the other boarders."[14]

"I know sometimes they were up at Mrs. Surratt's room," she replied, identifying Booth, Payne, and Atzerodt specifically. She had already been clear that John Surratt was not home very often, thus ruling out any confusion as to whose room she was referring. The detectives now had an unambiguous view of the importance of the Surratt boardinghouse, and a keener grasp of Mary's role. They realized that Mary could not have been uninformed or ignorant of the goings-on in her own room.

Anna Surratt, circa 1865. Courtesy Surratt House Museum, Clinton, Maryland.

Anna's interrogation followed. She, too, was uncooperative, though not as obstinate as her mother. It was obvious, however, that she was not very knowledgeable about activities in the house. Additionally, Anna's romantic interest in Booth was already known to the detectives, even though she tried to appear casual and disinterested in him. Her dreamy doodlings of his name, repeatedly swirled in her handwriting on papers found in her room, and the picture of him that she had hidden on the mantle betrayed her feigned disinterest.[15] She revealed, however, that Booth came frequently to the house, often when her brother was not there. This was what the detectives were looking for, and Anna's admissions only complicated her mother's case further.

They also asked Anna about Payne, who she had denied recognizing the night they were all arrested. She was caught in that lie when she explained in great detail how she first met Payne, known to her as Wood, the Baptist preacher, and then his return to the boardinghouse weeks later as Payne. He had changed his appearance then, but Anna had easily recognized him as Wood. How could she have not recognized him the night of the seventeenth?[16]

Anna clearly wanted to protect her mother and brother, and the authorities knew it. While imprisoned at Carroll Annex, she had daily contact with her mother, Nora Fitzpatrick, and other witnesses. How much her mother, or others, may have coached her is unknown, though she clearly had been prepped. The women could not have anticipated every question, however, or every angle of inquiry and where it would lead them. The women certainly did not know the breadth and content of information the detectives were collecting from other suspects.

These interrogations would help trap Mary. While she refused to divulge any information, remaining obstinate and evasive, the authorities were quickly gathering considerable evidence pointing to Mary's and John Jr.'s involvement in Booth's plans. It would take almost two weeks to place the evidence in any useful order, but once it was all collected and reviewed the government could not ignore Mary's deep complicity in Booth's plans. They had no choice but to keep her jailed.

The women's freedom to converse with other prisoners and potential witnesses proved problematic. Augustus Howell, imprisoned for months at Old Capitol, was put under close guard and refused outdoor privileges when he was caught trying to communicate with Mrs. Surratt in the common prison yard.[17] The authorities tried to infiltrate the prison with informants and government-paid spies, but they were not often successful in uncovering important information. In Mary's case, this was doubly so. According to Virginia Lomax, a young woman was brought into the prison and forced to spy on Mary Surratt and the others and to learn as much as she could from them. She ingratiated herself to gain Mary's and the other prisoners' trust. "She circulated freely among the inmates, and was very talkative, generally selecting the assassination as her subject. She was also very confidential, and would relate marvelous conversations which she had with H. [prison warden] and other officials, under the seal of secrecy," Lomax claimed. But when the young woman fell ill, Mary Surratt nursed her back to health. It was only then that the young woman revealed her assignment to betray Surratt and the others—for a bribe of twenty-five hundred dollars. She asked Mary's forgiveness, according to Lomax, and Mary

obliged.[18] Whether this story is true or
not is unknown, but Mary knew she had
to be on guard.

Mary Surratt, circa 1863. Courtesy
Surratt House Museum, Clinton,
Maryland.

Questioned by the authorities repeatedly, and many times by her lawyers,
Mary steadfastly maintained her innocence, refusing to divulge any information regarding her son or any of the other
accomplices.

Though well liked by her fellow female inmates, Mary remained cool and
collected, puzzling both her supporters
and accusers. She often tended to the
other inmates' needs when ill, and, Lomax wrote, nursed a dying Confederate
soldier, the son of a female inmate in the
prison infirmary. "An angel of Mercy,"
Lomax called her. Lomax speculated that Mary was about forty years
old, "a tall commanding figure, rather stout, with brown hair, blue
eyes, thin nose, and small, well-shaped mouth, denoting great firm-
ness." Mary rarely mingled with the other prisoners, "unless they were
sick," avoiding conversation as much as possible, and she never smiled
but exhibited "a calm, quiet dignity." Surratt "always retained her self-
possession, and was never in the least degree thrown off her guard,"
Lomax noted admiringly, although Mary did become indignant over
newspaper reports casting aspersions upon her character.[19] But according to Lomax, she suffered in silence, never uttering "one word of re-
proach or virulence."[20] That self-assuredness in her ability to
outmaneuver and obfuscate her interrogators may have been admirable
to another Confederate, but it would ensure her death sentence.

On April 15, the day following the assassination, federal authorities
in search of Booth and Herold in Piscataway, south of Washington,

received an important tip from an innkeeper named Nodley Anderson. Though some of his information proved wrong, Anderson had correctly surmised that John Lloyd, the tavern keeper in Surrattsville, may know something. His presumption was that if Booth and Herold had not traveled through Piscataway, they more than likely went through Surrattsville on their way south.[21] Soldiers were immediately dispatched to the Surratt Tavern to pursue the lead.

When the soldiers arrived and questioned Lloyd, he denied everything. He claimed that he had not seen the two men, nor did he know Booth or anyone else who may have been involved in the assassination. Within hours, a separate contingent of Washington police detectives arrived at the tavern and questioned Lloyd. He repeated what he told the federal officers: he saw and knew nothing. Once they left, Lloyd promptly packed his bags and fled to the village of Allen's Fresh, thirty miles south in Charles County, to stay with his wife's family.

By Sunday, officers and detectives had set up temporary headquarters in Surrattsville, beginning an extensive interrogation of residents in the area and coordinating ongoing searches throughout Southern Maryland. Delays in pursuing Lloyd and the repeated questioning of him wasted critical opportunities to glean important information. Soldiers and detectives were racing in different directions, following various clues, leads, and false tips. It was not until Tuesday, the eighteenth, that a small detachment of soldiers and detectives were sent to Allen's Fresh in pursuit of Lloyd.[22]

In the meantime, Lloyd was becoming more terrified with each passing hour. But he knew his time was running out; investigators were receiving tips from other witnesses who'd observed odd comings and goings at the tavern during the days and weeks leading up to the assassination. Union supporters, a silent minority in the region who had remained fearful of their pro-Southern neighbors throughout much of the war, finally felt empowered to divulge whatever knowledge they had. Some fingered Lloyd and the Surratt family, including Mary.[23]

Not realizing that law enforcement officials were on their way to arrest him, Lloyd, by coincidence, headed back to Surrattsville with his wife that morning. He had not made up his mind about what he was going to do, but he knew he had to return to the tavern. Along the road, the couple ran into the detectives and soldiers. They promptly arrested Lloyd and escorted him back to Surrattsville.

Lloyd was taken to a makeshift jail and interrogation room that had been set up in Robey's post office. Captain George Cottingham assumed custody of Lloyd and began what would become several days of back-and-forth questioning, stalling, intimidation, and obfuscation, manipulating Lloyd and wearing him down in the hopes of extracting a confession. Between the eighteenth and the twentieth, several other police detectives and army officers grilled Lloyd. He defied them, too.

On April 20, while Lloyd was undergoing heated questioning, Secretary of War Edwin Stanton issued a combined $100,000 reward for the capture of Booth and his two co-conspirators, John Surratt and David Herold. Additional rewards were offered for information leading to the arrest of accomplices. More of a threat than an enticement, Stanton added that "all persons harboring or secreting the said persons . . . or aiding or assisting in their concealment or escape, will be treated as accomplices in the murder of the President and the attempted assassination of the Secretary of State, and shall be subject to trial before a Military Commission and the punishment of DEATH."[24]

Lloyd was trapped and he knew it. Cottingham, in particular, kept at him, playing off Lloyd's love and concern for his family. Stanton's death threats may have tipped the scales, fueling Lloyd's fears. Finally, exhausted and still terrified, Lloyd blurted out to Cottingham:

"Oh, my God, if I was to make a confession, they would murder me!"

"Who would murder you?" Cottingham probed.

"These parties that are in this conspiracy," Lloyd cried out.

Cottingham seized the moment and pushed Lloyd over the edge. "Well, if you are afraid of being murdered, and let these fellows get out of it, that is your business, not mine."

Lloyd broke down crying.[25]

Back in Washington at the Carroll Annex, Mary had successfully withstood the first of several interrogations, revealing little while frustrating her interrogators. She had no idea that Lloyd was about to give her up.

Finally, Lloyd's resolve faded. He began telling Cottingham bits and pieces of what he knew, though it would still take days of further questioning before he would offer up most of the information he had. Lloyd revealed that John Surratt, George Atzerodt, and David Herold had come to the tavern near the middle of March and hidden some guns and other items inside a wall on the second floor. He had nearly forgotten about them, he claimed, until he ran into Mrs. Surratt on April 11 when they crossed paths on the road near Washington. She reminded him to have the "shooting irons" ready, as they would be "wanted soon." Three days later, he told detectives, Mary met him at the tavern and once again told him to have the guns ready, for they would be called for "that night."[26] Several hours later Booth and Herold arrived, demanding not only the guns, but other items, including the field glasses Mary had given Lloyd that afternoon, and whiskey. Booth was in pain and did not get off his horse, Lloyd recalled, but Herold took one of the two guns and a bottle of whiskey. Booth bragged to him, Lloyd claimed, "I am pretty certain that we have assassinated the President and Secretary Seward." The two men then set off toward the village of T.B.

Captain Cottingham raced over to the Surratt Tavern and looked for the remaining gun where Lloyd had indicated it would be. Unable to find anything, he returned with Lloyd and several colleagues in tow, threatening that he would burn the tavern down if he didn't find the weapons. Lloyd, seeing his wife for the first time in days, clutched her close to him, crying out, "Oh, Mrs. Surratt, that vile woman, she has ruined me! I am to be shot!"[27]

Lloyd had correctly surmised that the firearm had become dislodged from its hiding place. The rope used to suspend it between the walls from the floor joists on the second floor had snapped, and the gun had become wedged inside the wall on the main floor. The officers took an ax to the dining room wall and smashed open the plaster: there was the gun that Booth and Herold had left behind.

Over the next few days Lloyd cautiously revealed more information, all the while claiming that the Surratts had set him up. If he had never rented the tavern, he said, he never would have found himself mixed up in the assassination plot. Interestingly, he blamed Mary more than he blamed her son John.

The detectives transferred Lloyd to the federal headquarters set up at Bryantown, where he was interrogated by Colonel Wells. Lloyd's testimony helped fill in missing pieces of information about Booth's preparations for escape, and confirmed the participation of co-conspirators like Mary and John Surratt, Herold, and Atzerodt.

In the meantime, Dr. Samuel Mudd had been questioned and finally arrested. Mudd had failed to notify the authorities on Saturday, the fifteenth, that Booth and Herold were staying at his home. Days later, when detectives arrived at his farm to interrogate him, Mudd revealed that he had treated the broken leg of a mysterious guest in the early morning hours after the assassination. Mudd swore he had no idea who Booth was, and that the guests in his house could not have been in any way involved in Lincoln's death. Mudd failed to tell the detectives, however, that he had met Booth several times in the months leading up to the assassination. Mudd's demeanor seemed suspicious to the detectives, and they sensed he was hiding something. When Mudd finally produced the boot he had cut off Booth's broken leg, they were convinced Mudd was not revealing everything he knew. The boot bore the initials, "J.W.B."

On April 23, both Lloyd and Mudd were transferred to the Old Capitol Prison in Washington, which allowed for additional, more intensive and threatening interrogations. Miraculously, Lloyd would avoid prosecution; Mudd would not.

The search for Booth and Herold continued in Southern Maryland. Between the early morning hours of April 15 and the night of April 16, federal troops moving into the area had no idea just how close they were to the two men. But because of miscommunications and false tips given by Southern sympathizers, Booth and Herold remained undetected.

Ongoing interrogations and interviews of area residents, however, finally started to pay off. After questioning Mudd, the detectives now knew that Booth had a broken leg, which was probably slowing his escape. Broadly expanding their investigation, detectives were getting closer to nailing down Booth's route to Virginia. They realized that Booth would try to cross the Potomac, so directed thousands of Union troops to fan out through Southern Maryland and along the shores of the river.

With so many soldiers swarming the area, Herold and Booth were not able to make a swift crossing. Instead, they became trapped in the swampy pine thicket between Port Tobacco and Allen's Fresh. For five long days, Thomas Jones risked his life dodging constant Union patrols to secretly bring his charges food and news of the government's efforts to capture them. Finally, on the twenty-first, Jones guided the two men to a small boat, hidden along the river at Dent's Meadows, just east of Allen's Fresh. It was a calm, dark, and misty night. Though the Potomac seemed tranquil, the current ran strong, and when Herold tried to row Booth the two miles across the heavily patrolled river, the men got lost and failed to reach the other side. A second attempt two days later was more successful, and the men made it to Virginia on the twenty-third.

With the help of several former Confederate spies, secret agents, and soldiers, Booth and Herold traveled south from Gambo Creek on the Virginia shore to Richard Garrett's farm, a few miles northeast of Bowling Green. Garrett was a modest tobacco farmer whose two eldest sons had fought for the Confederacy. Garrett believed Booth was a wounded Confederate soldier, and allowed them to stay.[28] But their sojourn in Virginia was soon cut short.

During the early morning hours of April 26 the two men were found and trapped in Garrett's tobacco barn by the 16th New York Cavalry. Herold surrendered, but Booth refused to give up. After a two-hour standoff, and with tensions running high, one of the federal detectives accompanying the soldiers set fire to the barn to smoke Booth out. The soldiers had been tracking Booth for days; their growing exhaustion and mounting anger made them difficult to control, especially now that they had found Lincoln's assassin. In the mayhem, one of them, Sergeant Boston Corbit, spotted Booth through a gap in the door of the burning barn. Fearing Booth might escape or shoot his way out, Corbit disobeyed orders and took a clear shot, mortally wounding him. By seven o'clock that morning, Booth was dead and the manhunt was over.[29]

Booth's body was returned to Washington. On night of the twenty-seventh, it was transferred to the ironclad *Montauk*, where several of the conspirators were also being held. The public interest in catching a glimpse of Booth's corpse—even desecrating it—ran high, so extreme secrecy and high-security measures were the order of the day. The following morning, the body was transferred off the *Montauk* and taken to the Arsenal Prison. Booth was secretly buried in a storeroom at the prison, beneath the stone floor.[30]

With the chase for Booth over, the government now turned its full attention to the prisoners and suspected accomplices. The decision to prosecute eight of the suspects came on the twenty-ninth. By then, mountains of testimony had been taken and pored over. Stanton had concluded that the first course of action would be to indict Dr. Samuel Mudd, Ed Spangler, Sam Arnold, David Herold, Lewis Payne, George Atzerodt, Michael O'Laughlen, and Mary Surratt. Others who played varying roles in the plot—among them, Samuel Cox, Thomas Jones, John Lloyd, Louis Weichmann, Sarah Slater, Thomas Harbin—would be imprisoned for a while longer, but none would face charges. John Surratt was still at the top of Stanton's list of conspirators, but he remained frustratingly out of reach. Stanton was eager to get the trial underway and the full scope of the assassination exposed. He would deal with Surratt later.

Stanton had other angles to pursue. He was entirely convinced that the conspiracy plot had all the earmarks of Confederate President Jefferson Davis and his cabinet. Like many others in the government and public, he believed that the Confederate leadership had sanctioned, planned, and financed the assassination of President Lincoln. Operating under that assumption, Edwin Stanton and Brigadier-General Joseph Holt,

Judge Advocate General of the Union Army and chief of the Bureau of
Military Justice, pursued the leaders of the rebel government relentlessly. Davis had been running ahead of Union forces since April 2,
when he fled Richmond in front of General Grant's forces. Moving
stealthily through Virginia, North Carolina, and then into South Carolina, Davis refused to give up, in spite of Lee's surrender. While making his way further south toward Florida, Davis, his family, and several
rebel bodyguards were ambushed by Union troops near Abbeyville,
Georgia, on May 10. Davis was taken to Fortress Monroe in Virginia,
where he was held to await his own trial for treason. They finally captured Davis, but Confederate Vice President John C. Breckinridge and
Confederate Secretary of State Judah Benjamin remained at large.

Eventually, it became obvious to most investigators that if Davis
and his staff had been involved in the conspiracy, they had successfully
destroyed any and all documents linking them to it. Further, no material
witnesses could or were willing to substantiate those claims. While
Booth and Surratt had received funding from the Confederate treasury,
it appears that the assassination was not specifically paid for. Nevertheless, before Jefferson Davis's capture, and while the Confederacy's top
officials were still in hiding, President Johnson issued arrest warrants
and rewards for their capture, including a $100,000 bounty for Jeffer-
son Davis: twice the $50,000 reward offered for the capture of Booth.
With new information uncovered every day, Johnson, Stanton, and
many others believed from evidence collected by the military, "that the
atrocious *murder of the late President*, ABRAHAM LINCOLN, and the
attempted assassination of Hon. Wm. H. Seward, Secretary of State,
were incited, concerted, and procured by and between" top Confederate government officials.[31]

On April 29, Stanton ordered General Winfield Scott Hancock to remove Atzerodt, Herold, Payne, O'Laughlen, Arnold, and Spangler
from the ironclads *Montauk* and *Saugus*, both anchored in the Potomac

near Washington, and to bring them to the Arsenal Prison. The prisoners had been placed on the ironclads to prevent them from communicating with anyone and to thwart any possible escape attempts. Samuel Mudd, who was jailed in the Old Capitol, was transferred to the Arsenal at the same time.

The nation was still in deep mourning. Lincoln's funeral car was still slowly making its way to Illinois for final burial rites. Sporadic and violent attacks on pro-Southern citizens and businesses continued for weeks more. Stanton took every precaution. Recognizing the potential for vengeful mob action, he took great care in securing the removal of the prisoners under heavy guard.

Once he had them isolated at the Arsenal Prison, Stanton further ordered that these prime suspects not be allowed visitors nor to communicate with one another. He approved daily visits from a physician, Dr. George L. Porter, and prison superintendent Colonel Wells was instructed to check on them at least once a day. A sparse diet was ordered, with extra care being taken that no items be allowed in the cells that might provide a prisoner with tools to injure a guard or themselves. The transfer was quiet, orderly, and, in the words of one historian, "carried out with military precision and in the strict secrecy" demanded by Stanton.[32]

After the seven men had been secured in their cells at the Arsenal, Stanton ordered Superintendent William Wood of Old Capitol to "deliver . . . Mrs. Surratt, a prisoner in your custody, with any effects she may have."[33]

Mary's transfer did not proceed so smoothly. The following evening, April 30, soldiers arrived at the Carroll Annex of the Old Capitol Prison, calling for Mrs. Surratt to come with them immediately. The women of the prison were allowed time in the evenings to socialize, and it was during this social time that the soldiers burst into the room and ordered Mrs. Surratt to gather her "bonnet and cloak" and go with them.

Mary collected her things calmly and coolly; she softly said goodbye to her fellow prison mates, kissing a few on their cheeks as she left.

"Pray for me, pray for me," she told her friend Virginia Lomax.

Anna became hysterical, clinging to her mother and refusing to let her go.

A soldier pried Mary from her frantic daughter's grasp.

"Mother, oh Mother!" Anna repeatedly cried out.

Lomax noted that Mary was trembling.[34]

For weeks the women would endure Anna's grief, which veered from hysterical crying and outbursts to silent, sullen moodiness. Lomax recalled hearing the "patter" of Anna's "little slippered feet, as she restlessly paced the room above me. I fancy I can see her now, her light hair brushed back from her fair face, her blue eyes turned towards heaven, her lips compressed as if in pain, and her delicate little white hands clasped tightly, as she walked up and down that room, hour after hour, seeming insensible to fatigue, and speaking to no one. Sometimes she would be quite hysterical, then again perfectly calm, except for the constant walking. We all thought she would lose her mind if the strain were not relieved."[35]

Mary was swiftly transferred to the Arsenal Prison and escorted to a private cell. Her quarters were similar to those occupied by the seven other conspirators set for prosecution. The isolation of each room effectively prevented any possible collaboration with the other accomplices or witnesses who might, and eventually would, be called to testify for or against her. This, despite the fact that for nearly two weeks Mary had freely spoken with her daughter, with Nora Fitzpatrick, and with others at the Carroll Annex. Life, however, would change dramatically and irreversibly for Mary at the Arsenal.

Mary's cell was on the third floor, number 200. The others were scattered strategically throughout the prison: Herold was also placed on the third floor, while Payne and Atzerodt were confined on the second floor.[36] Mudd, Spangler, O'Laughlen, and Arnold were roomed elsewhere, far enough from each other to prevent any attempt at communication.

Major-General John F. Hartranft was commander of the penitentiary, and his regiment served inside and outside the prison. His guards were ordered to maintain no communication with the prisoners, and no one outside was allowed to speak to the prisoners from the street level. As one newspaper reporter described the scene outside the prison walls, "thick cordons of sentries surround the red brick building which confines the wretched criminals. . . ."[37]

The male prisoners were shackled with leg and wrist irons and were forced to wear heavy cotton hoods at all times—hoods that covered their eyes and ears, with only a small opening for the nose and mouth. The men complained bitterly about the discomfort they caused. Payne's hood was heavier and thicker than the others after more cotton padding was added to prevent him from injuring his skull when he began slamming it against his cell walls.[38] Mary was not required to wear a hood, nor was she shackled, as the men were.

Dr. Porter, the physician who was assigned to look after the prisoners, reported that he had little trouble with any of the prisoners—except for Mary Surratt. Mary refused to eat, posing a serious dilemma for the doctor, as well as for the secretary of war. Porter threatened her with forced feeding, which would have required restraining her and forcing liquid nourishment down her throat through a crude funnel. Such prospects convinced Mary to be more cooperative.[39]

President Andrew Johnson turned to U.S. Attorney General James Speed for advice on the how to proceed with a trial for the known conspirators. Speed undertook a highly systematic review of the evidence and legal precedent.[40] On April 28, Speed recommended that the co-conspirators be tried together by a military tribunal: a court composed of military officers of varying ranks who would sit as prosecution, judge, and jury. Speed was convinced that the actions of the conspirators was indeed a wartime act, that the conspiracy to kidnap, then kill President Lincoln was organized and executed to advance the Confederate cause, and was not a personal vendetta against Lincoln, but against the whole administration. Based partially on General Order 100, issued during the Civil

War by the army, the accused violated the "laws of war by acting as unlawful belligerents for the Confederacy."[41] The accomplices had colluded to kill President Lincoln, the commander-in-chief of the United States armed forces, to advance their own rebellious agenda. By violating these laws of war, even as citizens and not soldiers, the co-conspirators were subject to trial by a military tribunal or court. Therefore, Speed argued, they should be tried together by military tribunal. Johnson agreed.

On May 1, Johnson ordered Assistant Adjutant-General W. A. Nichols to "detail nine competent military officers to serve as a Commission for the trial." In issuing his decision, Johnson declared that "the persons implicated in the murder of the late President Abraham Lincoln, and the attempted assassination of the Honorable William H. Seward, Secretary of State, and in an alleged conspiracy to assassinate other officers of the Federal Government at Washington City, and their aiders and abettors, are subject to the jurisdiction of, and lawfully triable before, a Military Commission."[42]

The decision to try the conspirators in front of a military tribunal rather than a civil court created immediate dissent. Several of President Johnson's advisors disagreed with Speed's recommendation; others heartily endorsed it. Arguments for and against the legality of the trial proceedings have peppered the history of the assassination trials for almost 150 years. Nevertheless, many scholars have argued persuasively that Speed was right: although Lee had surrendered at Appomattox days before Lincoln was shot, the war was not over, physically, politically, or emotionally, for many Confederates. Skirmishes continued throughout the South until the end of May, and random and illegal guerrilla warfare continued for months more. Washington was still under de facto military control.[43]

In July, after the trial was over, Speed issued his official opinion on the constitutionality of the military "to try and execute the assassins of the President."[44] In a lengthy rebuttal to critics, Speed cited a vast array of legal, historical, and military sources and codes, outlining a compelling argument for holding a military tribunal:

Obedience to the Constitution and the law, then, requires that the
military should do their whole duty; they must not only meet and
fight the enemies of the country in open battle, but they must kill
or take the secret enemies of the country, and try and execute
them according to the laws of war. The civil tribunals of the
country can not rightfully interfere with the military in the performance of their high, arduous and perilous, but lawful duties.
That Booth and his associates were secret active public enemies,
no mind that contemplates the facts can doubt. The exclamation
used by him when he escaped from the box on to the stage, after
he had fired the fatal shot, *sic temper tyrannis,* and his dying message, "Say to my mother that I died for my country," show that
he was not an assassin from private malice, but that he acted as a
public foe.[45]

Speed argued that if the accused conspirators participated in the plot
to assassinate the President, they did so as "public enemies," who
"ought to be tried before a military tribunal." He further reasoned that
handing such conspirators over to the civil courts for offenses against
the laws of war would be as wrong as handing over soldiers who had
killed in the line of duty to civil courts to be tried for murder.[46]

Speed alluded to his belief that a military tribunal would be more
dispassionate and rational than a civil court for this trial. Given the
tremendous grief and rage over the murder of Lincoln, Speed may
have had a point. Military tribunals, Speed wrote, "prevent indiscriminate slaughter; they prevent men from being punished or killed upon
suspicion."[47] But the strong Southern sentiments of many of Washington's citizens may have precluded any concerns over "indiscriminate
slaughter." Indeed, Stanton and other Unionists feared that a civil jury
of local Washington and Maryland citizens would have been far more
sympathetic to the conspirators than citizens in more Northern and
loyal cities, like Boston and Philadelphia, negating the possibility of a
conviction. Nevertheless, Speed's arguments failed to convince those
who continued to believe that his decision was unconstitutional.

On May 4, a military commission was directed to meet on Monday, May 8, to begin the trial for Mary Surratt and the seven male conspirators. Nine officers, including Major-General David Hunter, Major-General Lewis Wallace, Brevet Major-General August V. Kautz, Brigadier-General Albion P. Howe, Brigadier-General Robert S. Foster, Brevet Brigadier-General Cyrus B. Comstock, Brigadier-General T. M. Harris, Brevet Colonel Horace Porter, and Lieutenant-Colonel David R. Clendenin were appointed to the commission as judges. Within days, however, Comstock and Porter were relieved of their position due to conflicts and replaced by Brevet Brigadier-General James A. Ekin and Brevet Colonel C. H. Tomkins.

Brigadier-General Joseph Holt was appointed judge advocate, or prosecutor, and recorder of the commission. It was his responsibility to ensure that court proceedings and testimony were correctly recorded, verbatim, and made available each day to the defense attorneys. Holt was deeply concerned about the precise recording of trial testimony. He called upon Benn Pitman, the brother of Isaac Pitman, who invented a widely used shorthand for taking such verbatim testimony, to be the official court stenographer.[48] Pitman was assisted by several other stenographers, collectively producing copies of each day's proceedings. These were distributed nightly to two major newspapers, the *National Intelligencer* and the *Philadelphia Inquirer,* and to the court and defense attorneys the following day. This record would be read in open court at the start of each session, where any errors could be noted and corrections made.[49] Copies of the daily proceedings, made available to major newspapers through the *Intelligencer* and the *Inquirer,* kept the public up-to-date with the trial. The *New York Times, New York Tribune, Boston Globe,* and *Washington Star* were among the many newspapers that also had their own reporters in the courtroom taking down testimony and observing the accused and the spectators. A lively competition sprang up between the reporters and their papers. Their stories, sent by telegraph nightly, vied for space in newspapers from coast to coast. In addition to providing verbatim copies of the trial, the

Inquirer and the *Intelligencer* provided their own reports of courtroom spectacle not part of direct testimony or official court proceedings. Daily courtroom dramas were frequently more exciting and interesting than the lengthy and often boring testimony of witnesses.

Holt, as prosecutor, was assisted by two other officers, Special Judges Advocate John A. Bingham and Henry L. Burnett, both of whom had extensive legal and government careers. They would be formidable adversaries for any defense counsel chosen by the accused. On May 9, Holt and the rest of the commission brought the co-conspirators into court and asked if they wished to be represented by an attorney of their own choosing. They all affirmed that that they did. The court gave them one day to secure representation.

The following day Holt read the charges against the co-conspirators:

> For maliciously, unlawfully, and traitorously, and in aid of the existing armed rebellion against the United States of America, on or before the 6th day of March, A.D. 1865, and on divers other days between that day and the 15th day of April, A.D. 1865, combining, confederating, and conspiring together with one John H. Surratt, John Wilkes Booth, Jefferson Davis, George N. Sanders, Beverly Tucker, Jacob Thompson, William C. Cleary, Clement C. Clay, George Harper, George Young, and others unknown, to kill and murder, within the Military Department of Washington, and within the fortified and intrenched lines thereof, Abraham Lincoln, late, and at the time of said combining, confederating, and conspiring, President of the United States of America, and Commander-in-Chief of the Army and Navy thereof; Andrew Johnson, now Vice-President of the United States aforesaid; William H. Seward, Secretary of State of the United States aforesaid; and Ulysses S. Grant, Lieutenant-General of the Army of the United States aforesaid, then in command of the Armies of the United States, under the direction of the said Abraham Lincoln; and in pursuance of in prosecuting said malicious, unlawful and traitorous conspiracy

aforesaid, and in aid of the said rebellion, afterward, to wit, on the 14th day of April, A.D. 1865, within the Military Department of Washington, aforesaid, and within the fortified and intrenched lines of said Military Department, together with said John Wilkes Booth and John H. Surratt, maliciously, unlawfully, and traitorously murdering the said Abraham Lincoln, then President of the United States and Commander-in-Chief of the Army and Navies of the United States, as aforesaid; and maliciously, unlawfully, and traitorously assaulting, with intent to kill and murder, the said William H. Seward, then Secretary of State of the United States, as aforesaid; and lying in wait with intent maliciously, unlawfully, and traitorously to kill and murder the said Andrew Johnson, then being Vice-President of the United States; and the said Ulysses S. Grant, then being Lieutenant-General, and in command of the Armies of the United States, as aforesaid.[50]

Specific or additional charges were applied to individual defendants. Payne faced attempted murder charges for his attack on William H. Seward. Herold was accused of helping to conceal John Wilkes Booth after he had assassinated the President. Atzerodt was accused of intending to murder then–Vice President Andrew Johnson. Michael O'Laughlen was charged with intent to kill General Ulysses S. Grant. Dr. Mudd faced charges that he, "on divers other days and times . . . [did] advise, encourage, receive, entertain, harbor, and conceal, aid and assist the said John Wilkes Booth" and the rest of the conspirators, and knowingly and willingly assisting in the escape of Booth and Herold.

In addition to being accused of conspiring to kill Lincoln and his cabinet in collusion with the rest of the defendants, Mary was singled out for her specific supporting role:

. . . in further prosecution of said conspiracy, Mary E. Surratt did, at Washington City, and within the military department and military lines aforesaid, on or before the 6th day of March, A.D. 1865, and on divers other days and times between that day and the 20th day of April, A.D. 1865, receive, entertain, harbor, and conceal, aid and assist the said John Wilkes Booth, David E. Herold, Lewis Payne, John H. Surratt, Michael O'Laughlen, George A. Atzerodt, Samuel Arnold, and their confederates, with the knowledge of the murderous and traitorous conspiracy aforesaid, and with the intent to aid, abet, and assist them in execution thereof, and in escaping from justice after the murder of the said Abraham Lincoln, as aforesaid.[51]

Mary and the other defendants pleaded not guilty. Some of the defendants had not yet retained legal representation, and the court extended the deadline yet another day. Securing counsel proved to be problematic for several defendants. Mudd had family wealth to support him, and Mary had her properties, but the others had few financial resources to cover legal services. In addition, early representation requests by some of the accused were rejected. David Herold approached Washington, D.C., attorney J. H. Bradley to represent him, but Bradley's current caseload prevented him from accepting the case. Herold also asked J. M. Carlisle, but Carlisle refused to take the required oath of allegiance to the United States and was therefore barred from appearing before the military court. Finally, Frederick Stone, a Southern sympathizer from Port Tobacco, agreed to take the oath and to take on Herold's case. In a strange twist, and unbeknownst to the military commission, Stone had been the judge who'd agreed to hold John Surratt's payment for Richard Smoot's boat back in January.[52]

Payne sought out Manson Campbell, a Baltimore attorney and the son-in-law of Supreme Court Justice Roger B. Taney. Considered a loyal Unionist, Campbell was a successful and experienced lawyer, and agreed to represent Payne. Most court observers questioned why Payne chose to avail himself of such qualified counsel, given that he had confessed his crime. Payne, did, however, plead not guilty, and was entitled to the best representation possible. Such sentiments probably made it even more difficult for the accused to obtain counsel. After all, even for successful and respected lawyers, the decision to defend the President's assassins would have been a difficult one.

Dr. Mudd had hoped to retain Robert J. Brent, another Baltimore attorney and a law partner of R. H. May, a Maryland congressional representative known for his strong Southern sentiments. Brent, however, was already trying an important case with J. M. Bradley. The *Philadelphia Inquirer* reported that Brent was willing to leave that case and "go to the rescue of Dr. Mudd," but his workload prevented him from joining Mudd's defense.[53]

Mary requested representation from her friend William Kirby, but Kirby was a mere constable, not a lawyer. The newspapers questioned his abilities, observing that while Kirby "may be ever so desirous of aiding her escape of the gallows that now seems to have the rope coiled round her neck, it is not likely he will attempt to play the lawyer before the court."[54] They were right; Kirby would be forced to stand aside.

Mary also hoped to retain Reverdy Johnson, a Maryland senator, a Union defender with Southern sympathies, and a nationally prominent attorney and politician. Johnson was seemingly a brilliant choice: his reputation was secure, he would not be intimidated by members of the military commission, and his courtroom experience could possibly save Surratt's life. The *Philadelphia Inquirer* reported shock, however, at "Mrs. Surratt's impudence" for requesting such a high-profile lawyer. Mary, they claimed, "the female fiend incarnate, who figures as the 'materfamilias' of these criminals, evinces her boldness in sending for Hon. Reverdy Johnson, senator from Maryland, too well known to need any explanation."[55] Johnson initially turned down Mary's request, citing prior commitments to other clients, but would ultimately appear in court on her behalf.

The *Philadelphia Inquirer*'s response was not surprising; on the contrary, it reflected the public's growing disdain for Surratt. The presumption of her complicity in the assassination plot, and the press's characterization of her criminal disposition, would escalate throughout the trial.

By the close of court on May 10, the rest of the defendants were still without counsel. Mudd's lawyer, Brent, backed out, so the following day, Mudd petitioned the court for change of counsel to Frederick Stone, Herold's lawyer. Mary arrived in court with new counsel as well: Frederick Aiken and John W. Clampitt, new associates in Reverdy Johnson's large practice in Washington. Aiken, born and raised in Massachusetts, had passed the bar in Vermont and was very active in Democratic Party politics. During the war he had worked as a correspondent for the *New York Times,* and had been practicing law only a short time when he was called upon to help defend Surratt. Clampitt was a Washingtonian, and had only recently begun practicing law with Aiken in Johnson's law office. He, too, was an active Democratic Party loyalist. Johnson, in the meantime, would remain Mary's lead counsel, in spite of his own heavy caseload.[56]

On Friday, May 12, the court reconvened at ten o'clock in the morning. Sam Arnold had successfully retained counsel: General Thomas Ewing, Jr., a Union officer and successful Washington lawyer. He would represent not only Arnold, but Ed Spangler and Samuel Mudd, too, as co-counsel with Frederick Stone. Michael O'Laughlen hired Walter S. Cox, a local attorney and professor at Columbia College, who would also assist Stone with Arnold's defense. George Atzerodt's family retained William E. Doster for him. Doster had been a former provost marshall in Washington, and would prove to be a contentious defense counsel. The court would prevail upon him to take Payne on as a client, too, after Payne's first lawyer backed out and no other was willing to represent him.

The court admitted the defendants' lawyers as counsel before the commission—with the exception of Reverdy Johnson. To argue before the military commission, each attorney had to take the oath of allegiance to the federal government. Johnson refused. As a senator during the Civil War, he'd had a long-standing argument about the constitutional validity of the oath. The commission noted that Johnson "did not recognize the moral obligation of an oath designed as a test of loyalty," and that Johnson had urged citizens to take the oath without really meaning it when Maryland sent its newly crafted constitution to public vote. Johnson argued that the Maryland Constitutional Convention, convened in mid-1864 to rewrite Maryland's constitution to end slavery, did not have the authority to require its citizens to take a loyalty oath. Fearful that heavily pro-Southern male voters would reject the new constitution, Maryland Unionists demanded that an oath of allegiance be required before one could vote. The requirement, Johnson claimed, merely disfranchised legal voters, making a mockery of loyalty to the Union. Johnson argued his points again in front of the commissioners, and finally they withdrew their objection. Johnson took his place as Surratt's lead attorney.

Reverdy Johnson was a longtime Union man and a friend of Lincoln's. He explained to the court that he was acting as Mary Surratt's attorney simply because she asked. He had no prior relationship with her or her family, and was representing her free of charge. He claimed that it was his professional obligation to protect her rights and that he was induced to come to her defense:

> [A]s a Maryland lady, protesting her innocence to me . . . she should not go undefended. I am now volunteering to do what evidence will justify me in doing for this lady, who is now being tried for her life. My detestation of everyone concerned in this nefarious plot, carried out with such fiendish malice, is as great as that of any member of this Court. I am not here to protect anyone who, when the evidence is heard, I shall deem to have been guilty—not even her.[57]

Whether Johnson ultimately decided that Mary was guilty or not remains unknown. However, within a few days, Johnson rarely appeared in court, leaving Mary's defense to his inexperienced associates Clampitt and Aiken.

With the commission's objections put aside, and defense counsel set for each conspirator, the trial commenced immediately. The defense attorneys had not yet been able to review the accusations and the extensive evidence against their clients. Holt's order to begin the trial immediately that day severely hampered the lawyers' initial efforts to familiarize themselves with their cases.

There must have been additional interrogations of Mary, but none have been uncovered. Her interviews with her attorneys, if recorded, remain a mystery, perhaps lost long ago. One of Mary's lawyers later claimed that they felt hamstrung by her uncooperative attitude.[58] Did she try to explain to them her role in the plot, or did she reconcile her claims of innocence with all the evidence mounting against her? Did she believe she was protecting her son, knowing that John's role as Booth's ally would link him to the assassination and put him at risk too? Had Booth lied to her by telling her that he had seen her son on the fourteenth, that John was a part of his plan that day, leaving her with the belief that her son was involved directly in the assassination?

Mary's attorneys—two inexperienced and unsure of themselves, the other mysteriously absent from court—prepared Mary as best they could for trial. Mary's attorneys and some family and friends steadfastly maintained she was innocent. But Mary refused to give plausible alternative explanations for her actions, making it very difficult to answer all the charges against her and frustrating her defense. All they had were her protestations of innocence, protests that mattered little as the evidence mounted against her. Perhaps she was confident that she would be acquitted. Booth was dead, after all, and the evidence against the other accomplices seemed far more damning.

CHAPTER EIGHT

THE CASE FOR THE DEFENSE

The courtroom was fashioned from a large hall on the second floor of the northeast corner of the penitentiary. New pine furniture—desks, chairs, and benches—was quickly manufactured to accommodate not only the twelve-member tribunal and the eight prisoners, but also their lawyers, court stenographers, newspaper journalists, and spectators. The room's freshly painted white walls stood in sharp contrast to the black iron bars on all the windows. The center of the room was reserved for the witness stand, while the prisoners' dock occupied a raised platform at the room's western end.

In 1865, no criminal defendant was allowed to testify in any court, military or civil, except in the state of Maine, so the defendants would never testify in their own defense. Allowing the co-conspirators to testify would not have necessarily improved their cases, and, in fact, could have hurt them even more. Nevertheless, the absence of their direct testimony in the courtroom only added to the deepening mysteries surrounding the case. Soon lurid speculation joined the already-dramatic proceedings.

Daily newspaper reports of the trial—throughout its full seven weeks and with its scores of witnesses—held the nation in thrall, and Mary's story got top billing. Vilified and caricatured in the mostly Northern newspapers that carried reports from the courtroom, Mary endured almost continual aspersions against her femininity, religion, age, physical appearance, and demeanor. Reporters seemed to take great satisfaction in demeaning her physical characteristics. In court, Mary appeared in a long black veil that shielded her face from spectators and the press. She sat nearly motionless, separated a few feet from her male co-conspirators on the prisoners' dock. Her stone-cold silence and seeming lack of emotion fed the most negative accounts.

On May 11, the first day of open court proceedings, reporters observed that Mary looked "very much broken down and humbled," showing the "first manifestations of fear." The *Philadelphia Inquirer* reported that she was "very slovenly dressed," and "weighs about two hundreds pounds."[1] The *New York Times* described her as a "stout, buxom widow, fitting Falstaff's ideal, 'fair, fat, and forty,' though ... she is far beyond that period of life." Some reporters countered that Mary did not exhibit the "cold, cruel gleam in her gray eyes" that other newspaper reporters had noted.[2]

Eager to increase readership, reporters sometimes strayed far from the truth to sensationalize their stories. The *Inquirer* intimated that Mary had long been a cruel and indifferent woman, who raised her son John, the "fugitive," in "idleness and crime." They suggested that Mary may have been responsible for the fate of her husband, John Sr., who "died suddenly and mysteriously" in 1862. Soon after Mary's move to Washington, her boardinghouse, they claimed, "became noted for its sesesh visitors and their obnoxious conduct until it was a terror to the whole neighborhood."[3]

Most of the other defendants were also caricatured in the newspapers, and so were some of the witnesses. As the trial progressed these caricatures subsided somewhat, and the newspapers focused more on the testimony presented each day. Descriptions of the defendants became more realistic and nuanced over time, probably as a result of reporters' growing familiarity with the accused during the many weeks together in the courtroom.

The simultaneous prosecution of all eight defendants proved confusing and protracted for attorneys on both sides. Witnesses called to

Courtroom scene from the trial of conspirators. Mary is seated in the far left corner, separate from the rest of the defendants. From *Frank Leslie's Illustrated Newspaper*, June 3, 1865.

the stand sometimes offered testimony pertaining to more than one defendant. Keeping track of all the testimony, and sitting through hours of questioning of witnesses that may or may not have had anything to do with their own clients, was tedious and wearisome for the attorneys. Yet they had to pay strict attention to all testimony, and to be ever ready to cross-examine any witness on even the smallest point.

Just as the trial was getting underway, newspapers reported that Confederate President Jefferson Davis had finally been captured, ending another dramatic manhunt. Transferred to the military prison at Fortress Monroe in Virginia, he would remain incarcerated for two years. While Davis's arrest in Georgia on May 10 generated great excitement, the lure of the assassination trial and daily testimony soon relegated his expected treason trial to the newspapers' back pages.

Louis Weichmann was among the first witnesses to testify. On May 13 he was called to the stand. Few could be sure of what the exact nature of Weichmann's testimony would be—including Mary. But she would soon learn that he had been an observant boarder.

Initially, Weichmann was hesitant to identify Mary as a co-conspirator. On the witness stand, he described her as a pious, sweet, and caring woman for whom he had much affection. He staunchly defended John Surratt, as well, claiming that John was a gentleman and a good friend.

Weichmann told the court he could not understand why Mary and John found Booth so alluring, nor why they were involved in Booth's plans to abduct, then assassinate, the President. But over time, he said, as he pieced together different parts of the story from other eyewitnesses, he began to realize that Mary and her son had been much more involved with Booth's plans than he imagined. He finally concluded that Mary had jeopardized his freedom—and his life. Living in her home, and escorting her to Surrattsville prior to the assassination, had placed him under serious suspicion. In fact, after the trial, Weichmann publicly announced, "I . . . don't believe that Mrs. Surratt was an innocent woman."[4]

Many harbored suspicions about Weichmann's level of involvement with Booth's plans. Nevertheless, his detailed testimony about several conspirators' comings and goings at Mary's boardinghouse, and Mary's trips to Surrattsville in the days leading up to the assassination, secured a strong prosecution case.

The prosecution brought John Lloyd to the stand directly after Weichmann. Lloyd, too, sat in a very precarious place: as a participant with a key supporting role in Booth's plan—albeit a role that was not entirely clear to him until the night of the assassination—Lloyd could have faced serious co-conspirator charges as well. But according to legal code at the time, a witness who testified for the prosecution could not be charged with the crime of co-conspiracy. Stanton and the detectives who interrogated the co-conspirators and scores of witnesses had to sometimes make difficult choices: potentially guilty parties who could provide important evidence about the assassination plot would have to be set free in exchange for their testimony. Lloyd's testimony, like Weichmann's, implicating John Surratt, Mary, Herold, Atzerodt, and Booth, was a trade-off the government was willing to make.

Lloyd told the court that John Surratt, Herold, and Atzerodt had come to the tavern during the middle of March and had left the guns and ammunition inside the walls and below the floor joists on the second floor. Though Surratt had told Lloyd he would come back for the items in a few days, he never did. Almost a month went by before Lloyd was approached by John's mother, Mary, about the guns and things hidden in the tavern's walls. In riveting testimony, Lloyd revealed that he met Mary near Uniontown, on the road to Surrattsville, on April 11, and then again at the tavern on the fourteenth. At both meetings, he told the court, she directed him to have the "shooting irons" and other items ready for pickup. He claimed, however, that Mrs. Surratt never alluded to a plot against the President, nor did she name those who would be coming for the guns and other items on the night of the fourteenth.[5]

Few in the courtroom questioned whether Mary knew who the guns were for and why. Lloyd's corroborating statements supported Weichmann's story, leaving little reasonable doubt as to Mary's role and motive. Indeed, they set the tone for the rest of the trial.

The following day brought a new round of questioning for Weichmann and a number of new witnesses. Mary's lead attorney, Reverdy Johnson, hoped to highlight inconsistencies in Weichmann's testimony, so had asked the court to recall Weichmann. Weichmann had not mentioned the April 11 meeting with Lloyd near Uniontown on the road to Surrattsville. Johnson was hoping to cast doubt on the significance of Mary and Lloyd's chance meeting that day, but Lloyd's damaging testimony caught Mary's defense counsel off-guard.

In responding to Johnson's new questions, Weichmann remained steady and cool. He testified that he did indeed remember the meeting, but that he never heard Mary's conversation with Lloyd that day. He was probably telling the truth: Lloyd, in fact, had testified that Mary's "language was indistinct, as if she wanted to draw my attention to something so that no one else would understand."[6] Weichmann told the court that Mary "put her head out [of the carriage] and made conversation with [Lloyd]" that was inaudible to him. He further claimed that after Mary was done talking with Lloyd, she yelled out to Emma Offutt that she was going to help secure the release of Augustus Howell, the Confederate spy and courier who had been arrested in March at her tavern and then imprisoned.[7]

Johnson's efforts to cast suspicion on Weichmann backfired. He not only failed to discredit Weichmann, he helped make Mary look guiltier.

Meanwhile, Mary continued to assert her innocence. She never seemed to offer credible explanations to refute the damaging testimony against her. Even though she refused to implicate herself, her son, or others during interrogations with detectives, she could have shared additional information with her attorneys that might have helped her case. Incredibly, two days later, co-counsel John Clampitt would ask Weichmann again about the conversation between Mary and Lloyd on the side of the road. "Mrs. Surratt leaned sideways in the buggy, and whispered, as it were, in Mr. Lloyd's ear," Weichmann reiterated, once more drawing attention to *Mary's* mysterious behavior, and not *his*.[8] Without her cooperation, her lawyers were unable to introduce any significant evidence to rebut the government's case.

The military trial had barely begun, but the press seemed certain of Mary's guilt. After Weichmann and Lloyd's extensive testimonies, Reverdy Johnson virtually gave up on Mary's defense. His absence was duly noticed. Rumors began spreading that Johnson knew Mary was guilty and had therefore deserted her. As early as May 16, the *Philadelphia Inquirer* reported that Johnson "had abandoned cross-questioning the witnesses, and is preparing an argument to prove that the court cannot try these cases, for lack of power."[9] Johnson's decision to not appear regularly in court as part of Mary's defense team, and to leave her in the hands of his inexperienced associates, Frederick Aiken and John Clampitt, would have tragic consequences.

Meanwhile, reporters observed that Mary seemed tired and weak. Though her face was covered with a black veil, her audible sighs and "broken down" look was enough to convince them that Mary knew she was in trouble.

From this point forward, Mary spent most of the trial with "her head resting on her hand," with a small handkerchief clutched close to wipe perspiration from her brow. Though not required to wear leg irons or other restraints, like the male co-conspirators, she seemed unable to walk without assistance. One reporter observed Mary leaning "heavily upon the arms of an officer, and trembl[ing] from head to foot," upon entering the courtroom every morning.[10]

Summer was fast approaching, and the temperature in the crowded courtroom climbed daily. The numbers of spectators grew too, creating an even more stifling atmosphere. More and more women began filling the spectator chairs, a phenomenon noted by several reporters. Some women came to offer support and encouragement to Mary, others to vilify her. Many were merely curious to catch a peek of the accused woman.[11] Eventually the crowd spilled out into adjoining rooms, aisles, doorways, and halls. General Hunter was finally forced to clear away some of the spectators, allowing the prisoners and their counsel to confer outside the courtroom privately and without obstruction.[12]

Almost every day, further negative testimony implicated Mary and her son John ever more deeply in Booth's plans. Reverdy Johnson's new associates, Aiken and Clampitt, now without their experienced lead counsel, seemed helpless to stem the flow of damaging evidence.

Defense counsel for the other witnesses faced similar problems. They were grossly unprepared for the volume of evidence collected by the government, plus their inexperience, the lack of cooperation from the accused, and the unquestionable guilt of their clients who could offer no alternative explanations for their actions, made a mockery of the trial. The *Philadelphia Inquirer* noted that when the defendants' lawyers "bring out any new point they are universally to their own injury, and generally their questions are totally irrelevant, and show they have no defense."[13]

Mary's counsel lost control of many of their witnesses. On several occasions witness testimony drew rounds of laughter—a sign of disrespect not only for Mary but for her defense as well. In one particularly awkward episode, police Captain W. M. Wermerskirch was questioned by Aiken about the night of Mary's arrest at her boardinghouse. While describing the scene when the officers were ready to take Mary and the other houseguests down to police headquarters, Wermerskirch commented that Mary "requested him to wait a while, and she knelt and prayed a little." Before Aiken could stop him, Wermerskirch added, "she knelt down, but whether she prayed or not I cannot say." The courtroom filled with laughs and snickers.[14]

Mary did not take this ridiculing lightly. According to one observer, Mary "turned quickly around for a moment, and for an instant her veil was thrown aside, displaying a pair of flashing eyes."[15]

Mary's veil was only lifted a few brief times during the trial. All eyes in the courtroom would turn to catch a brief glimpse of her face when she was ordered by the court to lift her veil for witness identification. Mary may have hoped to convey a proper, feminine, and genteel countenance by wearing the veil, but it only increased the public's suspicions about her.

In any event, on May 19, the day of Wemerskirch's testimony, any hope of capitalizing on Mrs. Surratt's piety was lost.

For the time being, the attention on Mary abated. Over the next few days, the prosecution focused on the other conspirators, though they also introduced irrelevant and prejudicial testimony regarding the terrible treatment of Union prisoners in Confederate prisons. This testimony had nothing to do with the accused, but passions were enflamed even more so against the co-conspirators.

On Thursday, May 25, the prosecution rested its case.

Mary's co-council Frederick Aiken announced to the court that the defendants' attorneys had met privately to discuss the order of presentation. They agreed that testimony relating to Mrs. Surratt would launch the first phase of the defense of the conspirators.

The first witnesses Aiken produced were priests. They were asked to testify to Mary's piety—as if the notion of good Christian character would exonerate her from any implication of guilt. Father Wiggett of Gonzaga College on F Street in Washington testified that he had known Mary for ten or eleven years and that she was regarded as a "lady and a Christian." The defense tried to show that Wiggett knew Surratt well; in fact, he did not. He was not her pastor, nor did he see her regularly. When cross-examined by Judge Holt, Wiggett admitted that he had no idea if she was loyal or disloyal to the Union, as he had never talked politics with her. Wiggett denied any knowledge of whether Mary's eyesight was poor—a point the defense would harp on continuously.

The next witness, Father Francis Boyle of Washington's St. Peter's Church, told the court that he had met Mrs. Surratt eight or nine years prior to the trial, but that he had only seen her perhaps three or four times since. He "heard her spoken of as an estimable lady," but when cross-examined, he admitted that he had little interaction with her and had no idea if she was loyal or a Confederate sympathizer.

Father Charles Stonestreet stepped into the witness stand after Boyle's brief testimony was completed. Stonestreet testified that he had met Mary "twenty years ago in Alexandria [Virginia]; after that I did not see her for ten years, and since then, only in transit as I was passing." He had "scarcely seen her" during the past two years. Though he thought of her as a "proper Christian lady," he could not vouch for her loyalty. In fact, when challenged by Holt, Stonestreet admitted he had actually not seen her since the beginning of the war four years earlier.[16]

Aiken then called Eliza Holohan to the stand. Eliza, with her husband John and two young children, had occupied the third floor suite in Mary's boardinghouse. Aiken questioned her about Lewis Payne, his arrival at the boardinghouse using the identity of Reverend Wood, the Baptist minister, and his intimacy with the Surratt family. Eliza told the court that she thought Payne was odd, but understood him to be a friend of the Surratts and, therefore, felt it was inappropriate to ask any questions about him. She added that she told Anna Surratt, however, that she did not think "he would save many souls." This elicited a good round of laughter throughout the courtroom. Even stone-faced Payne snickered.[17]

Eliza also described George Atzerodt's arrival and frequent visits to the house. She knew him only as "Port Tobacco." She supported Mary's claim that Atzerodt was not welcome in the house. Booth was there frequently, Eliza then admitted, though she seemed confused as to how often he came to the house. Aiken foolishly pushed her on this point.

"Did he spend most of the time when he came there in company with Mrs. Surratt?" he asked.

Yes, Eliza admitted, "he would ask for John Surratt, and if he was not there he would inquire for Mrs. Surratt."

More damning testimony. Granted, Aiken was a novice, but one has to wonder what sort of answer he was expecting.

Eliza mimicked Weichmann's earlier testimony, asserting that Mrs. Surratt was "a very kind lady to board with." She attended Lenten services with Mary during March and early April. When asked about Mary's eyesight, Eliza claimed that she never saw Mary read or sew by candlelight. When cross-examined by Judge Holt, Eliza noted that Mrs. Surratt never appeared to have difficulty recognizing people by gaslight in the parlor. Aiken's efforts to bolster Mary's claim that poor eyesight and dim light had prevented her from recognizing Payne on the night of her arrest were ineffectual.

The day had not gone well for Mary's defense.

Nora Fitzpatrick was next to take the stand. Aiken handled her more carefully. He concentrated on the issue of photographs of Booth, particularly the one hidden behind the picture of *Morning, Noon, and Night* found in Mrs. Surratt's room. Nora was no more helpful than Eliza Holohan. She declared that she knew nothing of that hidden photograph, except that a photo of Booth was usually displayed in Mrs. Surratt's room. Aiken then redirected Nora to comment on Mary's eyesight. She claimed that one time Mary failed to recognize Wallace Kirby's wife on the street. She also said that Mary "could not read or write at night on account of her eyesight." When cross-examined by Holt, Nora admitted Mary had no trouble recognizing her by gaslight in the parlor.[18]

Another poor defense examination.

B. F. Gwynn, a Surratt neighbor in Prince George's County and a well-known rebel sympathizer, was called next to testify.[19] Gwynn had been in Surrattsville, at the tavern, on the day of the assassination, and had seen Mary there. Mary had asked Gwynn to deliver and read a personal letter to John Nothey, who lived some three miles from Surrattsville. The note demanded payment of the thirteen-year-old debt Nothey owed her. Gwynn also testified that he had seen Lloyd earlier that day in Marlboro, and that Lloyd had been drinking.

"Did he seem to be considerably intoxicated?" Aiken asked.

"I could hardly tell that; he acted like a man who had been drinking some," Gwynn responded.

Gwynn's statements were hardly damaging enough to cast doubt on Lloyd's own testimony about that day.

Aiken then called Captain Cottingham, the officer who helped arrest and interrogate John Lloyd. The young attorney was wholly unprepared for what his defense witness was about to reveal. Cottingham swore that after arresting Lloyd and interrogating him over several days, Lloyd finally broke down. Lloyd feared for his life, Cottingham told the court, if he were to tell the truth. Lloyd believed that the co-conspirators—Booth, Herold, the Surratts, and Atzerodt, among others—would murder him.

Aiken foolishly allowed Cottingham to continue. Cottingham said Lloyd told him that on the afternoon of April 14, Mary had come to him and told him to have the guns and other items prepared for pickup that night. Booth and Herold arrived around midnight and demanded the items Mrs. Surratt had told him to have ready. Lloyd had also told Cottingham that one of the firearms remained hidden in the tavern—Booth was unable to take it due to his disabled condition. Booth's broken leg made it difficult for him to grip his saddle, and he needed both hands to hold on.[20] Cottingham told the court how he'd hurried Lloyd from Robey's post office back to the tavern, where the gun was discovered behind the dining room wall. Most damaging, however, was Cottingham's statement that Lloyd had directly blamed Mary Surratt for getting him into trouble. Cottingham swore that when they arrived at the tavern, Lloyd said, "Oh, Mrs. Surratt, that vile woman, she has ruined me!"

Aiken, stunned by this testimony, pushed Captain Cottingham further, unwittingly jeopardizing his client's defense even more.

"When did Mr. Lloyd state that Mrs. Surratt made the remark about the firearms?" Aiken asked.

"It was on Friday, between four and five o'clock," responded the Captain.

Lloyd had sworn to the same evidence several days earlier.

Aiken then pressed Cottingham again about Lloyd's comments, allowing the captain another opportunity to reiterate Lloyd's distress over being swept up into the conspiracy by Mrs. Surratt. The young attorney had given the prosecution a gift.

Judge Holt jumped at the opportunity to cross-examine Captain Cottingham.

"State whether at the time Mr. Lloyd mentioned the reasons why he had concealed his knowledge of this matter?" Holt asked.

"He said he was afraid of parties there, he said if he made this confession they would murder him."

"Who do you understand him to refer to?"

"To those engaged in this conspiracy," Cottingham responded.

"What was the precise language he used in reference to Mrs. Surratt?"

"It was, 'Mrs. Surratt, that vile woman, she has ruined me; I am to be shot! I am to be shot!' He meant by that, I suppose, that his guilt was so great there was no hope for him."[21]

Another terrible blow to Mary's plea of innocence.

The next several witnesses testified in defense of Michael O'Laughlen. Their testimony revealed that O'Laughlen had been in Washington the day of the assassination, and had even conferred with Booth. They did provide solid alibis for O'Laughlen's whereabouts the night of the assassination, however. This would help save his life, but his role in planning Booth's plot would send him to prison.

During these proceedings, Aiken was fuming. He had been led to believe that Cottingham would testify that Lloyd had *not* implicated Mary during his jailhouse interrogations. At least, that is what they had agreed. What the court did not know was that Aiken had met with Cottingham several hours earlier. He believed that Cottingham's testimony would reveal Lloyd to be a liar, thereby exonerating Mary Surratt.

As soon as Walter Cox had finished examining his witnesses for O'Laughlen's defense, Aiken demanded that Cottingham be recalled. He was convinced that Cottingham had perjured himself. What happened next proved to be one of the most dramatic yet fatefully foolish twists in the trial.

Aiken challenged Cottingham in front of the entire court. Cottingham boastfully related his meeting with Aiken earlier in the day at the nearby Metropolitan Hotel. Aiken told him he would be called as a defense witness, and then, curiously, asked him if he was a fellow Catholic. Cottingham said no, he was not. The question and its questionable relevance would come to haunt the defense. To many court observers Aiken's reason for asking appeared corrupt.

Cottingham explained to the court that Aiken asked him about the confession Lloyd had made to him, particularly about anything to do with Mrs. Surratt. Cottingham claimed he refused to reveal anything to Aiken. He said he would answer any question Aiken posed to him, but he did not say specifically what he would testify to on the stand. "I didn't think I was bound to tell him," Cottingham told the court.

Aiken was not getting the response he was looking for. He redirected Cottingham's attention.

"Did I ask you if Mr. Lloyd said anything in reference to firearms?"

"You asked me if Lloyd had made a confession to me, and I said yes, and you said what was it? I declined answering, but I said I would answer any question you would ask."

Frustrated, and obviously expecting a different answer, Aiken asked, "What did you tell me this afternoon?"

"I told you a lie; you were trying to pick it out of me, and I told you that you might call me into Court, and I would state what I had told you, a lie, and now state that I did do it."[22] Cottingham had clearly lied to Aiken at the hotel, leading the defense lawyer to believe his testimony might exonerate Mrs. Surratt.

Aiken was humiliated, and Mary's case was devastated still further. How could Aiken have allowed this to happen? Cottingham would have been a hostile witness at best; to assume he would give contradictory testimony about John Lloyd's earlier statements implicating Mrs. Surratt seems ludicrous.

Now Aiken called George Calvert to the stand. Calvert was told to read the letter he had written to Mary two days before the assassination requesting immediate payment for a debt she owed his father's estate. Calvert's testimony bolstered Mary's claim that she had legitimate business in Surrattsville on the day of Lincoln's murder. But it did little to soften the disastrous day in court.[23]

It was now less than two weeks into the trial, and Mary's lawyers had been unsuccessful in introducing evidence to exonerate their client. They could not substantiate Mary's claims of poor eyesight. They could not fully account for her actions during the week prior to the assassination. Most damaging, perhaps, was testimony from several sources that she entertained Booth frequently, welcomed his co-conspirators into her home, and, hours before the assassination, delivered vital messages and supplies to Lloyd at the tavern for Booth's eventual escape. Instead of boosting their case, Mary's lawyers and defense witnesses had actually confirmed the prosecution's case.

On the twenty-fifth and twenty-sixth of May, a new parade of irrelevant priests was called to testify to Mary's supposed piety, testing the patience of the court and spectators alike. None of the priests seemed to know Mary very well and none could vouch for her loyalty. Mary was pious, they all agreed, but no one knew her political or personal views. The focus on her Catholicism even irritated some observers.[24]

It was becoming obvious, now, that Mary's lawyers were having trouble finding friends and acquaintances that knew Mary well and were willing to testify on her behalf. Aiken even called W. L. Hoyle, a local shopkeeper, to vouch for Mary's good character. But Hoyle claimed he hardly knew Mary or her son John, and could not vouch for their loyalty. "It is only as a customer that I knew her," he said.[25]

During the morning of the twenty-sixth, Aiken turned the defense over to Walter Cox, legal counsel for O'Laughlen and Arnold. After a lengthy and confusing interrogation of several witnesses by Cox, the prosecution inexplicably and abruptly interrupted the defense's case to introduce more evidence of atrocities against Union captives in Confederate prisons. Once again the prosecution purposely redirected attention from the case at hand to inflame public passions. Testimony about the conditions at these prisons and the inhumane treatment of Union soldiers by Confederate guards should have been the business of another court.[26]

Once the witnesses for the prosecution were finished later that afternoon, Cox decided not to continue his case for the day, and Aiken resumed his defense. He called John Nothey to testify that he indeed did owe Mary Surratt money for seventy-five acres of land he purchased from her deceased husband some thirteen years before. He swore that he received the letter from Mary, delivered by Gwynn, on the day of the assassination. He did not personally see Mary, however, even though she had been in nearby Surrattsville for two hours that very afternoon.

The prosecution did not bother to cross-examine Nothey. Perhaps the timing of the series of letters between Mary, Nothey, and Calvert that week seemed too contrived to warrant a challenge by the court.[27]

Frederick Stone, counsel for David Herold and Dr. Mudd, took over from Aiken. He called a series of witnesses to give testimony relating to Mudd. As with Mary, Mudd, too, suffered from damaging statements made by knowledgeable witnesses. In spite of Stone's best efforts, defense witness testimony did little to help exonerate the doctor. Stone rested his case for the day and the court adjourned.

The following morning, Aiken called upon Confederate spy and blockade-runner Augustus Howell. In March Howell had been arrested at the Surratt Tavern for blockade-running; he'd been incarcerated at Old Capitol the entire spring. He had frustrated authorities with his obfuscation during prison interrogations, but Howell was a seasoned rebel; he knew what he was doing. Though he may have been knowledgeable about some details of the kidnapping plan, he was not part of the assassination attempt. Howell was clever enough to recognize that casting aspersions on Mrs. Surratt or anyone else helped him little. Protecting himself was his main objective, but he did have an honor code—honor among thieves and spies—and would respect it until it compromised his own freedom.

Howell testified that he had known the Surratts for about a year and a half, and that he had stayed at Mary's boardinghouse in Washington in late February, where he met Louis Weichmann. Aiken tried to use Howell to discredit Weichmann's earlier testimony and to impeach Weichmann's character. Howell testified that he had shown Weichmann a coded cipher, and that Weichmann had told him in confidence that he sympathized with the South and was eager to go to Richmond. He also claimed that Weichmann gave him confidential information regarding the numbers of Confederate prisoners in Union prison camps, numbers Weichmann supposedly had access to through the War Department where he worked.

Howell alleged that Weichmann expressed strong Southern feelings to him. He told the court that Weichmann had plans to study theology with the Catholic bishop in Richmond, but Howell insinuated that Weichmann was really looking to work for the rebel government, not the church. Fortunately, Weichmann had a long trail of evidence regarding his desire to study in Richmond; lengthy correspondence over several months clearly showed his long-term efforts to pursue his studies there. In spite of the war, such arrangements were not uncommon.[28]

Furthermore, Howell claimed, he and Weichmann "had some conversations in regard to the number of prisoners on hand, and he stated to me the number of Confederate prisoners the United States government had on hand, and the number they had over that of the Confederate government." Weichmann certainly had access to these types of figures, but revealing this information to Howell would not have compromised any secret Union plans. If Booth's plan to exchange a kidnapped Lincoln for Confederate prisoners had been known to Howell, knowledge of the exact numbers of prisoners would have made little difference to the overall scheme. The Confederacy was already aware of the location of most Union prisons, so even that information was not secret. Howell's own dubious character and background swayed the court against Mary more than his testimony impeaching Louis Weichmann.

Judge Advocate Burnett eagerly took over the cross-examination. The government knew that Howell had been in the Confederate army and had been arrested for blockade-running. Burnett wanted to get this information into the record—facts the defense did not want brought out. Careful to avoid incriminating himself further as a blockade-runner and spy, Howell stated that since leaving the Confederate army in 1862, he had "not been employed in any particular business," but that he was involved in "speculating a little bit in Virginia." He did admit that he often went to Richmond—to visit friends and to buy drafts. When asked to reveal his connections there, he refused. "That would be implicating others, and I do not wish to answer that question. Anything relative to myself I will answer willingly."[29] He did reveal that he knew Sarah Slater, claiming he met her first in Washington, then at the Surratt boardinghouse in February, then shortly thereafter in Richmond. He cleverly linked Slater with John Surratt, adding that he traveled with them to Virginia.[30] Howell intimated that Mary knew he was a rebel and that "she knew I was from Richmond." He then proudly admitted that he had never taken the oath of allegiance to the United States.

Thomas Ewing, one of Mudd's attorneys, asked for permission to reexamine Howell after the prosecutor's interrogations had prompted Howell to admit that he knew Dr. Mudd. This revelation was news to Mudd's attorneys. Howell assured Ewing that he had known Mudd before the war, but had not seen him since the start of the rebellion. This eased Ewing's obvious concern. But the dangerous alliances between conspirators and rebel agents were becoming more evident with each witness.

Burnett then continued his cross-examination. He found it curious that the conversations Howell claimed he had with Weichmann were recalled so clearly, and yet he could not remember details of conversations with Mrs. Surratt or anyone else in her house. It seemed suspicious.

Howell brushed aside the question, justifying he reason for his seemingly selective memory. He said the conversations with Weichmann "just came to my mind by the question being so pointed."[31]

Burnett was ready to play hardball.

"Did you know that [Weichmann] belonged to a company for the defense of Washington, and that he had a quarrel with one of the family on account of his Union regimentals?"

"No, I never heard a word about it," Howell responded.

"You didn't know that one of the ladies struck him in the quarrel because he wore a blue soldiers' uniform?" Burnett asked again.

"No, sir. I never saw him wear blue soldiers' pants," Howell claimed. He said he had only stayed at the Surratt home for a little over two days, and it would have been unlikely he would have seen Weichmann in his uniform.

"Didn't you know that he was turning you over to pick out of you [details] about your visits to Richmond? Don't you know he tried to find out what your objects were?" Burnett snapped back.

Howell remained cocky. "If he did, he did not succeed," he boasted.

The courtroom observers laughed.

Burnett would have the last word, though. "I rather think he did."

Aiken took up questioning next, trying to salvage his witness's testimony.

"Did Weichmann, in that conversation, or not, state that he had done all he could for the South?"

This time Howell was a little more cautious: "Yes, sir, but I can't recollect the exact words."

Howell's attempts to discredit Weichmann had failed.[32]

Howell's charges against Weichmann might have been partially true, but Weichmann was sure to quickly defend himself. Weichmann did have access to the rebel prisoner figures, and he did learn the cipher from Howell. He showed the cipher to his office mates, fooling around with it to play games and translate poems. If it was supposed to be so secret, why would he have shown it to other known Union men? Was Weichmann a Southern sympathizer? No one knew for sure, but in the end it mattered little in view of the preponderance of evidence he provided against Mary and the other conspirators.

Not surprisingly, Howell wallowed in prison for quite some time. What he really knew about Mary Surratt and her activities he never revealed. The defense's attempts to raise suspicions about Weichmann did not work, and only added to Mary's woes. In fact, Howell's association with Mary, even casually, probably hurt her.

By this time, spectators must have been asking themselves whether Mrs. Surratt had any loyal friends at all.

CHAPTER NINE

THE VERDICT:
SWIFT AND DEADLY

The heat in the crowded courtroom cast a heavy pall over the scene. Rising humidity and outdoor temperatures, combined with a growing number of spectators, sucked most of the oxygen out of the room by noontime. A parade of witnesses—both significant and inconsequential—gave long and tedious testimony, leaving the judges, lawyers, and tightly packed onlookers drowsy and inattentive. Women's dresses rustled, fans and newspapers flapped: at times the proceedings became nearly inaudible.

Mary's defense had taken a beating. By the time court adjourned that Saturday afternoon, Aiken and Clampitt had only succeeded in making the prosecution's case even stronger. Even at this early date, Mary's prospects looked bleak. Clampitt and Aiken needed to regroup. They returned to court on Monday ready to take a different tack.

The prosecution was first to call witnesses to the stand. The court spent the morning listening to more irrelevant and inflammatory testimony about Jefferson Davis and his supposed glee over the death of Lincoln. After a short break, the prosecution returned the floor to the defense. For the next couple of hours, witnesses testified in support of Ed Spangler, Samuel Mudd, and David Herold. In spite of defense efforts, however, the prosecution discredited the co-conspirators' witness testimonies and successfully linked these men more directly to the assassination scheme.

In the afternoon, the floor was turned over to Mary's defense team. In an attempt to discredit Lloyd's earlier damaging testimony connecting Mary to the "shooting irons," Aiken began by calling upon the Surratt Tavern barkeep, Joseph Nott, to testify about John Lloyd's drunkenness. Nott supported earlier testimony that Lloyd was indeed drunk on the afternoon of the assassination, but was still competent enough to deliver fish and oysters to the tavern kitchen and to help repair Mrs. Surratt's broken buggy.

Then the young lawyer made a calculated risk: he called Mary's brother John Zadoc Jenkins, a Confederate sympathizer, to the witness stand.

Jenkins told the court that he was at the tavern when Mary arrived with Weichmann on that fateful day. Mary's only purpose in going to Surrattsville that afternoon, Jenkins claimed, was to transact business with John Nothey. He confirmed what Lloyd, Ben Gwynn, Nott, and Weichmann had testified to: that Mary had lingered for about two hours at the tavern, never sending word to Nothey to come see her, nor making any attempt to go to him, even though he lived less than three miles away. Jenkins also confirmed that Lloyd arrived just as Mary was about to leave, and that he was "very much intoxicated."

Aiken then asked Jenkins to comment on Mary's loyalty to the Union. Jenkins said that Mary had provided food for Union soldiers and quartered their horses without fair pay or reimbursement.

"Have you, during the last year or two, been on intimate terms with Mrs. Surratt?" Aiken asked.

"Yes, sir," Jenkins replied.

"Have you, in all your intercourse with her, ever heard her breathe a word of disloyalty to the Government?"

"Not to my knowledge," Jenkins responded.

Rather than let Jenkins's testimony stand, Aiken continued his questioning.

"Was it not Mrs. Surratt's constant habit to express warm sympathy for the sick and wounded of our army?"

"I do not remember ever hearing her say anything about that," Jenkins replied.

Aiken quickly changed the subject. "Do you know of a defective eyesight on her part?"

"I have been present when she would be unable to read or sew by gaslight; this has been the fact for several years."

"Do you recollect on any occasion of her failing to recognize immediately friends who were near her?" Aiken asked.

"I do not recollect any," Jenkins responded.

This response should have been known by Aiken ahead of time, but now it was too late to retract.[1]

John Clampitt then took over the examination of the witness. He attempted to elicit more testimony supporting Mary's loyalty to the Union. He began leading his witness, directing Jenkins to recount a conversation he supposedly had with Mary in which she described her "loyal feelings" in response to the news of General Robert E. Lee's surrender. The prosecution objected, and demanded that the witness stick to his knowledge of Mary's "reputation for and acts of loyalty," not what she had said.

Clampitt rephrased his question: "You have never heard her express a disloyal sentiment?"

"No, sir."[2]

Assistant Judge Advocate Burnett stepped up to cross-examine the witness.

"What relation are you to the prisoner, Mrs. Surratt?" he asked Jenkins.

"She is my sister," he responded.

Aiken and Clampitt had avoided revealing that important point. It was a foolish, even perilous, attempt to mislead the court.

At Burnett's prompting, Jenkins admitted that he lived within a mile and a half of his sister's tavern, and that he had been brought from prison to testify: he'd been under arrest for weeks. The importance of Jenkins's testimony in supporting Mary's case was diminishing by the minute. Once again, the defense was in shambles.

Burnett took advantage of his control of the witness. He revealed to the court a troubling scene that had transpired at the Surratt Tavern. On April 17, Jenkins had apparently been drinking at the tavern when officers George Cottingham and Joshua Lloyd arrived there with Surratt neighbor Andrew Kallenbach and tavern keeper John Lloyd to look for the gun left behind by Booth. Kallenbach, a possible Southern sympathizer whose son had joined the Confederacy, had previously been in the tavern on April 14 when Mary was there, waiting for John Lloyd to come home. Kallenbach had seen Jenkins there on that date too. Kallenbach reported to the authorities that Jenkins had threatened him if Kallenbach testified against Mary or anyone else in Jenkins's family.

Kallenbach had reported entering the tavern with Cottingham and Lloyd on the seventeenth when, for reasons that were unclear to Kallenbach at the time, Jenkins had told him he would give him "the damnedest whipping [he] ever had," if he testified against Jenkins or "anyone connected with him."[3] Jenkins said he would look in the newspapers for any statement Kallenbach might make against Mary.

After intense cross-examination, Jenkins finally confessed: "[I]n reference to the public press, I told him I would look at his statement." Although Jenkins claimed he could not recollect specifically what he said to Kallenbach, he suggested that if he did call Kallenbach a liar, or "if there was any angry or excited conversation, I did not mean it anyhow."[4] Jenkins ended his testimony by defending his honor and claiming that he was "perfectly loyal" to the Union throughout the war.[5] A parade of witnesses would later challenge these claims, testifying that Jenkins was a notorious rebel and disloyal to the government.[6]

Aiken and Clampitt were once again caught unprepared by the testimony of their own defense witnesses. Rather than proving Mary's loyalty, they succeeded in raising more doubts about her real reason for going to Surrattsville before the assassination. They in fact bolstered the testimony of Weichmann and Lloyd, whose statements they had hoped to discredit. All in all, they were making the prosecution's case easy.

Aiken now called Mary's daughter, Anna Surratt, to the stand. Anna had been imprisoned since April 17 and had not seen her mother since the night of April 30, one month before. The extent of Anna's knowledge of the daily trial proceedings is unknown. Her testimony, however, revealed a little more coaching than her intense prison interrogation on April 28. She had clearly had time to rephrase her answers and to raise doubts about damaging testimony about her mother.

Aiken began by asking Anna about George Atzerodt, and her mother's opinion of him.

"Mama said she did not care to have strangers there, but we treated him with politeness, as we did everyone who came to the house." In fact, in December Mary had placed a newspaper ad for boarders. She must have expected that strangers would respond.

Anna went on to testify that Mary's eyesight was so poor that she did not recognize her friends on the street, and she could not read or sew in the evening by gaslight. Generally, people with vision problems are either nearsighted or farsighted. If Mary's vision was so poor that she could see neither close up nor far away, then she could not have functioned very well on a daily basis. But that was clearly not the case. Mary conducted daily business and went on outings into the city with no apparent problem in getting around. She recognized John Lloyd as they passed on the road near Uniontown on April 11. Anna's earlier and equally feeble testimony on this point had already been disputed by others, and in all it failed to produce results.

Anna was perhaps more successful in casting aspersions upon Weichmann. Weichmann, she claimed, was the real co-conspirator with Atzerodt and Payne, not her mother. While other witnesses clearly linked Atzerodt and Payne to John Surratt, Mrs. Surratt, and Booth, it was Weichmann's company, Anna claimed, that they ultimately sought.

"I have met Atzerodt," she testified. "I do not think he remained over-night but once. He called very often, and asked for Weichmann."[7] She further claimed that it was Weichmann who made arrangements for Atzerodt to spend the night; she saw the two make "private signs over to each other" in the parlor.[8] Weichmann, Anna snipped, was "but too kindly treated" by her mother. "[She would] sit up for him at night, when he was out of the house . . . the same as for my brother."[9]

Aiken asked Anna about Payne: when he first arrived, how long he stayed. Anna claimed it was "Weichmann who brought Payne" into the house. Once again, she asserted that her mother did not "like strangers coming to the house, but . . . treat[ed] him politely."[10]

She testified that Booth frequented the house, but "he never stayed long when he came." He did come on the day of the assassination, she said, just as her mother was about to ride off to Surrattsville "on a matter of business" she had been planning for "a day or two." She told the court that she had not seen her brother John since the beginning of April, and had no idea where he was. She also claimed that her brother thought Booth was "crazy, and he wished he would not come to [the house]."

Aiken and Clampitt asked Anna a number of trivial questions about her schooling and where her brother had gone to college. They also asked her if she had ever heard anyone in the boardinghouse discussing a conspiracy to assassinate the President. No, she told the court.

High-strung and nervous by nature, Anna now appeared to be agitated. She began to lose her composure on the witness stand. Aiken did not seem to notice.

"Did you ever hear any remarks made with reference to the assassination of any member of the Government?" Aiken asked her.

"No, sir," she said again. She began tapping her foot rapidly on the floor, glancing repeatedly at the clock on the wall, and searching the faces in the courtroom.

"Did you ever hear it discussed by any member of the family to capture the President of the United States?" Aiken asked again.

"No, sir. I did not. Where is mamma?" Anna cried out.

From her place on the witness stand, Anna could not see her mother on the prisoners' dock. One of the guards had been ordered to stand in front of Mrs. Surratt during Anna's testimony to prevent any sort of communication or signaling between the two.[11] Anna was becoming frantic with fear and concern, causing a stir in the courtroom. Spectators began to murmur, shifting uncomfortably in their seats.

Thomas Ewing, Mudd's attorney, stepped in and changed the line of questioning, perhaps in an attempt to calm Anna down.

"What year did your brother [John] leave college?" he asked.

Flustered, Anna replied, "In 1861 or 1862, the year my father died." John Surratt, Sr., had died in August of 1862, less than three years before. It is unlikely Anna would have forgotten the year.

Frantically, Anna began murmuring, "Where's mamma?" The guard did not move.

Ewing tried to distract her again, asking her if Mudd was ever a guest at her mother's house. "No, sir," Anna replied.

Anna was by now highly agitated. Recognizing the futility of questioning her under these circumstances, the prosecution declined cross-examining her and allowed her to step down.

Thomas Ewing located a guard to escort Anna from the witness stand. As she was led down, she cried out again, in what one reporter described as "a quick, sharp voice, 'Where is mamma?'"

Aiken quickly stepped forward and told Anna she would see her mother soon, then led her into an anteroom. On the way out of the courtroom, he shuffled her quickly past Mary, preventing them both from seeing each other. Perhaps he wanted to avoid a courtroom scene, an assumption that in hindsight proved correct.[12]

The *Philadelphia Inquirer* reported that the women spectators had "crowded forward with eager faces and devouring eyes." They noted that Anna had dropped a small handkerchief, which a soldier picked up and handed to her. "She snatched it from him quickly and rudely, without a word of thanks."[13]

Curiously, while on the stand, Anna was not asked about Payne's late arrival at her mother's door the night they were all arrested, even though she had been asked that during her prison interrogation weeks before. Given this oversight, it seems odd that the prosecution decided not to cross-examine her. Anna appeared to be handled more delicately than other witnesses. Perhaps her precarious condition on the witness stand prevented the prosecutors from challenging her in court. When a reporter from the *Inquirer* asked the judges why Anna was not questioned by them, he was told "it would have been cruel, the girl having a greater load of sorrow upon her than she could bear."[14]

At twenty-two years old, Anna was hardly the young child some members of the press conveyed in describing her to their readers. Anna's persona as a weak, fragile, nervous, and hysterical teenager may have spared her from an intensive and grueling cross-examination, but it did little to help her mother's case. As the daughter of the accused, trial observers viewed her testimony as tainted: her obvious attempts to draw attention away from her mother only served to make her testimony appear untrustworthy and deceptive.

Lieutenant-Colonel Christian Rath, who had been assigned responsibility for handling the prisoners at the Arsenal Penitentiary, later revealed that when Anna was escorted to the anteroom, Rath told her he was the one who had coordinated the ruse to hide her mother from view. Anna promptly fainted. She was carried down to General Hartranft's office, where Rath splashed cold water on her face. "She suddenly came to," he later recalled, "and then such a tirade of abuse I never heard in all my life. She gave me the worst tongue-lashing I ever had; but all I can remember of what she said was 'You mean old Yankees.'"[15]

Anna became hysterical, tearing at her hair and clothing. A doctor was called, and she was sedated. Everyone present was visibly shaken by the experience.[16]

Later that day, Anna was released from prison and allowed to go free. But freedom only brought her more woes. Anna had lost everything dear to her. Her mother, brother, home, friends, and hope for the future. The house on H Street had been seized by the government and Anna had no money. In the coming days, she would be forced to live temporarily with family members in Prince George's County, but her need to be near her mother for the duration of the trial made that unbearable. She finally found accommodating friends in the Washington area with whom she could stay.

Meanwhile, back in the courtroom, Mary had broken down crying. Her stoic and stern demeanor had finally shattered.

The day after her testimony, Anna was allowed to visit with her mother. From that day forward, she occupied a seat in the courtroom near Mary. Though mother and daughter were not allowed to speak to one another, reporters noted that Anna's presence had a "cheering effect" on Mary.[17]

Over the next couple of days of the trial, a few witnesses testified on behalf of Mrs. Surratt's loyalty and that of her brother John Zadoc. None could overcome the feeling in the courtroom or in the general public that neither were Union supporters, and therefore, their testimony seemed pointless. "The cross-examination of these witnesses," the *Inquirer* reported, ". . . brought to light very few facts beyond the existence of bitter political feeling in that section" of the state.[18]

The rest of the witnesses testified on behalf of the other defendants, who continued to suffer from a lack of solid alibis and daily revelations that compounded the evidence against them. Defense attorney William Doster sought to prove that Payne was insane and not responsible for his actions when he attacked and almost killed William H. Seward the night of Lincoln's assassination. The argument fell upon deaf ears, and only succeeded in irritating the judges. Doster was grasping at straws. Ironically, twenty years earlier, William H. Seward was one of the first lawyers in the country to use an insanity defense for a mentally ill client charged with murder. (Seward's defense failed, and his client died in prison.) But Payne was clearly not insane, and in spite of mid-nineteenth-century expert medical testimony declaring that the defendant exhibited signs of mental disorder (including severe constipation), Doster's insanity plea was doomed to failure.

On June 2, Frederick Stone, Herold's attorney, took the floor for Mary's defense. Mary had recruited Stone to join her defense team—she must have felt desperate for help as she witnessed her incompetent lawyers destroy her case. Taking another shot ar discrediting star witness Lloyd's reliability, Stone first called James Lusby, a farmer who lived about a mile and a half from Surrattsville, to the stand. Lusby had run into John Lloyd in Marlboro the day of the assassination. They had drinks together there before heading back to Surrattsville that afternoon, arriving as Mary and Weichmann were getting ready to leave.

Lusby testified that Lloyd was "very drunk" when they reached the tavern. Lusby described how Lloyd drove around to the front of the tavern, while he drove to the barroom door. He saw Mrs. Surratt, he claimed, "all ready to go home at the time Lloyd drove up . . . the buggy was there waiting for her, and she left about fifteen minutes afterwards."

Judge Holt then took the floor.

"You say Lloyd was drunk: how do you know that fact . . . did you see him drinking?" Holt inquired.

"Yes; and I took drinks with him," Lusby replied.

"Which drank the most . . . were you as tight as he was?" Holt pushed back.

"Not quite as tight," Lusby snapped back.

Judge Burnett stepped in to ask Lusby for clarification.

"Mr. Lloyd was sober enough, wasn't he, to drive his own horse and to take his fish, et cetera, into the kitchen?"

"He drove his own horse," Lusby responded; "I didn't see him go to the kitchen."

"Did you see him fix Mrs. Surratt's buggy?" Burnett pushed.

"No," Lusby responded, "I do not know anything about that."

"How far is it from Marlboro to Surrattsville?" Burnett asked.

"About twelve miles, it is a fast drive of about two and a half hours," Lusby told the court. They did not have drinks while on the road, he added.

Burnett and Holt had made their point. If Lloyd was so drunk, how could he drive his wagon from Marlboro to Surrattsville, deliver fish and oysters to the kitchen, and fix Mrs. Surratt's broken axle too? More defense claims discredited.[19]

On June 3, John Surratt's sometimes girlfriend, Anna Ward, was called to the stand. She testified that Mary had failed to see her on the street one day, although she quickly added that "I had also failed to recognize her; she made an apology to me and I made the same apology to her." Ward claimed that Mary had trouble reading by gaslight, but she was unaware of Mary's failure to recognize anyone else. Aiken asked her if she had received a letter from John Surratt the day of the assassination. The letter, mentioned by Mary to authorities when her house was first searched after Lincoln's murder, could have exonerated her son by placing him outside of the city when the assassination took place.

"I did," Anna replied.

"Where is that letter?" Aiken inquired. He should have known her response before asking.

"I gave it to his mother. I presume it has been destroyed."

Curiously, the letter had disappeared in the few hours since Anna Ward had received it. No one believed it was lost—and Ward confirmed that.

Judge Bingham took the cross-examination. He inquired again about the letters John had sent Ward. She confirmed that he had sent several letters from Montreal: two for her and two for his mother. She said that she gave them all to Mary on the day of the assassination, and had not seen them since.

Then Bingham briefly asked her about the day she inquired about a room at the Herndon House for John Surratt. She admitted checking on the availability of rooms there, but did not secure one.

Aiken hoped to end Ward's testimony on a better note. "Was Mrs. Surratt a lady?" he inquired.

Yes, Ward responded, a "Christian and a lady."[20]

Ward's examination was over. As was yet another devastating day for Mary.

Summer was drawing nearer. By early June, the heat and stale, odorous air in the courtroom had grown increasingly unbearable. "The air of the room during these hot summer days is positively sickening," the *Inquirer* reported. "At least three times as many persons are crowded into it as it should contain, and the result may be imagined." Women viewers seemed to trouble the lawyers and reporters the most. One reporter wrote that "the fair sex, faithful to their ancient reputation for curiosity, furnish daily the largest number of spectators, and fill every nook and corner and chair, and even invade the sacred precincts of the lawyers' tables, and that of the reporters without any compunction of conscience."[21]

In addition, General Hunter was forced to order the women to back away from the prisoners' dock, allowing the defendants more space to breathe and to confer privately with their lawyers and to see the court proceedings without obstruction.[22] These were but a few of the many complicating factors the defense teams faced in trying to represent their clients.

All of the defense attorneys faced significant disadvantages in the courtroom. The objections of defense lawyers were overruled by the military commissioners many times more than the prosecution's objections. When the defense teams challenged court proceedings and matters of law, they were often unable to soften the direct, damaging testimony revealing Mary's and the other defendants' active roles in

Booth's plans. Perhaps the most important disadvantage for the defense at that time was that they had no legal access to the interviews, interrogations, and other evidence collected by the government over the past two months. They relied wholly on the information provided to them by their defendants and defense witnesses. Unfortunately, neither group was completely forthcoming and, therefore, defense strategies were severely hampered, leaving defense lawyers often vulnerable to damaging testimony from their own witness's statements.

By the end of the first week in June, reporters began to note Mary's failing health. The heat, coupled with her heavy black dress and opaque black veil, were causing great discomfort. One female spectator had actually fainted because of the thick, hot air. Mary refused, however, to change her dress or remove the heavy veil.[23]

As the temperature increased, so did the disdain and disgust toward Mary. Daily press coverage of trial testimony revealing Mary's complicity in Booth's plot helped keep public rage against the conspirators at a high pitch. Some reporters sought to portray her as more motherly and feminine—but then used that as a travesty of accepted norms of motherhood and highlighted the depravations of Southern Confederate womanhood. One court reporter described Mary this way:

> The tigress in nursing the purpose of the assassins until it was fully ready for the deed; and when she was arrested in the small hours of the night, in her own house, asked permission to kneel and say her prayers before being marched away by officers. She actually did kneel, and no doubt repeated her "Hail, Mary!" But will the reader pause and take a view of this woman? She sits there, in the corner, the first row of the criminals—a position of honor to which both her age and her intelligence entitle her. The reader at first finds a vail [sic], a thin one, between him and the

object of his scrutiny. Wait a moment; this witness is called on to identify her, and her face must be uncovered. She is modest and reluctant, but justice is stern, and her shyness must give way. There, now, you see the face perfectly; and, between us, it is a fine one. Indeed, if there were nothing the matter, and we were called on at this distance of ten feet to give an opinion, we should pronounce her, for a woman of her age, handsome. She is tall and large, without being fat, weighing perhaps a hundred and eighty pounds. Her hair, seen in the shade of her bonnet, reveals no gray, and is a beautiful dark brown, well polished with a brush. Her face, as befits such a form, is broad, but not coarse—just the reverse. It is fair, the cheek slightly tinged by the interest of the circumstances; and her eye is bright, clear, calm, resolute, but not unkind. Her expression, for the several hours she was under our eyes, was that of deeply somber gentleness, which still bore a look of having been partly produced by the will, and for the occasion. Immersed as she is in crime, she does not forget the woman's art. She is doing her best to make a favorable impression, by dress and aspect, upon her judges. She was the very person to mold the material which fell into her hands. She no doubt ruled them like a queen. But the court, fortunately, is made of quite another metal.[24]

Another court observer noted that Mary presented an image of a "matronly woman of considerable force and decision, but not of overnice or delicate womanly character. There was something bordering upon the gross and repulsive in her countenance, and yet I hesitate to record it, knowing how much of our estimation of womanly beauty rests upon our faith in her beauty of soul."[25]

Some people did sympathize with Mary, however. Many were Southern apologists and rebels themselves who found her alleged actions admirable. Most cloaked their support in rhetoric about femininity and motherhood, as well as exaggerated claims of Catholic piety.

Jane Swisshelm was an exception. A former anti-slavery activist, women's rights proponent, and newspaper editor, Swisshelm attended the trial briefly. Observing Mary closely, she found herself defending the accused woman's honor:

> Her face, and indeed her whole figure, while on trial, was soft, rounded, tender and motherly. Her large grey eyes alone gave indications of reserved strength. Her behavior during that long and terrible ordeal, was full of delicacy and dignity. She made no scenes, as a weak and vain woman would have done. . . . All the long, hot days she sat with her heavy mourning veil down, a large palm leaf fan held between her face and the crowds who gathered and struggled, and crushed to gaze at her, as if she had been an alligator—hundreds of persons in these crowds making the most insulting remarks in her hearing.[26]

Though writing after Surratt's execution, when public sentiment had shifted in support of Mary's innocence, Swisshelm's defense of Surratt is peculiar. A supporter and friend to Mary Lincoln and Edwin Stanton, Swisshelm would seemingly have applauded the execution of a conspirator like Mary. Mary, as a Southern slaveholding woman and Confederate sympathizer, was the antithesis of a woman like Swisshelm. Nevertheless, Swisshelm may be representative of the broader public who found the hanging of a middle-aged mother unacceptable. In doing so, however, Swisshelm fell back on accepted notions of female virtue and piety as wholly incompatible with violence, murder, and conspiracy.

But some women were not trapped by such feminine conventions. Swisshelm identified women spectators as the most insulting among the courtroom visitors toward Mary. "She looks like a devil!" one woman snickered. "Hasn't she a horrid face?" another exclaimed. "I hope they'll hang her," yet another woman suggested, well within earshot of Mary and the other defendants.[27]

By the end of the first week of June, court observers began to notice that Mary was becoming ever more sickly and feeble. She had to be helped in and out of her chair on the defendants' dock, and relied on the guards' support when she walked to and from the courtroom. One reporter noted that the "lady visitors show very little consideration for her feelings, crowding around her closely and making impudent remarks in her hearing." He noted, however, that perhaps she would feel better if she took off her thick veil, before she "threaten[ed] herself with asphyxia."[28]

On June 7, the prosecution called John Holohan to the stand. Holohan had joined Weichmann and the detectives in searching for John Surratt in Canada; he had also been in the H Street house the night the detectives came looking for John Jr., Booth, and the other accomplices in the early hours after Lincoln's murder. Whose witness he was became a contentious issue, however. Both the prosecution and defense wanted to claim Holohan as their own. "The monotonous character of the proceedings was broken today by a spirited controversy," one reporter wrote excitedly.[29] The defense was hoping that Holohan would discredit Weichmann's testimony and support their contention that Weichmann was a liar and possibly a co-conspirator himself. The prosecution hoped to use Holohan to support the already-strong evidence against Mary, but also vouch for Weichmann's testimony.

Judge Burnett asked Holohan to describe his relationship with the Surratts and any of the defendants on trial. Holohan explained that he lived at the Surratt boardinghouse with his family and that over time he had seen several of the co-conspirators there, including John Surratt, Atzerodt, Payne, and Booth, as well as Sarah Slater. He explained that the last time he had seen John Surratt, on April 3, he had given him sixty dollars in cash in exchange for forty dollars in gold. So far, Holohan had only reiterated what had been said repeatedly in court before— the co-conspirators spent time at Mary's boardinghouse, and that John Surratt was last seen on April 3.

After some heated arguing between Judge Burnett and defense attorneys Ewing and Aiken, the defense was allowed to ask Holohan about Weichmann and the his actions the morning after the assassination. Aiken asked Holohan whether "Weichmann gave himself up after the assassination, or whether he was arrested and taken to the police office." The defense hoped to show that Weichmann had been arrested as a suspect, and that his testimony, therefore, could not be trusted. But in the end, Holohan could only claim that on the morning after the assassination, he "took Weichmann down myself" to the police station, and that the two of them had gone to Canada in search of John Surratt with federal detectives.[30]

The defense teams had tried, quite unsuccessfully, to bring in witnesses to discredit Louis Weichmann's testimony. When they could find no one to prove that Weichmann's description of events and activities were false, they tried to impugn his reputation and paint him as a rebel and possibly a spy. While it is entirely plausible that Weichmann may have harbored Confederate sympathies, his testimony was so specific and incontrovertible that his political views ultimately mattered little.

In truth, Weichmann had wavered back and forth before the trials, ambiguous at times while at others professing loyalty to one side or the other, apparently in deference to present company or to flatter those in positions of influence over his career and future aspirations. By the time he took the witness stand, Weichmann declared unwavering loyalty to the Union, leaving many to believe he was merely an opportunist out to save his own neck.

Nevertheless, it is Weichmann's testimony that has withstood intense scrutiny and reexamination over the past one hundred and forty years. His intimate relationship with John Surratt, his daily interactions with Mary and the rest of the H Street household, and his position on the periphery of Booth's inner circle of accomplices placed Weichmann in a difficult yet important position within the web of activities that resulted in the murder of Abraham Lincoln. Weichmann, in fact, came incredibly close to becoming a defendant rather than an eyewitness and informant. Moreover, for many witnesses, while the physical distance between the defendants' dock and the witness stand was but a few steps, the fine line between accomplice and informer was often indistinguishable.

But while the government had called a series of witnesses testifying to Weichmann's good character and loyalty to the Union, the defense could not produce solid and defensible counter-testimony. Weichmann, who was still being held at the Arsenal, learned of attempts to impeach his character, and when the court asked him to answer the charges made against him by the defense, Weichmann heartily complied. In lengthy correspondence to Judge Burnett, written from his cell at the Arsenal Prison, Weichmann countered some of the claims made by defense witnesses with hard evidence and more explicit detail than he had provided on the witness stand. When Howell, for instance, claimed that Weichmann was eager to move to Richmond and work for the Confederacy, Weichmann produced lengthy correspondence with the Catholic diocese and the bishop in Richmond regarding his desire to study at the theological school there. The government was not entirely sure of Weichmann's total innocence; in fact, they suspected he had known more than he was willing to reveal to protect his own life.[31]

Though Weichmann was able to answer all the charges against him, he suffered terribly because of his testimony. He would lose many friends and acquaintances, though most were Southern sympathizers to begin with and shunned anyone who testified against Mary and the others. But to have testified so specifically and in such a damning way about Mary's role left Weichmann more vulnerable. The trial would haunt him for the rest of his life.

Two days later Aiken recalled Nora Fitzpatrick to the witness stand. She explained that she did not realize it was Payne who had come to the boardinghouse on the night they were all arrested, because she had remained in the parlor the whole time. She swore that it was not until they were all sitting in General Augur's office later that night that she noticed Payne was there. She told the court that she did not think Mary or Anna denied knowing Payne, only that he was not John Surratt. Anna had become indignant, Nora recounted, when someone suggested that Payne was her brother and the assailant who had tried to murder Secretary Seward. Nora also supported Mary's claim that her eyesight was poor.[32] When Nora had been interrogated by Detective Wells later that night, she said nothing to him about Payne. But after several interrogations later, Nora had revealed the truth, claiming she lied out of fear, not to protect a killer. Unlike some witnesses and suspects, incarceration had succeeded in making her more cooperative.

The prosecution also called a series of witnesses to testify, again, to the disloyal sentiments harbored by Mary and her brother John Zadoc. And, as expected, the defense produced more witnesses asserting the Surratt family's loyalty to the Union. Rachel Semus, one of Mary's former slaves, testified in Mary's favor, claiming that Mary treated her "servants" well, and that she had been exceedingly kind to Union troops coming through the area. Henry Hawkins, another former slave, also testified on Mary's behalf. Both supported the defense's contention that Mary had poor eyesight. The focus on Mary's eyesight had become tiresome and, in context of all the evidence against her, seemed at this point merely a distraction, serving no purpose.[33]

Finally, after four weeks, the trial was drawing to a close. The defense teams begged for more time to call in more witnesses and present new facts to counter the astounding body of evidence the government had compiled. "The counsel for the Government feel that their case is strong enough, and they can afford to be generous in granting opposing counsel any reasonable time they ask for," the *Inquirer* reported.[34] The paper also noted, once again, that Reverdy Johnson had not appeared in court since the first week of the trial.

John Lloyd and Emma Offutt were recalled by the defense. Why Lloyd was put back on the witness stand is a mystery. Aiken and Clampitt already knew his testimony. This time, when Aiken asked Lloyd to testify about the guns John Surratt brought to the tavern for safekeeping, Lloyd recounted how the guns were "put between the joists, where they remained until Mrs. Surratt called to give directions in regard to them, which was Friday, the fourteenth of April." He then reiterated that "in accordance with her directions I took them out from where they had been secreted, and kept them ready for whoever would call for them. . . ."[35] Was Aiken expecting a different answer? Was he trying to refocus attention on John Surratt's important role? Whatever his intentions, he only succeeded in reinforcing Mary's complicity.

Emma Offutt testified next. She asked the court if she could adjust her testimony from her previous statements made to the court in May. She had told the court then that Mary did not give her a package on the day of the assassination. In correcting her statement, Offutt swore she had been ill that day in court and had misspoken. She testified that she did, in fact, receive a package from Mrs. Surratt, and though she had no idea of what was in it, she saw Lloyd holding a similar package later that evening. Offutt stated that Mary told her she had business to transact that day. She also asserted that she knew Mary had poor eyesight.[36] Overall, Offutt's adjusted statement did not help Mary. But it supported John Lloyd's testimony about Booth's field glasses, wrapped in brown paper, which Mary had given him that day. Why Aiken brought Offutt back to the stand to revise her previous statement is also puzzling.

On June 13, Aiken and Clampitt rested their defense. With the exception of Doster, who was still pulling together a list of witnesses to support Payne's insanity plea, most of the other defendants' lawyers had completed their cases as well. After a few more days of testimony relating to Payne's physical and mental state, and after court-appointed doctors visited with Payne in his cell, Doster's strategy fell apart. Long and boring medical testimony irritated the judge advocates, but the government's physicians admitted they found no evidence of insanity. Payne was probably relieved. As one historian has noted, it was one thing to be called a murderer, something Payne had admitted to doing—and doing for the rebel cause—but to be called insane was entirely different. Many of the doctors fixated on the fact that Payne had been constipated for weeks—a sign, they believed at that time, of insanity. The prison doctor, Porter, who spent time with Payne every day, swore that Payne was "sane and responsible."[37]

The government pressed on with its effort to link a larger, more co-ordinated Confederate conspiracy with Lincoln's assassination. But they could not provide a positive link to the highest levels of the Confederate government, and the statements of various shady characters who gave perjured testimony hurt the government's case. Though Payne had claimed that there were many more people involved in the plot than the government knew of or had in custody, it did not change the weight of evidence condemning Mary and the others.

On June 19, the court was preparing for summation arguments. Reverdy Johnson had written an extensive closing argument, which was presented by John Clampitt and took hours to read. Much of it harangued the court for conducting the trial illegally. Reverdy argued that a military tribunal could not try and convict civilians in peacetime. These were the same arguments Johnson had made before, and every time he had argued these points he was overruled and dismissed. Johnson claimed that the tribunal was unconstitutional, and in pages and pages of summation, Johnson outlined ancient and contemporary legal traditions throughout the world. He dedicated just a few sentences to Mrs. Surratt, his client, and even those select words neglected to make a case for her innocence. In closing, he wrote:

> As you have discovered, I have not remarked on the evidence in the case of Mrs. Surratt, nor is it my purpose. But it is proper that I refer to her case in particular for a single moment. That a woman, well educated, and, as far as we have it in evidence, a devout Christian, ever kind, affectionate, and charitable, with no motive disclosed to us that could have caused a total change in her very nature, could have participated in the crime in question it is almost impossible to believe.
>
> Such a belief can only be forced upon a reasonable unsuspecting, unprejudiced mind by direct and uncontradicted evidence,

coming from pure and perfectly unsuspected sources. Have we these? Is the evidence uncontradicted? Are the two witnesses, Weichmann and Lloyd, pure and unsuspected? Of the particulars of their evidence I say nothing. They will be brought before you by my associates. But this conclusion in regard to these witnesses must have in the minds of the court, and it's certainly strongly impressed upon my own, that if the facts which they themselves state as to their connection and intimacy with Booth and Payne are true, their knowledge of the purpose to commit the crimes and their participation in them, is much more satisfactorily established than the alleged knowledge and participation than Mrs. Surratt. As far, gentlemen, as I am concerned, her case is now in your hands.[38]

It would be another two days before Aiken and Clampitt would provide their own closing summation, even though Johnson knew that they were inexperienced attorneys and it could prove disastrous to leave Mary's final defense arguments in their hands. Just as he did through most of the trial, he left Mary's life—and left Mary's life in their hands. He used up hours of the court's time to once again challenge the jurisdiction of the military court, knowing that those same arguments had failed repeatedly in the past. Why didn't he engage in the evidence and defend his client? Why did he not present his summation in person? Mary Surratt was being tried for treason, conspiracy, and murder, all of which were punishable by death. The court was unimpressed by his efforts, and the public knew it.

Mary was doomed. She suddenly took ill and was escorted from the room. Closing arguments for the other defendants consumed the few minutes left to the day, and the court adjourned until the next morning.[39]

On June 21 William H. Seward's wife, Fanny, died. Ill for several years, the tragic sequence of events that spring had taken a tremendous toll on her, physically and emotionally. Secretary Seward was still recovering from his own near-fatal wounds, and the nation mourned with him. The tragic consequences of Booth's mad scheme seemed endless. It cast its shadow over the courtroom that day, and when Mary reappeared, she, too, was weak, worn out, and depressed.

Noting Mary's declining health, the court ordered that Mrs. Surratt be given extra privileges. Her daughter, Anna, was allowed to be with her in her cell during the day. This had an uplifting effect on Mary, though it brought Anna to the brink of a nervous breakdown.

On the twenty-second, Aiken would present his summation to the court. It was his last chance to redeem himself and Mary. After lengthy summations by William Doster on behalf of his two clients, Payne and Atzerodt, Aiken took the floor. He began with broad oratorical comments about honor and obligation to protect the weak and dependent.

"Profoundly impressed," he told the court, "with the innocence of our client, we enter upon this last duty in her case with the heartfelt prayer that her honorable judges may enjoy the satisfaction of not having a single doubt left on their minds in granting her acquittal, either as to the testimony affecting her or by the surrounding circumstances of the case." He alluded to Reverdy Johnson's argument that the court had no constitutional jurisdiction.

Then, he very carefully argued a case for reasonable doubt, an argument governed by the rules of law in civil courts, where, he argued again, this trial should have taken place. Quoting "judicial wisdom," and the accepted "administration of criminal law" in civil courts, Aiken claimed that if Mrs. Surratt could be found guilty in a civil court, then she must be found guilty in this court; however, he stressed, she could not be found guilty in a civil court because of the standards of reasonable doubt.

In an almost threatening and certainly prescient way, Aiken told the court that "for private and public reasons it was highly desirable that the findings of the Court should be sustained by sufficient evidence. If they were," he warned the military commissioners, "the public would overlook any irregularities that might be supposed to exist." The commissioners were undoubtedly irked by this implied threat or scolding in open court. Aiken was taking a big risk.[40]

Aiken continued to argue the finer points of law concerning conspiracies, and whether those conditions applied to Mrs. Surratt's case. No, he claimed, because there was reasonable doubt that she participated in any crime, and the claim of a general conspiracy had not been proven by the government. Aiken was right. The government had failed to prove the existence of a general Confederate conspiracy to assassinate Lincoln, conceived and supported at the highest levels of the rebel government. So if according to the law no conspiracy existed, Mary could not have been part of one. This argument seemed ineffective at best, but at least Aiken was trying to cover all the charges in Mrs. Surratt's indictment.

Finally, Aiken recounted the evidence against Mary, charging that it was all weak and circumstantial. Oddly, Aiken read directly from the court transcript the testimonies of John Lloyd, Louis Weichmann, officers and policemen who arrested Mary and searched her house, and assorted other prosecution witnesses. Though he was trying to discredit those witnesses' statements, he also reminded the court of the preponderance of evidence against Mary.

Aiken also tried to lay more of the blame on John Surratt, who remained missing and in hiding. Still sheltered by priests and friends in Canada, John made no attempt to come to his mother's aid. The trial reports he received may have been a few days old, but by the time the trial was well under way, it was obvious that Mary's defense was weak and that she was at great risk of being found guilty. John would later claim he did not know his mother was in such deadly trouble.[41] A letter, a telegram, a written confession, sent through intermediaries, could have made a difference for his mother's case. But John said and did nothing.

Aiken concluded his summation by reminding the court of Mary's piety, the sanctity of motherhood, and virtues of true womanhood. He declared Mary "widowed of her natural protectors," and left vulnerable to "revenge" and "retribution." He trusted the court to preserve its dignity by finding her not guilty.[42] In an extravagant closing, Aiken pleaded that the court "not let this first State tribunal in our country's history, which involves a woman's name, be blazoned before the world with the harsh hints of intolerance which permits injustice. . . ."[43]

Throughout the next week, defense counsel for the remaining defendants presented their summary arguments, followed by the prosecution's lengthy summation. Mary did not attend the last few days of the trial. She was very ill, clearly breaking down under the stress of the trial and its negative direction.

The case ended on June 28. The nine commissioners, Judge Holt, and Holt's two assistants, Bingham and Burnett, prepared to deliberate the trial proceedings and render a decision on each charge for each defendant. It would be a short deliberation, and the verdicts would be swift and deadly. Four of the eight conspirators would be executed; four would serve prison terms. Mary would be among the four to be hanged; Payne, Herold, and Atzerodt would hang with her. Mary, however, would bear a singular distinction: she would be the first woman ever to be executed by the United States government.

CHAPTER TEN

SCENES AT THE SCAFFOLD

John Clampitt and Frederick Aiken were sitting in their offices, awaiting the announcement of the verdicts when they were "suddenly startled by the cry of the newsboys on the street:

THE EXECUTION OF MRS. SURRATT![1]

Aiken and Clampitt had not been informed ahead of time of their client's sentence. Incredibly, newspapers had gotten hold of the story before the War Department had officially announced it, and had published extra editions to accommodate the fresh news. "So sudden was the shock, so unexpected the result . . . we hardly knew how to proceed," Clampitt would later recall.

The two lawyers had truly believed that their defense of Mrs. Surratt had been a good one. In spite of rumors circulating the day before that some of the conspirators would hang, Aiken and Clampitt were confident that Mary would be acquitted, or at worst, endure "a temporary confinement."[2]

The twelve members of the commission had deliberated for two full days in total isolation until they reached their verdicts: death for Mary Surratt, Lewis Payne, David Herold, and George Atzerodt; life sentences for Samuel Mudd, Michael O'Laughlen, and Samuel Arnold; and a six-year prison term for Ed Spangler. Each case required a two-thirds majority vote before a sentence could be passed. The decision to sentence a woman to death was unprecedented, and required extremely careful consideration. Mary's execution would be a profound milestone in American criminal history.

The commissioners found Mary Surratt's case an extraordinary challenge. Overwhelming evidence, coupled with an incompetent defense team, destroyed any possibility of acquittal. Mary's inability or refusal to offer plausible alternative explanations for her actions in the weeks and days leading up to the assassination, and a stunning lack of supportive and believable character witnesses, left few doubting her guilt. In addition, her black lace veil, shielding her from public scrutiny during the trial, added fodder to the sinister view of her. Her steely resolve and stoic demeanor throughout most of the trial also confirmed, for some observers, the depth of her callousness. Perhaps a little arrogant and overconfident, Mary contributed to her own negative public image, helping to reinforce notions of her guilt.

The judges must have known their decision would evoke strong reactions. Nevertheless, they bravely voted against historical tradition, determining that Mary must hang. Based on the evidence, they believed that she was just as guilty as Payne, Herold, and Atzerodt, accomplices who shared equally in supporting Booth's deadly plan:

> After mature consideration of the evidence adduced in the case of the accused, MARY E. SURRATT, the Commission find the said accused—
>
> Of the Specification . . . [Conspiracy to Murder] . . . GUILTY
>
> Except as to "receiving, sustaining, harboring, and concealing Samuel Arnold and Michael O'Laughlen," and except as to "combining, confederating, and conspiring with Edward Spangler;" of this . . . NOT GUILTY

Of the Charge . . . [Aiding and Abetting] . . . GUILTY

Except as to "combining, confederating, and conspiring with Edward Spangler;" of this . . . NOT GUILTY

And the Commission do, therefore, sentence her, the said Mary E. Surratt, to be hanged by the neck until she be dead, at such time and place as the President of the United States shall direct; two-thirds of the members of the Commission concurring therein.[3]

The twelve-person commission determined that Mary was guilty of conspiring not only with Payne, Atzerodt, Herold, and Mudd, but also with her son John Surratt, John Wilkes Booth, the leaders of the Confederacy, and "others unknown . . . who were then engaged in armed rebellion against the United States," to "combine, confederate, and conspire together, at Washington City, within the Military Department of Washington, and within the entrenched fortifications and military lines of the United States" to "unlawfully, maliciously, and traitorously . . . kill and murder Abraham Lincoln, then President of the United States . . . and Commander-in-Chief of the Army and Navy thereof; Andrew Johnson . . . William H. Seward . . . and Ulysses S. Grant."[4] In addition, Mary's charges also included aiding and abetting the escape of Booth, Herold, Payne, Atzerodt, and John Surratt after Lincoln's murder.[5]

In spite of their collective decision finding Mary guilty and recommending she hang with the three other co-conspirators, five of the twelve commissioners, including David Hunter, August Kautz, Robert Foster, James Ekin, and C. H. Tomkins, recommended leniency for Mary:

The undersigned members of the military commission detailed to try Mary E. Surratt and others for the conspiracy and the murder of Abraham Lincoln, the late President of the United States, do respectively pray the President, in consideration of the sex and

age of the said Mary E. Surratt, if he can upon all the facts in the
case, find it consistent with his sense of duty to the country to
commute the sentence of death to imprisonment in the penitentiary for life.[6]

The recommendation to commute Mary's death sentence, rather
than to give her a life imprisonment sentence in the first place, is curious. The commissioners believed she was as culpable as Payne, who
attempted to assassinate Seward; Atzerodt, who had been assigned the
murder of Vice President Johnson; and Herold, who aided Booth in
his escape. The weight of the historical and legal precedent they were
about to set may have tempered their decision. By offering an alternative to sending her to death, they placed the final decision in their
commander-in-chief President Johnson's hands. Johnson would have
to approve the verdicts and sentences, and now it would be up to him to
decide Mary's final fate.

The commission gave their separate clemency petition to Judge Advocate Burnett, who then attached it to the written statements detailing
the prisoners' sentences, and prepared them for Judge Advocate General Joseph Holt to present to the President.

Johnson had been ill for several days, and had therefore delayed reviewing the findings of the court. On July 5 he requested that Judge
Holt meet him at the White House to discuss the verdicts and sentences. Johnson told his private secretary, General R. D. Muzzey, that
he needed to be alone with Holt and that he was not to be disturbed.

For three hours, Holt and Johnson discussed the findings of the
court and each prisoner's sentence. When the two men emerged from
their meeting, Johnson remarked to Muzzey, "The papers have been
looked over and a decision reached." Muzzey later recalled that Johnson told him that several commissioners recommended leniency for
Mrs. Surratt "on the grounds of her sex (and age, I believe)." He also
remembered that Johnson "thought the grounds urged [were] insuffi-
cient, and that he refused to interfere; that if she was guilty at all, her

sex did not make her any the less guilty." Later, Johnson reiterated his feelings on the subject, telling Muzzey that "there had not been 'women enough hanged in this war.'"[7]

After meeting with Holt, President Johnson met with several members of his cabinet, including William Seward, Secretary of War Edward Stanton, Secretary of the Interior James Harlan, and Attorney General James Speed. They discussed the findings of the court, the sentences, and the recommendation of mercy for Mrs. Surratt. While cabinet meetings are secret, Assistant Judge Advocate John Bingham later confirmed with Stanton and Seward that the petition for clemency had been seen and discussed by the President and his cabinet. They both agreed. "The petition was presented to the President and was duly considered by him and his advisors before the death sentence upon Mrs. Surratt was approved." Bingham later wrote that Stanton and Seward also told him that "the President and the cabinet, upon such a consideration, were a unit in denying the prayer of the petition."[8]

Holt, who would later come under intense attack for his role in the trial and would face charges that he never showed Johnson the clemency plea, told fellow jurist General James Ekin that he made a point of drawing Johnson's attention to the petition. Johnson, however, told him that he "could not accede to or grant the petition, for the reason that there was no class in the South more violent in the expression and practice of treasonable sentiments than the rebel women."[9]

After meeting with President Johnson, Holt went directly to Secretary Stanton's office at the War Department. Judge Advocate Burnett was meeting with Stanton at the time and remembered the encounter this way:

"I have just come from a conference with the President over the proceedings of the military commission," Holt announced to the two men.

"Well, what has he done?" Stanton asked.

"He has approved the findings and sentences of the court," Holt replied.

When asked what Johnson had decided about the plea for mercy, Holt told them that Johnson said, "She must be punished with the rest; that no reasons were given for his interposition by those asking for clemency in her case, except age and sex."[10]

In approving the sentences, Johnson ordered Major General Hancock to carry out the executions immediately.

"The President of the United States has approved the foregoing sentences in the following order, to wit,"

Executive Mansion, July 5, 1865

The foregoing sentences in the cases of David E. Herold, G. A. Atze-rodt, Lewis Payne, and Mary E. Surratt, are hereby approved; and it is ordered that the sentences in the cases of David E. Herold, G. A. Atzerodt, Lewis Payne, and Mary E. Surratt, be carried into execution by the proper military authority, under the direction of the Secretary of War, on the seventh day of July, 1865, between the hours of 10 o'clock, A.M., and 2 o'clock, P.M., of that day.

Andrew Johnson,
President[11]

The following morning Hancock gave the orders for the death sentences to Major-General Hartranft at the prison. At noon, both men climbed the stone steps to the cells of the four co-conspirators scheduled to be hanged the next day, July 7.

Payne was the first to receive the news, taking the sentence "as if he fully expected it." He told the generals that he was sorry for what he had done, and though he believed he was doing his duty for the Southern cause at the time, he realized he was wrong.[12] Atzerodt was next. He began to shake and shiver. He asked to be allowed to see some family and friends, and a minister. Hancock and Hartranft then went to Herold's cell on the floor below Atzerodt. Upon hearing the sentence, Herold, too, began to "tremble like a leaf." Herold then admitted that he was a party to Booth's kidnapping plans, brought into it, he told the generals, by John Surratt. When he discovered Booth's murderous plan, he told them, he objected to it, but then agreed to help Booth escape. His "sympathies had been with the South, head, and heart." He, too, asked that his family be brought to him.[13]

Mary was alone when Hancock and Hartranft arrived at her cell, also on the third floor. She was completely unprepared for the verdict and sentence. She became hysterical, screaming and sobbing uncontrollably. Collapsing on the floor, she could not be comforted. Fearing she might die then and there, the generals called for the prison physician immediately. He gave her wine and sedatives, which succeeded in calming her temporarily.[14] Swearing her innocence, she begged for Father Jacob Walter and Father Bernadin Wiggett, John Brophy of St. Aloysius College, and her daughter.[15] Anna, who had been visiting her mother, had not yet left the prison grounds when she heard Mary's sentence. She, too, became hysterical, and was taken off the grounds until she could regain her composure.[16]

Oddly, the people Mary asked to come to her in her final hours were relatively unknown to her. She did not ask to see her mother or brothers, nieces or nephews, Washington neighbor and friend Wallace Kirby, or even female friends. Instead, Father Walter, who had never met her, and John Brophy, who barely knew Mary, came to see her. Brophy had met her only briefly once or twice before the trial. He later revealed that he had been trying for weeks to help Mrs. Surratt's defense, believing wholeheartedly that she was innocent. He surmised, probably correctly, that Clampitt and Aiken had told her of his efforts, and that she felt he could be trusted. Still, of all her family, friends, and acquaintances she should call for, her request to see two near-strangers seems peculiar. It appears to say a lot, however, about the lack of personal support Mary actually had.

Coincidently, during the morning of July 6—and before the verdicts were publicly announced—Father Walter had been trying to get a pass to visit Mary. Early on during Mary's incarceration she had sent a note to Father Walter asking him to come see her at the prison. By the time he received her request, she had been moved to the Arsenal and was not allowed any visitors. It was a moot point, however, because he did not want to see her: he feared being associated with an alleged conspirator.[17]

But when Mary requested to see him, again, on the sixth, he believed it was his duty as a priest to meet with her if she so desired. He had not attended the trial, nor, according to his own admission, had he followed the trial proceedings and testimony very closely. When he heard the rumors of her death sentence, he went to the War Department and asked for a pass to visit her. General James Hardie, assistant to Secretary of War Stanton, was in charge of handling the many requests put before Stanton. Hardie agreed to let Walter see Mary, and within a few hours a pass, signed by Hardie in Stanton's place, was delivered to Walter by special messenger.

What happened next was widely disputed for years. According to most accounts, after Father Walter received the pass from the messenger, he remarked that he thought Mrs. Surratt was innocent, and that the trial clearly was unfair. In fact, he was so angry in his tone that the messenger hurried back to Hardie's office to report the disturbing encounter to Hardie.

In the meantime, Hardie had been informed of the official verdicts. Suddenly, he realized that the pass he had signed and sent to Walter would no longer be sufficient to gain an audience with Mrs. Surratt. Tighter security and greater caution would now be protocol at the prison. Hardie immediately procured a new pass with Secretary Stanton's signature and was about to have it sent to Walter when the messenger returned and reported Walter's angry words.

Troubled by what the messenger told him, Hardie immediately left to deliver the pass to Walter himself.

When Hardie appeared at Walter's door, Walter became belligerent, shouting that Mary was innocent and unjustly tried and convicted. Hardie told him he must temper his emotions and refrain from agitating Mary by discussing his personal belief in her innocence. Walter accused Hardie of anti-Catholic bias, and in doing so, carelessly accused the wrong man; Hardie was a devout Catholic, converted years earlier, and had been especially helpful to Catholics in their pursuit of favors from the secretary of war.

Hardie was deeply shocked and insulted by Walter's behavior, and told him he would not give him the pass after all. As Hardie turned to leave, Walter backed down and promised to hold his tongue. Hardie accepted Walter's apology and reluctantly gave him the pass. He would later come to regret it. Even though Walter was allowed access to Mary, and stayed with her until her execution, he would spend years falsely claiming that Hardie and Stanton had purposely tried to prevent him from seeing Mary in her final hours. He would also deliberately misinform the public by spreading disinformation and outright lies about the trial, including promoting false evidence in defense of Mrs. Surratt, and feeding the public unfounded conspiracy theories regarding the military commission and Secretary Stanton's influence upon them.[18]

Mary's other surprising visitor, John Brophy, an old school friend of Lou Weichmann's who now taught at St. Aloysius College in Washington, was another relatively unknown character who emerged during the trial and execution as a champion of Mrs. Surratt's innocence. During the early part of the trial, Brophy later claimed, Lou Weichmann had come to him, confessing that he knew Mrs. Surratt was innocent. Weichmann had met Brophy through John Surratt sometime during their years together at St. Charles College. Weichmann's friendship with Brophy had never been close, but they shared a common interest in the Catholic church and ministry.[19]

According to Brophy, the day after Weichmann had been released from prison on May 31, he went to visit Brophy. Brophy even claimed that Weichmann had admitted to being threatened with death if he did not testify against Mrs. Surratt. He said Weichmann told him that Mary had no knowledge of Booth's intentions to either kidnap the President or kill him. Brophy further said he asked Weichmann to write a letter to President Johnson, stating that Mrs. Surratt was innocent, but Weichmann refused.

Weichmann, in turn, publicly disavowed all of Brophy's claims and accusations. He pointed out that Brophy had been called by both the defense and prosecution to testify to their meeting and to Weichmann's statements. But Brophy had somehow avoided being interrogated and he was never placed on the stand.[20] Brophy did not publicly reveal this supposed conversation until the day of the execution, when he sent a telegram to the press, outlining his accusations.[21]

Considering what Brophy alleged to know about Weichmann's supposedly false testimony during the trial, it is curious that he waited until Mary Surratt was hanged before publicly acting upon it. During the trial, President Johnson had received an anonymous list of accusations against Weichmann that was strikingly similar to the ones Brophy would later also level against Weichmann. Stanton and Burnett had demanded that Weichmann answer all the charges against him—which Weichmann did to their satisfaction. Some of the charges were spurious, others more serious. Most suggested that he was a Confederate rebel, sympathetic to Booth's cause. But that was all determined to be untrue. More serious charges claimed Weichmann had been threatened with death if he did not testify against Surratt and the others, but that, too, was proved false. In the end, Weichmann never wavered from his belief that Mary was guilty, and his testimony has never been proven to be false.

In spite of Brophy's claims about what he knew about Weichmann, Brophy said nothing of Weichmann's testimony or his alleged confession to him when he published a pamphlet in mid-June, defending Mrs. Surratt's honor and condemning the press for its biased and unflattering coverage of her as a person. While his protest is well taken—the press was often cruel and overly preoccupied with describing Mary in the most unflattering terms—Brophy, in a flourishing and breathless literary style, called upon the return of gallant and chivalrous men to protect Mary, "alien among her own people, torn from her home, separated from her children, stricken in her affections, blighted in fame and hopes, dispossessed of liberty and all that makes life estimable." He alluded to her Christ-like behavior, eliciting imagery of Christian martyrdom, reminding readers that Christ had been condemned by false witnesses who called for his crucifixion. The commissioners, he argued, were better suited to charge against "enemies in the battlefield, than to receive charges against a weak, unprotected woman in a courtroom." Mary was but a "simple woman, much too weak to oppose" the "cunning" of the court and witnesses against her.[22]

The pamphlet was originally published in Washington's *Constitutional Union* on June 14, and then reprinted in other newspapers. The court took little notice of Brophy's claims—claims that offered no new evidence in defense of Mrs. Surratt.

After the sentences had been read to the four condemned prisoners, they were escorted to new cells on the first floor, closer to the prison yard. Brophy, the two Catholic priests, and Anna crowded into Mary's new cell, hoping to comfort her and to decide what their next steps would be.

In the meantime, stunned and unsure of what to do, Aiken and Clampitt hurried over to the White House and requested an audience with President Johnson. They hoped to plead for mercy—if not to stay Mary's execution, at least to give them a few more days to help them prepare another argument in her defense. Less than twenty-four hours was not enough time to begin an appeals process. But Johnson refused to see them. Guards with "fixed bayonets" were a firm deterrent to anyone seeking to push their way through to see the President.[23]

Confused, angry, and perhaps feeling shame and guilt for not preparing their client for the possibility of a death sentence, Clampitt and Aiken rushed to the prison to meet with Mary. Mary had not called for them, but as her attorneys, they were allowed unrestricted access to her. They hoped to use Anna to convince Judge Advocate General Joseph Holt to help them get an audience with the President to plead their case.

With little time to spare, and with Anna in tow, Clampitt and Aiken hurried by carriage the two miles to Judge Holt's War Department office near the White House. They believed that a personal plea, and the "unutterable woe" of Anna, might help them secure a few days' reprieve. On "bended knees, bathed in tears," Anna begged Holt to go to the President and ask for a three-day delay in the execution order. Holt acquiesced and agreed to meet them all later that morning at the White House.

When Clampitt, Aiken, and Anna arrived at the White House, Holt was just leaving. Holt had met with the President, he told them, and said, "I can do nothing." The President was unmoved; the execution would be carried out as planned.

Deeply distraught, Aiken and Clampitt wired Reverdy Johnson in Baltimore, requesting immediate advice on their next move. Johnson wired back and told them to apply for a "writ of habeas corpus and take her body from the custody of the military authorities. We are now in a state of peace—not war."[24] Johnson was still convinced that the military trial was illegal. Since the war was officially over, the civil courts should have handled the prosecution of the co-conspirators, not a military tribunal, he believed.

By now it was two o'clock in the morning, less than twelve hours until the execution. Clampitt and Aiken rushed to the home of Judge Andrew Wylie of the Washington Supreme Court to request a writ of habeas corpus for Mrs. Surratt. He invited them into his study, where, sitting attentively in his nightshirt, Wylie listened to them argue their cause. When they were done, Wylie excused himself to think. After a few short minutes, Wylie emerged from his study and agreed to sign the writ. According to Clampitt, Wylie told them, "I am about to perform an act which before tomorrow's sun goes down may consign me to the Old Capitol Prison."[25]

At four o'clock in the morning, the two lawyers stood before United States Marshall David S. Gooding, with the order from Judge Wylie, commanding General Hancock "to have the body of Mary E. Surratt, detained under your custody ... [brought] before the Criminal Court of the District of Columbia, now sitting at City Hall ... at the hour of ten o'clock." Gooding delivered the writ to General Hancock, whom he found at the Metropolitan Hotel at eight-thirty that morning.[26]

News of Clampitt and Aiken's attempts to stay the execution "spread like wildfire" throughout the city. Rumors that Mary would be pardoned began to float around. By ten o'clock, however, Hancock had not arrived at the courthouse with Mrs. Surratt, as the writ had ordered. Judge Wylie, who was in court to hear another case, and District Attorney Edward C. Carrington were at a loss as to how to proceed. Never before had they been forced to test a civil court's power against a federal military power. By ten-thirty, Wylie and Carrington concluded that if Hancock had decided to ignore the order, they could do nothing. They issued the following statement:

> The Court acknowledges that the laws are silent, and that it is without power in the premises, and therefore decline to make any order whatsoever ... The court therefore must submit to the supreme physical power which now holds the custody of [Mrs. Surratt], and declines to issue an ... order in this case.[27]

Instead, Carrington and Wylie proceeded with another trial already in progress.

At noon, General Hancock burst into their courtroom, accompanied by Attorney General James Speed. Speed apologized to the court for their late arrival. He asked for forgiveness for the appearance of disrespect for not honoring the writ of habeas corpus. He explained that General Hancock was bound by the orders of his commander-in-chief,

President Andrew Johnson, who, at ten o'clock that morning, had suspended the writ for Mrs. Surratt, and had ordered Hancock to proceed with the execution. Not surprisingly, the court acknowledged that it was powerless to act in this case. Speed thanked the court and made a brief speech justifying the military tribunal and its findings.

All avenues for legally delaying the execution were now closed.

The scene at the prison was quite frantic. Anna had determined she could not wait for the court to make a decision. The stress of the day's news had brought her to the edge of her sanity. She had spent most of the night with her mother, Fathers Wiggett and Walter, and John Brophy, hoping and praying for an intervention on Mary's behalf. At one point, Brophy accompanied her to the boardinghouse, which by now had become a morbid tourist attraction. Since the announcement of the verdicts, hundreds of people had flocked to the H Street home, standing outside in the hopes of seeing something, hearing something. Anna entered with Brophy, quickly gathered a few personal items, and left, overwhelmed by the lurid spectators keeping vigil at her home.[28]

It was a restless night for all of the condemned, but particularly for Mary. She suffered greatly from intestinal problems and was beset with grief. As the other three prisoners sentenced to death spent time with their families and with clergy brought in to attend to their final spiritual needs, Mary continued to profess her innocence, crying out loudly enough for the others to hear. Her protestations and outbursts that night affected the other prisoners measurably. Atzerodt and Herold became so irritated by Mary's wailing that they both reiterated to the guards and visitors that she was as guilty as they were.

In his brief memoir published in 1915, William E. Doster, attorney for George Atzerodt and Lewis Payne, revealed that co-defendant David Herold had complained during the trial that Mary Surratt "is as deep in as any of us." Doster claimed Herold said this out of jealousy because, as Doster tried to argue, positive and seemingly persuasive defense arguments on Mary's behalf were winning her case for her. But that was hardly so. Mary's defense team was incompetent: their strategy only highlighted the overwhelming preponderance of evidence against her. Most people who observed Mary's defense in court knew she was doomed. Herold hardly would have been envious of her.

Doster also claimed that Atzerodt and Payne were clear in their defense of Mrs. Surratt, and never wavered from their claims of her innocence. "Payne and Atzerodt . . . constantly and repeatedly stated that Mrs. Surratt was entirely innocent of the conspiracy."[29] Perhaps fifty years had clouded his memory. For all those years, Doster had been in possession of Atzerodt's confession, taken in Doster's presence on the night of May 1, 1865, but never admitted into evidence during the trial. In that confession, Atzerodt had clearly implicated Mary Surratt as a co-conspirator.[30] In addition, on the day of the hangings, Atzerodt swore that Mary was as guilty as the rest of them—an outburst reported in the news and no doubt heard by or reported to Doster at the time.[31]

Doster's motives in claiming Mary's innocence are unclear, but fit a pattern. In his memoir, Doster also asserted that Atzerodt was innocent, knowing full well that Atzerodt had confessed to participating in the kidnapping plans and had learned of the decision to kill Lincoln hours before the assassination. But rather than acknowledging Atzerodt's confession and the evidence presented at the trial against all the defendants, Doster blamed the military commission for conducting an illegal trial outside of its jurisdiction. He said that the conspirators' executions were "but a lynching," and that Mary Surratt's death was "judicial murder!"[32] That Doster would knowingly distort the facts, even fifty years later, when he held evidence implicating Mary, indicates the level of bitterness and partisanship involved in this trial and the profound and lasting implications of the decision to execute a woman.

Payne was the only conspirator who finally asserted, though in qualified terms, that Mary was innocent of the conspiracy charges. He did so in a statement made during the early morning hours on the day of the hangings, but only after dramatic and repeated demands by Mary's supporters. On the night before the execution, a hysterical Anna Surratt, joined by John Brophy and Fathers Walter and Wiggett, visited with Payne to convince him to make a statement exonerating Mary. Payne, who felt great sympathy for Anna, was badgered by her and the others for hours until he finally acquiesced.

Hampered by Payne's own admission of guilt, Doster tried fruitlessly to convince the court that his client was insane. But he knew Payne to be more stable than most of the defendants. In fact, after Payne learned of his death sentence on July 6, he freely described his role in the assassination scheme and his subsequent escape to Reverend Dr. A. D. Guillette and several guards. Dr. Guillette had been sent by Edwin Stanton to comfort the prisoners in their last hours. An Associated Press reporter later wrote that Payne told Guillette and the guards that he regretted going to Mary's boardinghouse the night of April 17. Payne said he had only gone there because he "believed Mrs. Surratt knew about the plot and would help him through, but was not sure she would not give him up, that he was almost indifferent to his fate, and had even confidentially given himself up on the following morning, and would not therefore have blamed Mrs. Surratt if she had caused him to be arrested. He [Payne] never has either said she was guilty or innocent, but has more than once said that the conversations of Booth and John H. Surratt led him to believe that she knew in general terms what the plot was. He condemned John H. Surratt in the strongest terms for running away, and said he was sorry if any act of his had proved harmful to Mrs. Surratt." When asked why he participated in Booth's scheme and attempted to kill William Seward, he claimed that he "considered it his duty, that he had no ill will toward Mr. Seward personally, that he had believed that it was God approved of his course; but that within a short time he had received enlightenment about the matter, was convinced that the North had not heretofore meant what he had supposed they did, and now felt he had done wrong, and that his punishment was just."[33]

A reporter for the *Washington Chronicle* was more specific: "Payne . . . regretted more than anything else the part he had taken in bringing Mrs. Surratt into trouble, and declared that he had no conversation with her at her house the night he was arrested there. His object in going to her house was to obtain a suit of clothes that would enable him to make his escape into Virginia. He censures her son, John H. Surratt, in the severest terms for deserting his mother in the hour of her direst extremity."[34] But Father Wiggett, it was later revealed,

> embraced the favorable moment to ask [Payne] a question unheard of by the others: "Laying my hand on his shoulder, so, I said in a low tone, 'Tell me my friend, is Mrs. Surratt guilty?'" Just as quick he answered, "No, she is not!" Then, suddenly leaning forward and putting his lips to my ear he whispered, "She might have known something was going on, but she did not know what."[35]

An article in the *New York Times* on the day of the execution noted that Payne, "noticing the kind consideration of Miss [Anna] Surratt toward her mother, expressed regret that they should be compelled to part. He said he would do anything, say anything, which could help Mrs. Surratt, who is an innocent woman. . . . Payne, last evening, informed Col. Dodd, who has special charge of the prisoners, that so far as he knew, Mrs. Surratt had nothing to do with the plot for assassination. Certainly, she had never said a word to him on the subject, nor had any of his co-conspirators mentioned her in connection with the matter. She may have known what was going on, but to him she never disclosed her knowledge by word or act."[36]

After two days of listening to a hysterical Anna sobbing and pleading for her mother's life, one can imagine how Payne may have wanted to ease her pain and suffering, regardless of Mary's guilt. Payne told Reverend Dr. Guillette that Mary, "at least, does not deserve to die with us. If I had no other reason, Doctor—she is a woman, and men do not make war on women."[37] Payne's position here is interesting, given that he was arrested several months earlier for brutally beating a black maid in Baltimore.

Payne's confession clearly indicates that he knew he would be safe returning to the Surratt household, that Mary could provide a change of clothing for him, and that he could trust her. Like Howell, Payne respected an honor among rebels. Though repentant over his role in the attempted murder of Seward, he had believed deeply in the rebel cause and in Booth's plan; indeed, he believed the plan was sanctioned by God. Mary played a role in that scheme, and Payne knew it, but her role was not as violent as his was. To Payne, Mary Surratt was a rebel supporter, respected for her dedication to the cause. Payne would die a chivalrous man, protecting Mrs. Surratt's reputation.

On the day of the scheduled executions, several key players escalated their all-out efforts to stop the hanging. Anna went to see President Johnson early in the morning to plead mercy once again for her mother. Brophy, meanwhile, convinced General Hartranft to record Payne's statements about Mrs. Surratt's innocence and rush them to the President. Hartranft wrote out Payne's statement, signed it, and had Brophy take it to Johnson.

When Brophy arrived at the White House at around nine-thirty in the morning, he ran into Anna. Anna had been rebuffed by Johnson's secretary, General Muzzey, and refused an audience with the President. This made her hysterical. General Muzzey had no idea who Anna was when she begged and pleaded with him to let her see the President. According to Johnson, Muzzey told him there was a "crazy woman . . . downstairs [who] wanted to see me and she wouldn't give her name, but was crying and tearing her hair out and exhibiting all the evidence of insanity."[38] Anna was forced out of the building and left on the White House steps.

Just as Brophy was trying to get past the guards who were restraining Anna to enter the White House, Mrs. Stephen A. Douglas arrived on the scene. A close friend of Lincoln's who was highly respected in Washington's political and social circles, Mrs. Douglas listened to Anna and Brophy's pleas. She agreed to try to see the President in their stead and to argue for Mary's commutation.

Mrs. Douglas took Hartranft's affidavit and pushed past the guards and their bayonets. Inside, she was admitted to the President's office. The discussion that ensued has never been revealed. Within a few minutes she reappeared outside on the White House steps, reporting to Brophy and Anna that she was helpless to change the President's mind.[39] Later, David Herold's sisters also tried to see the President, but as with Anna, they too, were refused.

Word of the sentences had spread throughout the greater Washington area on July 6. With lightning speed, thousands who wished to watch the hanging descended upon the city. Hancock made a list of approximately one hundred persons who could be issued passes to witness the execution in the prison yard: mostly dignitaries, court officials, and reporters. More than a thousand eager spectators who applied for passes were denied.[40] The rest of the witnesses in the prison yard would be Union soldiers.

Outside the prison walls, thousands of people waited in the intense heat, in the hopes of seeing or hearing something. One reporter who was disgusted by the spectators' macabre curiosity described the scene thusly:

> The hotels were thronged Thursday. The streets were filled with restless, impatient people. The headquarters were surrounded by crowds of anxious men, who desired above all things to witness the execution, and who were willing to spend hundreds of dollars for the poor privilege. All day long, the trains came in loaded with people from the North; all night long the country roads were lined with pedestrians, with parties hurrying on to

the city, where they might at least participate in the excitements of the occasion.

Officials of every grade and name, with or without influence, were pestered by applications for tickets ... by those whose idle or morbid curiosity impelled them to come to this hot and sweltering city in search of food for gossip and remembrance. Of course, all endeavor was futile.[41]

General Hartranft called on Captain Christian Rath to build a gallows and prepare the nooses for the four prisoners. Rath ordered the prison carpenter to begin construction in the prison yard immediately. As Rath later recalled, the carpenter became deeply troubled with the task. Apparently, up until this time, he had only built furniture and coffins. Rath thought the carpenter might faint, and ordered several soldiers to help him. They eagerly complied.

The scaffold platform was about twenty feet high and thirty feet across: large and sturdy enough to accommodate the simultaneous hanging of the four conspirators. The gallows required two large, hinged drops, each drop designed to hold two of the accused. Space was needed behind the drops for the prisoners' spiritual advisors, the soldiers standing guard, and the hangman. When finished, its presence in the yard would be a haunting specter; a tainted spirit watching the final horror of the country's bloody sectional conflict.

Rath took a length of Boston hemp rope, brought from the Navy Yard, and tied four nooses. Three nooses were tied carefully with seven knots each for strength. The fourth, Mary's noose, he left for last: he tied five knots in it and then set it aside. Convinced in the last hours before the execution that Mary's sentence would be commuted, Rath believed he would not need to finish tying her noose.[42]

Rath commanded several more soldiers to dig four graves next to the gallows. The civilian laborers who were initially asked to perform the job were "superstitious," according to Rath, and refused to carry out the task.

After the hanging, the accused would be buried immediately in the prison yard, and would remain there indefinitely. The government wanted to ensure that the bodies, like Booth's, would not be accessible to random members of the general public—among them, relic hunters who might desecrate the graves. In addition, they wanted to prevent any sort of memorialization by Southern sympathizers eager to celebrate the co-conspirators' treasonous deeds.

Rath assigned several additional soldiers the task of leading the prisoners out of the prison and up the scaffold stairs to their respective places on the gallows platform. Four more soldiers were stationed beneath the platform drops to knock the support posts from under the scaffold when the order for the execution was called out.

At about eleven-thirty that morning, the soldiers began to test the drops with one hundred-and-forty-pound weights. One of the drops failed to fall, so the testing was repeated over and over again until both drops worked evenly and simultaneously. The snap and crack of the heavy platform drops as they fell must have unnerved the prisoners, whose cells were so close to the yard.[43] Indeed, Atzerodt could be seen through his barred window, trying to concentrate on the words of his minister, Dr. J. G. Butler.

Four plain pine coffins were piled randomly near the open graves. In spite of the refusal of civilian workers to dig the graves, there was no shortage of military volunteers eager to participate in the "gruesome" work of the execution. Many viewed it as an "honor to serve in any capacity in avenging the death of Lincoln."[44]

Vaguely aware of the numerous and frantic efforts by supporters throughout the night and morning, some spectators had fully expected that President Johnson would grant Mary a reprieve. As an additional precaution, Hancock ordered cavalrymen to guard and clear specific points along the roadways from the White House to the penitentiary. For in the event the President *did* grant Mary a reprieve, he wanted to be sure the message would reach him swiftly.

Others were not so sure that Mary would get a reprieve. Rumors began circulating that a bold attempt was under way by an unknown number of persons to rescue Mrs. Surratt from the penitentiary. In response, Hancock ordered several hundred soldiers into position in and around the prison to prevent any possible attacks. The Twelfth Regiment Veteran Volunteers took their places around the scaffold, while a portion of the regiment stood guard on top of the prison wall. One eyewitness observed batteries of artillery positioned strategically around the penitentiary.[45]

After her fruitless attempt to meet with President Johnson, Anna returned to the prison to say good-bye to her mother. Her anguished wails filled the prison hallways, affecting the guards deeply. Mary struggled to maintain her composure, but was overwhelmed by her weakened state and terror over her impending death. Still, she managed to consult with Brophy over Anna's care, the disposition of her estate, and other personal matters. Fathers Wiggett and Walter listened to Mary's final claims of innocence, while helping to prepare her to "meet her God."[46]

The unbearably hot July morning wore on. The waiting proved trying for some of the soldiers stationed in the prison yard. One Union officer later reported that the carpenters, still putting the final touches on the scaffold, tossed leftover bits and pieces of wood to the loitering soldiers. Such construction trash was eagerly snatched up and fought over by "relic hunters." A rat racing across the prison yard was caught and summarily hanged on a miniature gallows, its body tossed into the open graves nearby.[47]

Finally, the death machine was ready, but the execution could not move forward without General Hancock. At twelve-thirty, Hancock arrived after making his way from the courthouse through the jammed streets.[48] As Rath recalled, Hancock's late arrival gave hope to some that Mary's sentence would finally be commuted. But with Hancock on the scene, the order stood firm: Mary must die.

Hancock turned to Rath and said, "All is ready, Captain, proceed."
Rath, surprised, said, "Her too?"
"Yes," Hancock replied, "she cannot be saved."[49]

The crowds inside and outside the prison yard bore the searing heat with impatient excitement. One reporter noted that it was "one of the hottest and most oppressive days ever known in Washington," with temperatures nearing one hundred degrees.[50] The newly built gallows dominated the northeast wall of the prison yard. Mounds of deep red earth lay near the four open graves beyond the scaffolding, eerily beckoning the rough pine coffins stacked haphazardly nearby. Scores of soldiers stood shoulder to shoulder along the top of the prison yard wall, keeping a watchful eye on the hundred or so spectators within the walls and the thousands standing in wait outside. Final inspections were made of the scaffold, trap floors, and nooses. At 1:12 P.M., the hangman gave the signal, and the heavy wooden penitentiary door swung open. The procession of the condemned to the gallows, fifty feet away, began.

Mary Surratt emerged from the dark and dank prison first, sending an immediate hush over the crowd. They turned to gape at the infamous woman. Her black veil and bonnet shielded her eyes from the bright midday sun. For nearly two hours she had listened to the sharp clap of the gallows's twenty-foot-long trap floor as the hangman repeatedly tested it to assure its flawless performance. She had prepared herself for the scene, but the sheer size of the gallows overwhelmed her. Two soldiers, Lieutenant-Colonel McCall and Sergeant W. R. Kennedy, accompanied her. Fathers Wiggett and Walter, both carrying crucifixes and reciting the church's last rights, walked with Mary too. Her legs weakened, forcing her to lean heavily upon the soldiers as they approached the scaffold stairs. When she saw the freshly dug graves, she lost her composure. The two soldiers had to carry her up the fifteen steps to a chair atop the gallows.[51]

The four condemned conspirators (left to right), Mary Surratt, Lewis Payne, David
Herold, and George Atzerodt, with officers, priests, and others on scaffold.

Mary was followed by Atzerodt, Herold, and Payne, each guarded
by more soldiers and additional clergy members. Four armchairs had
been placed on the platform behind the two matching hinged drops.
Mary would need the support more so than the others. The nooses
hung before them, swaying slightly in the soft hot breeze, taunting the
condemned in their final minutes of life. Though still veiled, Mary's
lips could be seen moving rapidly, as if reciting a prayer. She kissed a
crucifix held by one of the priests.[52]

Hartranft called for umbrellas to shield the condemned from the
blazing sun. He could not afford to have any of them faint. He read the
charges and sentences to the conspirators.

The hangman paused before Mary. He had never executed a woman
and was somewhat reluctant to proceed. For four hours, he had waited
for word from the President that Mary Surratt's sentence would be
commuted. Now, he had no choice but to carry out the jury's order.
First he bound her hands and arms. But her legs, hidden beneath a
large black skirt, posed an embarrassing dilemma. After a long pause,

General John F. Hartranft reading the death warrant to the conspirators.

the hangman wrapped the cotton ties around her billowing skirt, tightening it awkwardly against her legs. William Coxshall, one of the soldiers stationed beneath the platform and responsible for knocking out the large wood beam drop supports when the hanging order was shouted out, recalled hearing Mrs. Surratt complain about the tightness of the restraints around her wrists. "It won't hurt long," she was told.[53]

When the hangman removed Mary's veil and bonnet and slipped the noose around her neck, the crowd became visibly agitated. One spectator turned away from the scaffold and confronted the crowd, throwing his hands into the air and shouting, "Gentlemen. I tell you this is murder; can you stand and see it done?" When no one responded, he silently turned back to the scaffold.

The knot of the noose was tight against Mary's left ear. Now the hangman slid the white cotton hood over her head, masking her face from the restless crowd below.

Photographer Andrew Gardner had been called by the War Department to record the historic event. A Lincoln favorite, Gardner had been

Adjusting the ropes for hanging; hangman tying Mary Surratt's arms and legs.

chosen to photograph several of the co-conspirators after they had been arrested and confined to the *Montauk*. He also photographed John Wilkes Booth's body when it was returned to Washington. Gardner had visited the prison in advance to determine where he could find the best views of the execution and to set up his cameras. His photographs remain the most vivid and haunting images of the end of Booth's accomplices.[54]

The priests recited their final prayers for the condemned and, with the exception of Fathers Walter and Wiggett, thanked the soldiers and General Hartranft for their kind treatment. Captain Rath readjusted and tightened Payne's noose around his powerful neck.

"I want you to die quick," Rath told him.

"You know best," Payne replied.[55]

Mary turned to Father Walter.

"Shall I say anything?" she asked.

Walter inquired as to what she wanted to say.

"I wish to say to the people that I am innocent," Mary replied.

The hanging bodies of the conspirators, with crowd departing and soldiers mingling. The bodies were left for a little more than twenty minutes before being taken down and buried.

Walter told her it would be "useless" to say that at this moment, but Mary persisted. "I am innocent, but God's holy will be done."[56]

The condemned were ordered to stand and move forward onto the trap floors. Their chairs were removed. Mary barely made it beyond the hinges in the floor. "Don't let me fall," she called out. Payne stood strong and "straight as an arrow" next to Mary, advancing well out toward the brink of the drop, placing "his toes right on the edge."[57] They would fall together when the execution order was made.

Herold and Atzerodt stood to Payne's left. Herold shook uncontrollably. Atzerodt called out to the crowd, "Gentlemen, take warning." Pausing for a moment, he continued, "Good-by gentlemen who are before me, may we all meet in the other world."[58]

Below the scaffold and underneath the trap floors, the four soldiers waited patiently for the signal to dislodge the platform props. One of them, William Coxshall, became nauseated by the strain of the heat and the "interminally" [sic] long prayers spoken by the priests. Moments before Rath came down the scaffold steps to give them the signal, he vomited. Then Rath clapped three times. On the third clap, Coxshall and the three other soldiers swung the support beams out from under the drops, and all four conspirators fell with a loud thud and a "heavy slam," straining the wooden beams supporting the four nooses.[59] Their bodies "swayed backward and forward" briefly.

At 1:22 P.M., July 7, 1865, forty-two-year-old Mary E. Surratt was hanged for conspiring to murder President Abraham Lincoln. Mary was the first woman executed by the United States government.

She died instantly; Herold and Atzerodt's deaths also seemed to be swift. Payne was not so lucky. As Captain Rath had feared, Payne's thick neck was not broken by the fall. He struggled for what some estimated to be as long as five minutes.[60]

The bodies were left hanging for at least twenty minutes to be certain they were all lifeless. Then the corpses were cut down. The prison physician inspected them and pronounced them officially dead. Captain Rath personally handled Mary's body, "not being willing that any hand should desecrate her." He lifted her body carefully and removed the noose from her neck. Carrying her slowly to the unmarked, predug graves, he placed her gently into a readied coffin. Her name, written on a small piece of paper and sealed in a glass vial, was placed in the coffin with her. She was buried next to the other conspirators in the yard.

AMERICAN TRAGEDY OR AMERICAN JUSTICE?

P ublic disgust and outrage over Mary's execution was immediate. Despite the strong negative feelings toward Mary throughout the monthlong trial, public sympathy swelled dramatically and instantaneously after her execution. During and immediately following the hanging, many Southern sympathizers maintained the illusion that Mary was an innocent victim of a vengeful and vindictive Northern political machine. Her name rallied the cause of defiant Southerners reluctant to rejoin the Union. Even Napoleon III of France, hoping to install a French-backed ruler in Mexico, used Mary Surratt's execution as a tool to recruit disaffected Southern Confederate soldiers to his army units, which were battling Mexican and Spanish interests in the Southwest for control of Mexico.[1] In response to Mary's execution, rebels and Confederate sympathizers in Canada "manifested their feelings by wearing crape on their arms, singing secession songs, and threatening the President with terrible retribution."[2] Portraying Mary as the poster child for wronged Southern womanhood, sympathizers carried on the call for justice and vengeance for her hanging for decades.

Louis Weichmann came under intense public attack within days of the execution. His onetime classmate and now-nemesis John Brophy wrote a lengthy critique of Weichmann's testimony and published it in the *Constitutional Union* on July 11.[3] Claiming that Weichmann had perjured himself and was more deeply involved in the plot than he admitted, Brophy attacked Weichmann's character. He outlined a series of statements and inconsistencies in Weichmann's testimony, revealing, he claimed, a duplicitous and devious ploy to protect himself at the expense of an innocent woman.

Brophy nitpicked at several inconsistencies in Weichmann's testimony, but most had been challenged in court. In any event, Weichmann had already defended himself fully to the court's satisfaction. Brophy also charged that Weichmann had tried to escape from federal custody when he was in Canada searching for John Surratt. Officer William Kelley, who had accompanied Weichmann and Holohan to Canada in the days after the assassination, answered that Weichmann had willingly gone to Canada, that he was not restrained nor under arrest, and that he could have escaped easily if he had wanted to.[4]

In addition to attacking details of Weichmann's testimony, Brophy claimed that Weichmann had reneged on his promise to tell the world that Mary was innocent. Weichmann later clarified that supposed promise, arguing, "I partly made a promise to her friends, which on account of circumstances I do not deem it prudent to fulfill."[5] Some people were suspicious of this statement, believing that Stanton, Holt, and others desperate for conviction had threatened Weichmann if he did not lie on the stand. But Weichmann was clear: "I . . . don't believe that Mrs. Surratt was an innocent woman."[6]

In a lengthy rejoinder to Brophy's charges, Weichmann responded by not only defending his character and loyalty, but also spelling out in detail, once again, all the evidence against Mrs. Surratt. His response, reprinted across the country, reminded people that his was not the only damaging testimony against Mary, and that the preponderance of evidence from multiple witnesses had sealed her fate. Newspapers headlined the controversy with titles such as "Weichmann Vs. Brophy!! Refutation of Certain Slanders," titillating readers still eager for more trial gossip.[7]

Within days of the execution, Mary's final confessor, Father Walter, swore out an affidavit claiming that Secretary of War Stanton and his assistant, General Hardie, had refused to let him see Mrs. Surratt when she requested spiritual counsel during her last hours. He alerted the press, which ran a sensational story about Walter's struggles to provide Mary with religious counseling in her final hours. He charged that General Hardie refused to give him a pass unless he promised not to discuss Mrs. Surratt's innocence at the prison. Hardie fired back with his own version of meeting with Walter, exposing Walter as a liar. Walter, Hardie wrote, was first summoned by Mary to the prison in early May, but he refused, not wanting to "have his name connected" with the trial. Hardie also revealed that he had helped facilitate Walter and Anna Surratt's desperately-hoped-for access to the President on the day of the execution, even though it proved futile.[8]

Both Brophy and Walter would continue their efforts to discredit Weichmann, the trial, and the key players well into the 1890s and early 1900s. Joined by attorney John Clampitt and theater owner John Ford, an unlikely supporter on whose property Lincoln was shot, these trial and execution critics kept up the attacks for years.[9] As time passed and memories faded, their public condemnations became more bizarre and contorted, misleading the public with misinformation and faked facts concocted to dramatize Mrs. Surratt's innocence and Weichmann's supposed duplicity.[10] As one writer observed, "Her sex appears to have blinded the judgment of many who did not follow the trial with attentiveness."[11] He might have added that some very close trial observers were blinded to the truth as well. In 1895, John Clampitt's home in Chicago was destroyed by fire. At the time he claimed that the fire destroyed thirty years of evidence he had collected proving Mrs. Surratt's innocence. Oddly, in those thirty years he never produced any of this hard evidence, and after the fire he was never able to tell the public exactly what that evidence was.[12]

But Lou Weichmann would bear the greatest burden in trying to reclaim his reputation and defend his character. He would battle Brophy,

Walter, and John H. Surratt, Jr., among others, until his death in 1902. Weichmann never wavered nor changed his testimony, but that never stopped his critics, who continued to berate and harass him. He spent the last few decades of his life collecting evidence, correspondence, and testimony to write a narrative of the "truthful history of the whole affair."[13] He died before publishing it, and for some unknown reason, his family never attempted to do so for him. Decades later, Floyd Risvold, a collector of Americana, acquired the manuscript from one of Weichmann's nieces, publishing it in 1975 under Weichmann's original title: *A True History of the Assassination of Abraham Lincoln and the Conspiracy of 1865*. The book brought to light the many well-researched details Weichmann had hoped to share with the public about the case. Weichmann's narrative clearly shows a man deeply wounded by his critics, but also a man who, over time, became more and more convinced of Mrs. Surratt's guilt.

Throughout Mary's trial, John Surratt, Jr., had been moving about eastern Canada, safely hidden by sympathetic Catholic priests in Montreal and elsewhere. After his mother's execution, he was secretly shipped off to Europe through the aid of Canadian Confederate agents, where he evaded United States authorities for two years. He joined the Papal Zouaves (the pope's guards) in Vatican City under an assumed name, then, remarkably, was recognized by an acquaintance from Maryland who happened to be in Rome. He was arrested, but managed to escape the prison where he was being held. He fled to Egypt, where in 1867 he was finally apprehended by U.S. marshals.

When John was forcibly returned to the United States, he was placed on trial by the government. Much of the same testimony from the 1865 trial of the co-conspirators was resurrected. Tried in a civil court and not a military court, John's defense was successful in demonstrating that he had been in Elmira, New York, spying for the Confederacy when the assassination took place, and was therefore unaware of Booth's final plan. As with his mother and fellow co-conspirators before him, John by law was not permitted to testify at his own trial. Still, much more evidence was introduced shedding light on the extensiveness of the conspiracy, as well as new details about Mary's complicity in it. But despite the new evidence, John's case ended in a mistrial—the civilian jury was packed with Southern sympathizers. All charges were then dropped because the statute of limitations of two years on a charge of treason had passed, and, in February 1868 John was set free.

In reality, however, the nation had tired of the emotional, political, and economic costs of the Civil War and the turmoil generated by Lincoln's murder. Few Americans were interested in revisiting this national tragedy and avenging yet another of its perpetrators. The drama and difficulties of federal Reconstruction and efforts to promote reconciliation between the North and South dominated the nation's political and economic interests.

Arrogant, unapologetic, and confident he would not be tried again, John hit the lecture circuit in 1870, rewriting his mother's and his own historical participation in Booth's plot. Claiming his mother was innocent, John helped promote the goals and interests of other Southern apologists and Mary Surratt sympathizers who would not let Mary's memory fade, nor give up on clearing her name.

After a brief and unsuccessful attempt to cash in on his notoriety, John married and settled into a mundane life working as a clerk for a Baltimore shipping company. His older brother, Isaac, had fled to Mexico after being discharged from the Confederate army, where he served as a soldier for hire for a time. When, exactly, he learned of his mother's fate is unknown. He eventually returned to Baltimore and moved in with John and his family, where he worked for a shipping company too. By the mid-1870s, both men had faded into obscurity. Isaac, who never married, passed away in early November 1907. John died in April 1916.

After the execution, the bodies of the co-conspirators were disinterred and moved to another location within the prison walls. For several

years, the families were denied claim to them. On Anna Surratt's be-
half, Father Walter kept up the pressure on the government to release
Mary's body to the family; in February 1869, he was finally successful.
Mary's remains were taken to Baltimore and reinterred in Mt. Olivet
Catholic Cemetery. They reside in a small plot marked with a simple
headstone.[14]

Anna Surratt moved in with the Brophy family after the trial. She
married William P. Tory, a former government clerk who went on to a
career as a chemist. They moved to Baltimore and raised several children there. She died in October 1904, and was laid to rest in a plot next
to her mother at Mt. Olivet.[15] Isaac lays buried next to them.[16]

The Surratts' personal effects were sold at auction to pay the family's numerous debts; they ended up mostly in the hands of curiosity
seekers and relic hunters. The sale of both the H Street house and the
inn and tavern in Surrattsville elicited much attention from the press.[17]
Reports that the boardinghouse was haunted popped up periodically
too.[18] The tavern is now a house museum in Clinton, Maryland (for-
merly Surrattsville); a Chinese restaurant occupies the former boardinghouse in Washington, D.C.

The remaining four conspirators—Dr. Samuel Mudd, Michael
O'Laughlen, Samuel Arnold, and Ed Spangler—were not told of their
sentences until after the hanging of the others, leaving them to wonder
in terror and isolation what their fates might be. They were sent to
serve out their sentences in a prison in the Dry Tortugas in the Florida
Keys. Mudd's family worked tirelessly through the appeals court system to overturn Mudd's conviction—to no avail. In 1867, an outbreak
of yellow fever at the prison killed numerous guards and inmates, including O'Laughlen. Dr. Mudd worked endless days treating the sick
and dying. The survivors at the prison sent a petition to President
Johnson asking him to pardon Mudd. In February 1869, Mudd received
that pardon and returned to Maryland. One month later, on President

Johnson's last day in office, both Arnold and Spangler were also pardoned. All of them lived out the rest of their lives in relative obscurity.

The repercussions of Mary's execution reverberated throughout the
Johnson administration, threatening careers and damaging the reputa-
tions of a variety of witnesses. President Andrew Johnson became em-
broiled in a bitter dispute over his role in finally deciding Mary's death
sentence. In 1867, after two years of battling with Congress over how
best to rebuild the South and assist the newly freed slaves, Johnson
had managed to offend nearly every powerful Republican and some
Democrats in Congress. Frustrated by Johnson's efforts to pardon all
Southern rebels, and his lack of support for voting and civil-rights leg-
islation for African Americans, members of Congress and other powerful Republicans began circulating unfounded rumors that Johnson
was involved in Lincoln's assassination. In his defense, Johnson began
to claim that Judge Holt had never shown him the clemency plea for
Mary written and endorsed by five members of the commission.
Though many eyewitnesses testified that Johnson had indeed seen it,
and that Johnson was firm that Mary's sex was no reason to stop her execution, Johnson now claimed otherwise. The controversy peaked in
1873 when a very public argument erupted between Holt and Johnson
over the clemency plea. Johnson continued to claim that he never saw
the plea, while members of his cabinet, his secretary, and several other
associates with intimate knowledge of the execution order in July 1865
assured the public otherwise. Nevertheless, for those true believers in
Mary's innocence, Holt had duped Johnson into signing Mary's death
warrant without considering the commutation recommendation.[19]

In 1895, David Miller DeWitt, a judge from New York, wrote a
book on the trial of the co-conspirators. Entitled *The Judicial Murder of
Mary E. Surratt*, DeWitt denounced the government's handling of the
trial and its decision to hang Mary Surratt, resurrecting the same old
arguments about the legality of the military tribunal and rehashing the

trial testimony. Like those before him, DeWitt conflated, misstated, and refashioned evidence to support his contention that Mary was innocent and railroaded to the gallows. But as one reviewer noted, "The side taken in the controversy appears in the title chosen by the writer, who weakens his cause very materially by sweeping denunciation of everyone, high or low, connected with the government at the time of the trial. . . . The strongest case imaginable [is] weakened by the vehement abuse that comes so readily from the pen of the . . . author."[20] DeWitt's work helped frame arguments in favor of Mary's wrongful conviction for the next hundred years.

By the turn of the century, more people who had been involved in the trial came forward with their own stories. Surviving witnesses and government officials linked to the trial were compelled to continue publicly defending their roles in Mary's conviction and execution. However, just as Brophy, Walter, Clampitt, and others tried to clear Surratt's name, many other people associated with the trial defended the conduct of the military tribunal and the execution. Even a few Booth accomplices who were unknown to the authorities in 1865 came forward with stories about their role in Booth's complicated plans and Mary's involvement with him.[21]

Today, at the beginning of the twenty-first century, the evidence cannot be ignored. Mary Surratt did indeed keep "the nest that hatched the egg." She could have chosen not to help Booth, but she decided to assist him in whatever way she could. In providing a warm home, private encouragement, and material support to Abraham Lincoln's murderer, she offered more than most of Booth's other supporters. For that, Mary Surratt lost her life and must forever be remembered as the assassin's accomplice.

ACKNOWLEDGMENTS

This book would not have been possible without the research completed by many historians and part-time assassination buffs over the past several decades, who have doggedly pursued every lead in the hopes of uncovering new historical evidence. One of my biggest debts is to James O. Hall, an assassination scholar who perhaps did more than anyone to advance scholarship and research into the conspiracy to kidnap and then assassinate President Lincoln. Though I never met him, I share in the fruits of his labor. Housed at the James O. Hall Research Center at the Surratt House Museum in Clinton, Maryland, Hall's voluminous research files remain the core of any historian's investigation into the complex web of John Wilkes Booth's fatal scheme.

I am also indebted to the many assassination scholars who have recently published excellent books on the conspiracy, assassination, and trial, and who have also made available trial transcripts and long-lost interviews with conspirators and trial participants alike, and who have generously shared their own weighty and important finds. The Surratt Society in particular is a wonderful example of a small museum's ability to provide the public and scholars with the most up-to-date research, promoting an amicable and nonjudgmental forum for debating the many conspiracy and assassination theories, and providing a venue for open discussion of historical research and resources. The Surratt Museum's director, Laurie Vergie, and her staff of professionals and volunteers have not only preserved Mary Surratt's tavern home, but also encouraged ongoing scholarship and debate on Mary's specific role in Booth's plans.

I have also profited from the tremendous historical resources now digitized and available online. The Library of Congress and the National Archives have made available many assassination documents and photographs through their websites. Google Books, Making of America, Documenting the American South, the Gutenberg Project, and numerous universities, libraries, archives, and museums have also digitized assassination- and trial-related materials and books, making them accessible to everyone. Digitized newspapers from the time period have proved most useful. The Early American Newspapers and Imprints project sponsored by the American Antiquarian Society and Newsbank provides instant online access to fully searchable period newspapers. What would have taken months of painstaking page by page research is now done with the stroke of a few keywords targeting specific people, places, and events. NewspaperARCHIVE, Ancestry.com, Accessible Archives, and Proquest are just a few of the online databases offering historical and contemporary news sources, invaluable for any historical research and analysis. I am grateful for the vast collections related to the Civil War and Lincoln at the Boston Athenaeum and the Winchester Public Library, and the important historical sources at the Maryland State Archives.

Thanks to my friends and colleagues far and near who have encouraged this project and offered their valuable insight. Kieran McAuliffe's *John Wilkes Booth Escape Route Map,* proved invaluable as I tried to follow the details of Booth's escape, and his early encouragement helped inspire me to dig deeply into the mystery of Mary Surratt's involvement with Booth. Special thanks go to my agent, Doe Coover, and Basic Books Vice President and Editorial Director, Lara Heimert, who both recognized the importance of Mary Surratt's story and my ability to tell it. I am deeply indebted to my editor Ruth Greenstein, whose sharp eye and inquisitive mind pushed me to write more clearly and thoughtfully, making this a far better book than I could have imagined. And to Wayne Weber, whose keen attention to detail helped tie up those pesky loose ends and clarify some of the more complicated minutiae of this historical drama.

And lastly, thank you to Spencer, Rebecca, and Trevor for your patience and forbearance as I became absorbed with telling the story of a woman long dead but still tantalizing and mysterious. I am truly blessed and I love you all.

NOTES

INTRODUCTION

1. Elizabeth Leonard, "Mary Walker, Mary Surratt, and Some Thoughts on Gender in the Civil War," in Catherine Clinton and Nina Silber, eds., *Battle Scars: Gender and Sexuality in the American Civil War* (New York: Oxford University Press, 2006), 104–119.

2. David Miller DeWitt, *The Judicial Murder of Mary Surratt* (Baltimore: J. Murphy & Co., 1895), title page.

3. Leonard, "Mary Walker, Mary Surratt, and Some Thoughts on Gender in the Civil War," *Battle Scars*, 116.

4. Ongoing research by members and friends of the Surratt House Museum in Clinton, Maryland, continues to spotlight the question of Mary's role in the assassination. The Surratt Society, a volunteer group that works with the Surratt House Museum, publishes *The Surratt Courier,* a monthly newsletter featuring the latest research and interpretations of the assassination and the trials of the conspirators. *Courier* articles defending Mary's innocence share space with those claiming her guilt. Some of this work has uncovered significant details of Mary's activities in the days, weeks, and months before the assassination. During the latter part of the nineteenth century and throughout most of the twentieth, most assassination scholarship that even mentioned Mary Surratt usually defended her innocence. Recent scholarship on the Lincoln assassination, however, has taken a new view of Mary's role. Among others, works that have challenged those claims of Mary's innocence are Edward Steers's *Blood on the Moon: The Assassination of Abraham Lincoln* (Lexington: University Press of Kentucky, 2001). Michael Kauffman's *American Brutus,* Elizabeth Leonard's *Lincoln's Avengers,* James L. Swanson's *Manhunt: The 12-Day Chase for Lincoln's Killer,* Steers's edited volume of the assassination trial transcripts, *The Trial: The Assassination of President Lincoln and the Trial of the Conspirators,* and

Roy Z. Chamlee's deeply researched and detailed study, *Lincoln's Assassins: A Complete Account of the Capture, Trial, and Punishment.*

The exception to this is Elizabeth Steger Trindal's 1996 biography, *Mary Surratt, an American Tragedy.* Trindal explores the full context of Mary's life, from her birth, to her Catholic conversion, marriage, motherhood, and wartime struggles. Broadly researched, Trindal's work follows generations of scholarship that presents Mary as innocent and unjustly murdered by rapacious and immoral Northern Republicans and Unionists. Trindal interprets Mary's life and her role in Booth's plot through the lens of Lost Cause mythology and memory, situated squarely within a pro-South, pro-Confederate perspective. This and similar works invariably ignore the strongest evidence against Mary, while often making claims and highlighting testimony and evidence long discredited by historians.

CHAPTER ONE: "DEVOTED BODY AND SOUL TO THE CAUSE"

1. "Mrs. Surratt. Card from L. J. Weichmann—Additional Testimony as to Mrs. Surratt," *Chicago* Tribune, July 20, 1865.

2. "John H. Surratt's Lecture. Given at the Courthouse in Rockville, Maryland, on December 6, 1870," in Mark Wilson Seymour, ed., *The Pursuit & Arrest of John H. Surratt: Dispatches from the Official Record of the Assassination of Abraham Lincoln* (Austin, TX: Civil War Library, 2000), 93–101.

3. Louis Weichmann, *A True History of the Assassination of Abraham Lincoln and the Conspiracy of 1865*, Floyd E. Risvold, ed. (New York: Alfred A. Knopf, 1975), 20.

4. Weichmann, *A True History*, 105–106.

5. "The Assassins! Their Trial at Washington," *Philadelphia Inquirer*, May 15, 1865.

6. Weichmann, *A True History*, 127.

7. Weichmann, *A True History*, 170.

CHAPTER TWO: CREATING A LIFE, BUILDING THE NEST

1. For a detailed biographical treatment of Mary's early life, see Elizabeth Steger Trindal, *Mary Surratt: An American Tragedy* (Gretna, LA: Pelican Publishing Company, Inc., 1996). Also, the Surratt House Museum in Clinton, Maryland, is an important resource for information on Mary Surratt and her family.

2. Trindal, *Mary Surratt*, 19–20.

3. Trindal, *Mary Surratt*, 22–24. Isaac was born June 2, 1841; Anna, January 1, 1843; and John Jr., April 10, 1844.

4. Trindal, *Mary Surratt*, 24–25.

5. Trindal, *Mary Surratt*, 29.

6. Trindal, *Mary Surratt*, 35.

7. Trindal, *Mary Surratt*, 36.

8. Trindal, *Mary Surratt*, 21.

9. Barbara Jeanne Fields, *Slavery and Freedom on the Middle Ground: Maryland during the Nineteenth Century* (New Haven, CT: Yale University Press, 1985), 6–7. In 1850, Prince George's County was nearly 60 percent black, but only 5.3 percent of the black population was free; neighboring Charles County was 65 percent black, with 5.6 percent free; St. Mary's County nearly 55 percent black, with nearly 12 percent free. See pages 10–12.

10. The Fugitive Slave Act of 1850 supplanted an earlier law passed in 1793 that addressed the problem of increasing numbers of runaway slaves and their helpers—many of whom had been inspired by the promise and the rhetoric of the American Revolution, in addition to vigorous moral and religious authorities who called for an end to the inhumane and brutal system of slavery.

11. The Christiana Riot, in Christiana, Pennsylvania, in 1851, in which a Maryland slave master chasing his enslaved man was attacked and killed by local black and white abolitionists, is a case in point.

12. Trindal, *Mary Surratt*, 35.

13. "Surratt House Insurance Policy," File 382, Drawer 13, Surratt House Museum, Clinton, Maryland.

14. Trindal, *Mary Surratt*, 35–39.

15. Trindal, *Mary Surratt*, 39.

16. Bertram Wyatt-Brown, *Honor and Violence in the Old South* (New York: Oxford University Press, 1986), 131–133.

17. Trindal, *Mary Surratt*, 41–44. See also 1860 Slave Census, Prince George's County, Maryland, District 9. U.S. Bureau of the Census, *Eighth Census of the United States, 1860*.

18. Trindal, *Mary Surratt*, 42–46.

19. "House Divided," speech presented by Abraham Lincoln in Springfield, Illinois, June 16, 1858. See David Herbert Donald, *Lincoln* (New York: Simon & Schuster, 1995), 206.

20. Several other border slave states—Missouri, Kentucky, and Delaware—also remained in the Union, even though many of their citizens were avidly pro-South.

21. "Slave-Hunters," *Christian Advocate and Journal,* December 26, 1861. "Whipped to Death," *Saturday Evening Post,* February 8, 1862. "Progress," *New York Independent,* April 3, 1862. "Mr. Cox and the Slave Who Was Whipped to Death," *Liberator,* April 4, 1862.

CHAPTER THREE: REBELS, SPIES, AND COURIERS

1. For an excellent discussion of the Confederate Signal Corps and the Confederate Secret Service, see William A. Tidwell, James O. Hall, and David Winfred Gaddy, *Come Retribution: The Confederate Secret Service and the Assassination of Lincoln* (Jackson: University Press of Mississippi, 1988).

2. Tidwell, Hall, and Gaddy, *Come Retribution,* 80–91.

3. Tidwell, Hall, and Gaddy, *Come Retribution,* 72.

4. Weichmann, *A True History,* 30. See also Weichmann's reprint of John Surratt's "Rockville Lecture" from December 1870, where Surratt reveals his rebel mail and courier service to the Confederacy, 430. Surratt had long been a suspect in Lincoln's assassination, but he fled to Europe to evade arrest in the summer of 1865. He was captured in 1867 and extradited back to the United States for trial, which ended in a mistrial. In 1870 Surratt hoped to capitalize on his notoriety by giving public lectures on his role in Booth's plans.

5. Trindal, *Mary Surratt,* 62–63. Gwynn's son Clarence, a contemporary of John Jr., had with thousands of other young Maryland men enlisted in the Confederate army early in the war, later dying in battle in Virginia.

6. James A. Mudd, Robert A. Burch, Y. Posey, Thomas Smith, George W. Smith, and Luther Allen were but a few of the local residents involved in this activity. See United States War Department, United States Record and Pension Office, *The War of the Rebellion: A Compilation of the Official Records of the Union and Confederate Armies,* 2d Ser., 2 (Washington, DC: Government Printing Office, 1897), 868–881.

7. "The Surratt Family & John Wilkes Booth," compiled from the research of James O. Hall (Clinton, MD: The Surratt Society, n.d).

8. "The Surratt Family & John Wilkes Booth."

9. James M. McPherson, *Battle Cry of Freedom: The Civil War Era* (New York: Ballantine Books, 1988), 492–493.

10. Robert J. Brugger, *Maryland: A Middle Temperment, 1634–1980* (Baltimore: Johns Hopkins University Press, 1988), 286–289.

11. McPherson, *Battle Cry of Freedom,* 602–603.

12. Roy Z. Chamlee, Jr., *Lincoln's Assassins: A Complete Account of Their Capture, Trial, and Punishment* (Jefferson, NC: McFarland & Company, Inc., Publishers, 1990), 102–103.

13. Chamlee, *Lincoln's Assassins*, 102–103.

14. "Townsend Interviews Weichmann," *The Lincoln Assassination: From the Pages of The Surratt Courier (1986–1999)*, Vol. 2 (Clinton, MD: The Surratt Society, 2000), IX-18–IX-19.

15. Weichmann, *A True History*, 19.

16. Weichmann, *A True History*, 20.

17. "Townsend Interviews Weichmann," *The Lincoln Assassination*, Vol. 2, IX-19. No further information was provided about these two men.

18. "Townsend Interviews Weichmann," *The Lincoln Assassination*, Vol. 2, IX-19.

19. Weichmann, *A True History*, 27.

20. Chamlee, *Lincoln's Assassins*, 165.

21. Weichmann, *A True History*, 30.

22. Weichmann, *A True History*, 28. How these two girls became friends is unclear. Nora was younger than Anna, and no known relationship between the two families has been uncovered. Weichmann believed they had been friends, but he may have been mistaken. If a courier or spy, Fitzpatrick's relationship to the Surratts would make sense.

23. Chamlee, *Lincoln's Assassins*, 342.

24. Chamlee, *Lincoln's Assassins*, 175. Weichmann, *A True History*, 27–28. Trindal, *Mary Surratt*, 82–84.

25. Weichmann, *A True History*, 28. Chamlee, *Lincoln's Assassins*, 104. McPherson, *Battle Cry of Freedom*, 600–611. Trindal, *Mary Surratt*, 96. Bounty brokers negotiated bounties paid by states, counties, and municipalities to entice young men to enlist in the Union army. Bounty brokering had become a flourishing profession since the Lincoln administration's enforced draft system. Local and regional quotas demanded by federal authorities needed filling, creating tremendous pressure and competition between different communities, counties, and states eager to enroll eligible young men. Bounty and substitute brokers found a lucrative and brisk business filling those muster rolls as the war dragged on, but the profession lacked respectability and was looked down upon as unsavory and unpatriotic.

26. Chamlee, *Lincoln's Assassins*, 166.

27. Chamlee, *Lincoln's Assassins*, 165.

28. Weichmann, *A True History*, 29.

Chapter Four: Keeper of the Nest

1. Edward Steers, Jr., *His Name Is Still Mudd: The Case against Dr. Samuel Alexander Mudd* (Gettysburg, PA: Thomas Press, 1997), 64–65.

2. Steers, *His Name Is Still Mudd*, 61–67.

3. Steers, *His Name Is Still Mudd*, 39–42. See also Tidwell, Hall, and Gaddy, *Come Retribution*, 5–6, 337–341, and Chamlee, *Lincoln's Assassins*, 102.

4. Steers, *His Name Is Still Mudd*, 39–48, 60–62. Steers has thoroughly investigated Mudd's story and determined the timeline of meetings between Booth, Mudd, Surratt, and others involved in Booth's plans.

5. Weichmann, *A True History*, 33.

6. Weichmann, *A True History*, 34.

7. Weichmann, *A True History*, 34.

8. Benn Pitman, *The Assassination of President Lincoln and the Trial of the Conspirators* (New York: Moore, Wilstach & Baldwin, Publishers, 1865), 114, 133, 139.

9. Pitman, *Assassination*, 114.

10. Chamlee, *Lincoln's Assassins*, 345.

11. Weichmann, *A True History*, 104.

12. Weichmann, *A True History*, 105–106.

13. George Parnell Fisher, *The Trial of John H. Surratt in Criminal Court for the District of Columbia* (Washington, DC: Government Printing Office), 372, 436–437.

14. Fisher, *The Trial of John H. Surratt*, 372, 436–437.

15. Richard Mitchell Smoot, *The Unwritten History of the Assassination of Abraham Lincoln* (Clinton, MA: Privately printed, Orra L. Stone, 1908), 7–8.

16. Tidwell, Hall, and Gaddy, *Come Retribution*, 339.

17. Fisher, *The Trial of John H. Surratt*, 1267–1268.

18. Smoot, *The Unwritten History*, 10.

19. Edward Steers, Jr., *Blood on the Moon: The Assassination of Abraham Lincoln* (Lexington: University Press of Kentucky, 2003), 81.

20. Steers, *Blood on the Moon*, 62–63. "Statement of Samuel Bland Arnold Made at Baltimore, Maryland, April 18, 1865," in *From the War Department Files: Statements Made by the Alleged Lincoln Conspirators Under Examination, 1865* (Clinton, MD: The Surratt Society, 1980).

21. Chamlee, *Lincoln's Assassins*, 162–163.

22. Steers, *Blood on the Moon*, 83–85. Chamlee, *Lincoln's Assassins*, 163–164, 474–475.

23. Weichmann, *A True History*, 13, 14, 74.

24. Weichmann, *A True History*, 75.

25. Michael W. Kauffman, *American Brutus: John Wilkes Booth and the Lincoln Conspiracies* (New York: Random House, 2004), 164.

26. Chamlee, *Lincoln's Assassins*, 104.

27. Chamlee, *Lincoln's Assassins*, 190–191, 164, 169–173.

28. "Headquarters MD. Dist. of the Patuxent. Port Tobacco, MD, May 2, '65. Confession of Geo. A. Atzerodt in the Matter of the Murder of the President Taken by Col. H. H. Wells," in Laurie Vergie, ed., *From the War Department Files: Statements Made by the Alleged Lincoln Conspirators Under Examination, 1865* (Clinton, MD: The Surratt Society, 1980), 60–62. Atzerodt's confession was actually taken on April 25, 1865, and forwarded to Wells's superiors on May 2, 1865. Anna Surratt later testified that Weichmann intervened on Atzerodt's behalf to allow him to stay at the house, but Atzerodt himself recalled being brought to the house by John Surratt. Regardless of the initial introduction, Atzerodt became a frequent visitor to the H Street home.

29. Pitman, *Assassination*, 71.

30. Pitman, *Assassination*, 119.

31. Chamlee, *Lincoln's Assassins*, 115. Pitman, *Assassination*, 119. Fisher, *The Trial of John H. Surratt*, 435–436.

32. Tidwell, Hall, and Gaddy, *Come Retribution*, 200–206.

33. "Atzerodt's Confession in the 1/18/1869 *Baltimore America*," "Unpublished Atzerodt Confession Revealed Here for the First Time," and "Atzerodt's Confession in the 7/9/1865 *National Intelligencer*," in Joan L. Chaconas, ed., *The Lincoln Assassination: From the Pages of the Surratt Courier (1986–1999)*, Vol. 1 (Clinton, MD: The Surratt Society, 2000), III-19–III-28.

34. Pitman, *Assassination*, 134.

35. Pitman, *Assassination*, 119.

36. Chamlee, *Lincoln's Assassins*, 501.

37. Pitman, *Assassination*, 134.

38. Tidwell, Hall, and Gaddy, *Come Retribution*, 340–341.

39. Pitman, *Assassination*, 115–133.

40. "Statement of Mrs. Mary E. Surratt, Mother of Jno. Surratt. Carroll Prison, Ap'l 28 '65," in *From the War Department Files*, 44–52.

41. "Affidavit of Louis Weichmann," in Pitman, *Assassination*, 421.

42. Weichmann, *A True History*, 87. See also *Boston Daily Advertiser*, February 28, 1865; *New Haven Daily Palladium*, February 28, 1865; and *Milwaukee Daily Sentinel*, February 28, 1865.

43. Tidwell, Hall, and Gaddy, *Come Retribution*, 408.

44. Pitman, *Assassination*, 161. Testimony of Margaret Kaighn.

45. Pitman, *Assassination*, 133–134.

46. Pitman, *Assassination*, 133.

47. Pitman, *Assassination*, 115.

48. Pitman, *Assassination*, 115.

49. Weichmann, *A True History*, 97–98.

50. Weichmann, *A True History*, 98.

51. Weichmann, *A True History*, 97–98.

52. "Statement of Samuel Bland Arnold Made at Baltimore Maryland April 18, 1865," in *From the War Department Files*, 20–22.

53. Kauffman, *American Brutus*, 183–185.

54. Weichmann, *A True History*, 101.

55. Pitman, *Assassination*, 118.

56. Weichmann, *A True History*, 102–103.

CHAPTER FIVE: THE ASSASSIN'S ACCOMPLICE

1. Pitman, *Assassination*, 85.

2. Kauffman, *American Brutus*, 191. Weichmann, *A True History*, 377.

3. Pitman, *Assassination*, 118. Fisher, *The Trial of John H. Surratt*, 381.

4. Pitman, *Assassination*, 113, 135.

5. Kauffman, *American Brutus*, 192. See also Fisher, *The Trial of John H. Surratt*, 715, 719.

6. Tidwell, Hall, and Gaddy, *Come Retribution*, 416.

7. Fisher, *The Trial of John H. Surratt*, 386–387. Why John Zadoc did not take the public coach remains a mystery.

8. Fisher, *The Trial of John H. Surratt*, 387.

9. Fisher, *The Trial of John Surratt*, 670.

10. "John H. Surratt's Lecture. Given at the Courthouse in Rockville, Maryland, on December 6, 1870," Mark Wilson Seymour, ed., *The Pursuit & Arrest of John H. Surratt. Dispatches from the Official Record of the Assassination of Abraham Lincoln* (Austin, TX: Civil War Library, 2000), 93–101.

11. Tidwell, Hall, and Gaddy, *Come Retribution*, 419–420.

12. Steers, *Blood on the Moon*, 89–91. See also Tidwell, Hall, and Gaddy, *Come Retribution*, 417–421. According to Atzerodt's own testimony, Booth believed that the support for this scheme came from Confederate Secret Service operatives in New York. Steers, Tidwell, Hall, and Gaddy have not

been able to discern a link between the New York rebel networks and the Torpedo group assigned to blow up the White House, but the plan may have been known to several branches of the Confederate Secret Service. Tidwell, Hall, and Gaddy further speculate that it was John Surratt, Jr., who actually had firsthand knowledge of the plan, based on his frequent visits to Richmond and New York.

13. "Unpublished Atzerodt Confession," in *The Lincoln Assassination*, III-19–III-21.

14. Weichmann, *A True History*, 168. Chamlee, *Lincoln's Assassins*, 260–261. Kauffman, *American Brutus*, 208–209.

15. Kauffman, *American Brutus*, 209, 443 n. 32.

16. Pitman, *Assassination*, 85.

17. Pitman, *Assassination*, 119.

18. Pitman, *Assassination*, 85.

19. Kauffman, *American Brutus*, 209. Weichmann, *A True History*, 134–135, 472–474 nn. 7–8.

20. Fisher, *The Trial of John H. Surratt*, 1285.

21. Pitman, *Assassination*, 116. Fisher, *The Trial of John H. Surratt*, 389–390.

22. Kauffman, *American Brutus*, 209.

23. Smoot, *The Unwritten History*, 10–12.

24. Smoot, *The Unwritten History*, 12.

25. "Atzerodt's Confession in the 7/9/1865 *National Intelligencer*," in *The Lincoln Assassination*, III-23–III-25.

26. Weichmann, *A True History*, 163–164.

27. Pitman, *Assassination*, 126.

28. Fisher, *The Trial of John H. Surratt*, 391; Pitman, *Assassination*, 116.

29. "Confession of Geo. A. Atzerodt," in *From the War Department Files*.

30. Pitman, *Assassination*, 420. Weichmann, *A True History*, 165–166.

31. Pitman, *Assassination*, 126.

32. Pitman, *Assassination*, 126. Weichmann, *A True History*, 168–170.

33. Pitman, *Assassination*, 121, 125.

34. Pitman, *Assassination*, 85–86, 121, 125.

35. Pitman, *Assassination*, 121, 125–126.

36. Pitman, *Assassination*, 85, 121, 125–126, 129.

37. Pitman, *Assassination*, 85–87.

38. Pitman, *Assassination*, 420.

39. Weichmann, *A True History*, 172. Pitman, *Assassination*, 420.

40. Weichmann, *A True History,* 174–175. See also Weichmann's affidavit in Pitman, *Assassination,* 420.

41. Fisher, *The Trial of John H. Surratt,* 689–690.

42. Smoot, *The Unwritten History,* 12–13.

43. Weichmann, *A True History,* 175.

44. For complete descriptions of Booth's murder of Lincoln, see Kauffman, *American Brutus;* Steers, *Blood on the Moon;* Chamlee, *Lincoln's Assassins;* Elizabeth D. Leonard, *Lincoln's Avengers: Justice, Revenge, and Reunion After the Civil War* (New York: W. W. Norton & Company, 2004); and James L. Swanson, *Manhunt: The 12-Day Chase for Lincoln's Killer* (New York: HarperCollins, 2006).

45. For complete descriptions of Payne's brutal attack, see Kauffman, *American Brutus;* Steers, *Blood on the Moon;* Chamlee, *Lincoln's Assassins;* Leonard, *Lincoln's Avengers;* and Swanson, *Manhunt.*

46. Weichmann, *A True History,* 175. Pitman, *Assassination,* 140.

47. Fisher, *The Trial of John H. Surratt,* 394–395.

48. Fisher, *The Trial of John H. Surratt,* 697.

49. Fisher, *The Trial of John H. Surratt,* 672.

50. Fisher, *The Trial of John H. Surratt,* 698.

51. Weichmann affidavit, in Pitman, *Assassination,* 421.

52. Weichmann, *A True History,* 179.

CHAPTER SIX: A SHREWD WITNESS

1. Chamlee, *Lincoln's Assassins,* 11.

2. Chamlee, *Lincoln's Assassins,* 79.

3. Fisher, *The Trial of John H. Surratt,* 1310.

4. Pitmann, *Assassination,* 121–122. See also Chamlee, *Lincoln's Assassins,* 80–81.

5. Pitman, *Assassination,* 121–124. See also Chamlee, *Lincoln's Assassins,* 80–81, and Steers, *Blood on the Moon,* 174–177.

6. Pitman, *Assassination,* 122–123.

7. Kauffman, *American Brutus,* 268–269.

8. Pitman, *Assassination,* 122–123.

9. "Statement of Mrs. Mary E. Surratt In the Matter of the Murder of the President, April 17, 1865, Related to Booth, Jno. E. Surratt, Atzerodt, Wood, Harold [sic] and Payne," in Laurie Vergie, ed., *From the War Department Files: Statements Made by the Alleged Lincoln Conspirators Under Examination, 1865* (Clinton, MD: The Surratt Society, 1980).

10. Chamlee, *Lincoln's Assassins*, 85.

11. "Washington April 28th, 1865. Anna Surratt," in Laurie Vergie, ed., *From the War Department Files: Statements Made by the Alleged Lincoln Conspirators Under Examination, 1865* (Clinton, MD: The Surratt Society, 1980).

12. The War Department stenographer misspelled Weichmann's name.

13. Atzerodt would later identify a Confederate spy named Kate Thompson, alias Sarah Slater, as a visitor to the Surratt house.

14. "Statement of Mrs. Mary E. Surratt In the Matter of the Murder of the President. April 17, 1865," in *From the War Department Files*.

15. Chamlee, *Lincoln's Assassins*, 67–76. Leonard, *Lincoln's Avengers*, 53–62.

CHAPTER SEVEN: THE "MATERFAMILIAS" OF THE CRIMINALS

1. David Heidler, Jeanne T. Heidler, and David J. Cole, *Encyclopedia of the American Civil War: A Political, Social, and Military History* (New York: W. W. Norton & Co., 2002), 1433–1434.

2. "Arrest of the Surratt Family," *Chicago Tribune*, April 22, 1865.

3. "Some Notable Trials. The Case of Mary Surratt," *New York Times*, February 16, 1896, 30.

4. "Riotous Proceedings in Fall River," *Liberator*, April 21, 1865.

5. "A Friend of the Assassins Tarred and Feathered at Swampscott," *Liberator*, April 21, 1865.

6. "Punishment of Secessionists," *Liberator*, April 21, 1865.

7. Dorothy Meserve Kunhardt and Philip B. Kunhardt, Jr., *Twenty Days: A Narrative in Text and Pictures of the Assassination of Abraham Lincoln and the Twenty Days and Nights that Followed—The Nation in Mourning, the Long Trip Home to Springfield* (New York: Harper & Row, 1965), 139.

8. For a lengthy and descriptive narrative of the Lincoln funeral procession, including many photographs, see D. M. Kunhardt and P. B. Kunhardt, *Twenty Days*.

9. See Virginia Lomax, *The Old Capitol and Its Inmates: By a Lady, Who Enjoyed the Hospitalities of the Government for a "Season"* (New York: E. J. Hale & Son, 1867).

10. Lomax, *The Old Capitol*, 83–84.

11. Lomax, *The Old Capitol*, 66, 70–72.

12. Lomax, *The Old Capitol*, 93.

13. Chamlee, *Lincoln's Assassins*, 174–175.

14. Chamlee, *Lincoln's Assassins*, 175.

15. Chamlee, *Lincoln's Assassins*, 176.

16. Chamlee, *Lincoln's Assassins*, 179.

17. Chamlee, *Lincoln's Assassins*, 171.

18. Lomax, *The Old Capitol*, 136–137.

19. Lomax, *The Old Capitol*, 134–135.

20. Lomax, *The Old Capitol*, 133–136.

21. Kauffman, *American Brutus*, 233.

22. Kauffman, *American Brutus*, 256, 261.

23. Chamlee, *Lincoln's Assassins*, 126–127. See also Pitman, *Assassination*, 141–143.

24. Swanson, *Manhunt*, 222–223.

25. Pitman, *Assassination*, 124. Kauffman, *American Brutus*, 286–287.

26. Pitman, *Assassination*, 85.

27. Pitman, *Assassination*, 124.

28. Kauffman, *American Brutus*, 309.

29. For a detailed description of Booth's final hours at the Garrett farm, see Swanson, *Manhunt*, 287–343.

30. Chamlee, *Lincoln's Assassins*, 158–160. Kauffman, *American Brutus*, 325. Booth's body would remain under the storeroom floor throughout the conspirators' trial and executions, and for several years afterward. Its whereabouts were even kept secret from the Booth family.

31. "The Assassins. Important Proclamation by President Johnson," *New York Times*, May 4, 1865.

32. Chamlee, *Lincoln's Assassins*, 195.

33. Chamlee, *Lincoln's Assassins*, 195.

34. Lomax, *The Old Capitol*, 172.

35. Lomax, *The Old Capitol*, 173–174.

36. "The Great Conspiracy: The Execution of the Condemned," *Daily National Intelligencer*, July 8, 1865. On the eve of the hanging, they would all be removed to cells on the ground floor of the penitentiary.

37. "The Assassins and Conspirators. The Arsenal Building, Washington, Where the Culprits Are on Trial," *Philadelphia Enquirer*, May 13, 1865.

38. "The Assassins Captured," *New York Observer and Chronicle*, May 4, 1865. John A. Gray, "The Fate of the Lincoln Conspirators. The Account of the Hanging, Given by Lieutenant-Colonel Christian Rath, The Executioner," *McClure's Magazine*, October 1911.

39. Chamlee, *Lincoln's Assassins*, 200.

40. For more detailed examinations of this issue and arguments surrounding the decision to conduct a military trial of the co-conspirators, see Edward

Steers, Jr., *The Trial* (Lexington: University of Kentucky Press, 2003), xi–xxviii; Steers, *Blood on the Moon;* Chamlee, *Lincoln's Assassins;* Kauffman, *American Brutus;* and Leonard, *Lincoln's Avengers.* For a transcription of Speed's opinion, and General Order 100, see Steers, *The Trial,* 403–419.

41. Steers, *The Trial,* xcviii.

42. Steers, *The Trial,* 17.

43. Steers, *Blood on the Moon,* 211–213.

44. Steers, *The Trial,* 403–409.

45. Steers, *The Trial,* 409.

46. Steers, *The Trial,* 409.

47. Steers, *The Trial,* 409.

48. Steers, *The Trial,* xvi.

49. Steers, *Blood on the Moon,* 214–215.

50. Steers, *The Trial,* 18–19.

51. Steers, *The Trial,* 20.

52. Kauffman, *American Brutus,* 397.

53. "The Great Conspiracy!" *Philadelphia Inquirer,* May 11, 1865.

54. "The Great Conspiracy!" *Philadelphia Inquirer.*

55. "The Great Conspiracy!" *Philadelphia Inquirer.*

56. Steers, *The Trial,* 21–22.

57. "The Assassins! Their Trial at Washington," *Philadelphia Inquirer,* May 15, 1865.

58. Chamlee, *Lincoln's Assassins,* 362.

CHAPTER EIGHT: THE CASE FOR THE DEFENSE

1. "Washington. The Treason Trials!" *Philadelphia Inquirer,* May 13, 1865.

2. "The Assassins," *New York Times,* May 14, 1865.

3. "Washington. The Treason Trials!" *Philadelphia Inquirer.*

4. "Mrs. Surratt. Card from L. J. Weichmann—Additional Testimony as to Mrs. Surratt's Guilt," *Philadelphia Inquirer,* July 17, 1865.

5. "The Assassins! Their Trial at Washington," *Philadelphia Inquirer,* May 15, 1865.

6. Pitman, *Assassination,* 85.

7. "Trial of the Assassins. Mrs. Surratt Abandons Hope," *Philadelphia Inquirer,* May 16, 1865.

8. Pitman, *Assassination,* 119.

9. "Trial of the Assassins. Reverdy Johnson on a New Track," *Philadelphia Inquirer,* May 16, 1865.

10. "Trial of the Assassins," *Philadelphia Inquirer*, May 16, 1865. See also "Washington. Mrs. Surratt Meditating," *Philadelphia Inquirer*, May 19, 1965.

11. "Trial of the Assassins," *New York Times*, May 20, 1865.

12. "Interesting Incidents of the Trial," *Philadelphia Inquirer*, May 20, 1865.

13. "Interesting Incidents of the Trial," *Philadelphia Inquirer*.

14. "The Trial. Yesterday's Proceedings," *Philadelphia Inquirer*, May 20, 1865. See also "Sharp Hits at Mrs. Surratt," *Philadelphia Inquirer*, May 20, 1865.

15. "Sharp Hits at Mrs. Surratt," *Philadelphia Inquirer*.

16. "Opening of Testimony for Defense," *Philadelphia Inquirer*, May 26, 1865.

17. "Opening of Testimony for Defense," *Philadelphia Inquirer*. Chamlee, *Lincoln's Assassins*, 344.

18. "Opening of Testimony for Defense," *Philadelphia Inquirer*.

19. Gwynn and his brother Andrew were well-known rebels in the region. See B. F. Gwynn's testimony in regards to his rebel activities and his testimony related to Dr. Mudd in "The Trial," *Philadelphia Inquirer*, May 29, 1865, and Pitman, *Assassination*, 182–183 (Pitman incorrectly dates the testimony as May 20, but Gwynn's testimony was given on May 25).

20. Swanson, *Manhunt*, 105.

21. "Opening of Testimony for Defense," *Philadelphia Inquirer*.

22. "Opening of Testimony for Defense," *Philadelphia Inquirer*.

23. "The Trial of the Conspirators!" *Philadelphia Inquirer*, May 27, 1865.

24. "The Trial of the Conspirators!" *Philadelphia Inquirer*.

25. Pitman, *Assassination*, 136–137.

26. On the twenty-sixth, Aiken and Clampitt asked the court to recall a prosecution witness, Henry Von Steinacker, who had testified to a grand rebel plot linking Booth to top Confederate leaders. Taken in a secret closed-door session without defense counsel present, Von Steinacker's testimony had convinced many in Washington of a larger, Confederate-sanctioned plot to kill Lincoln, and that Booth and his accomplices were but foot soldiers to carry out the scheme. Von Steinacker was a fraud and rebel spy, and his testimony was completely false. But his testimony had no direct bearing on Mary's case, and the justices were puzzled as to why Aiken and Clampitt were so adamant about cross-examining this witness. Von Steinacker would be one of several fraudulent prosecution witnesses who gave false testimony during the trial.

27. Chamlee, *Lincoln's Assassins*, 350.

28. People traveled back and forth between Northern and Southern states under the "Flag of Truce" system to engage in educational, business, and personal affairs.

29. Pitman, *Assassination*, 134.

30. Pitman, *Assassination*, 114, 133–135.

31. "The Trial. Saturday's Proceedings," *Philadelphia Inquirer*, May 29, 1865.

32. "The Trial. Saturday's Proceedings," *Philadelphia Inquirer*.

CHAPTER NINE: THE VERDICT: SWIFT AND DEADLY

1. "Infamy! Testimony of J. Z. Jenkins," *Philadelphia Inquirer*, May 31, 1865.

2. "Infamy! Testimony of J. Z. Jenkins," *Philadelphia Inquirer*.

3. Pitman, *Assassination*, 141.

4. Pitman, *Assassination*, 128.

5. "Infamy! Testimony of J. Z. Jenkins," *Philadelphia Inquirer*.

6. Pitman, *Assassination*, 138–143.

7. Pitman, *Assassination*, 130–131.

8. "The Trial of the Conspirators," *Philadelphia Inquirer*, May 31, 1865.

9. Pitman, *Assassination*, 130–131.

10. "The Trial of the Conspirators," *Philadelphia Inquirer*.

11. Gray, "The Fate of the Lincoln Conspirators," 633.

12. Chamlee, *Lincoln's Assassins*, 380.

13. "The Trial of the Conspirators," *Philadelphia Inquirer*.

14. "The Trial of the Conspirators," *Philadelphia Inquirer*.

15. Gray, "The Fate of the Lincoln Conspirators," 633.

16. Chamlee, *Lincoln's Assassins*, 380–381.

17. "Mrs. Surratt and Her Daughter," *Philadelphia Inquirer*, June 3, 1865.

18. "Rebutting Evidence," *Philadelphia Inquirer*, June 3, 1865.

19. "Examination of Witnesses for the Defense . . . Testimony of James Lusby," *Philadelphia Inquirer*, June 3, 1865.

20. "The Trial of the Conspirators," *Philadelphia Inquirer*, June 5, 1865.

21. "How Much the Ladies Are Interested," *Philadelphia Inquirer*, June 5, 1865.

22. Washington . . . Gen. Hunter Compelled to Interfere," *Philadelphia Inquirer*, June 5, 1865.

23. "Mrs. Surratt's Failing Health," *Philadelphia Inquirer*, June 8, 1865.

24. "Signs of Character. Physiognomy. The Conspirators. A Personal Description of the Assassins on Trial at Washington," *American Phrenological Journal*, July, 1865, 19.

25. "Letter From Washington," *Zion's Herald and Wesleyan Journal*, June 14, 1865.

26. "Mrs. Swisshelm on Mrs. Surratt," *Baltimore Sun*, July 17, 1865.

27. "Mrs. Swisshelm on Mrs. Surratt," *Baltimore Sun*.

28. "Mrs. Surratt's Health Failing," *Philadelphia Inquirer*, June 8, 1865.

29. "Incidents of the Great Trial," *Philadelphia Inquirer*, June 8, 1865.

30. "Testimony of John Holohan," *Philadelphia Inquirer*, June 8, 1865.

31. Chamlee, *Lincoln's Assassins*, 424–426.

32. Pitman, *Assassination*, 132.

33. Pitman, *Assassination*, 129–138, 247.

34. "News of the Day. Advantages Offered to the Counsel for the Defense," *Philadelphia Inquirer*, June 13, 1865.

35. "The Conspiracy!" *Philadelphia Inquirer*, June 14, 1865.

36. "The Conspiracy!" *Philadelphia Inquirer*. See also, Pitman, *Assassination*, 125–126.

37. Chamlee, *Lincoln's Assassins*, 422–423.

38. "The Conspiracy! Reverdy Johnson on the Jurisdiction of the Commission," *Philadelphia Inquirer*, June 20, 1865.

39. "Washington . . . Severe Illness of Mrs. Surratt," *Philadelphia Inquirer*, June 21, 1865.

40. "The Conspiracy! The Argument for Mrs. Surratt," *Philadelphia Inquirer*, June 22, 1865.

41. Fisher, *The Trial of John H. Surratt*, 813, 896.

42. Pitman, *Assassination*, 299.

43. Pitman, *Assassination*, 299.

Chapter Ten: Scenes at the Scaffold

1. John W. Clampitt, "The Trial of Mrs. Surratt," *North American Review*, September 1880, Vol. 131, Issue 286, 235.

2. Clampitt, "The Trial of Mrs. Surratt," 235.

3. Pitman, *Assassination*, 248.

4. Pitman, *Assassination*, 18–19.

5. Pitman, *Assassination*, 18–22.

6. Chamlee, *Lincoln's Assassins*, 442.

7. Horatio King, "Judge Holt and the Lincoln Conspirators," *The Century: a Popular Quarterly*, April 1890, 956.

8. King, "Judge Holt," 956. Attorney General James Speed also admitted to seeing the petition during that cabinet meeting, but refused to discuss what was actually said during the meeting, claiming he was bound to never disclose cabinet-meeting discussions.

9. King, "Judge Holt," 956.

10. King, "Judge Holt," 957.

11. Pitman, *Assassination*, 249.

12. "Extra. The Execution." *Washington Evening Star*, July 7, 1865.

13. "Extra. The Execution," *Washington Evening Star*.

14. "End of the Assassins," *New York Times*, July 8, 1865.

15. "Extra. The Execution," *Washington Evening Star*.

16. Chamlee, *Lincoln's Assassins*, 445.

17. Chamlee, *Lincoln's Assassins*, 448.

18. "The Surratt Case . . . by Rev. J. A. Walter . . . Read before the U.S. Catholic Historical Society, May 25, 1891," Vertical File 362, Folder 1, Surratt House Museum, Clinton, Maryland.

19. Joseph George, Jr., "Trial of Mrs. Surratt: John P. Brophy's Rare Pamphlet," *Lincoln Herald*, Vol. 93, No. 1 (Spring 1991).

20. "Weichmann vs. Brophy!!" *Philadelphia Inquirer*, July 24, 1865. See also "Affidavit of Mr. John P. Brophy," *Daily Index*, July 17, 1865; Weichmann, *A True History*, 292, 486–487 n. 13; and Chamlee, *Lincoln's Assassins*, 424, 452–453, 457.

21. "Weichmann vs. Brophy!!" *Philadelphia Inquirer*.

22. George, "Trial of Mrs. Surratt," 17–22.

23. Clampitt, "The Trial of Mrs. Surratt," 235.

24. Clampitt, "The Trial of Mrs. Surratt," 236.

25. Clampitt, "The Trial of Mrs. Surratt," 236.

26. "Attempt to Stay the Execution," *Daily Index*, July 10, 1865. "The End of the Assassins," *New York Times*, July 8, 1865.

27. "Last Expedient of Mrs. Surratt. Important Proceedings in the District Court," *Philadelphia Inquirer*, July 8, 1865. "Attempt to Stay the Execution," *Daily Index*, July 10, 1865.

28. "Extra: The Execution," *Washington Evening Star*, July 7, 1865.

29. William E. Doster, *Lincoln and Episodes of the Civil War* (New York: Putnam and Sons, 1915), 277.

30. "Unpublished Atzerodt Confession," in *The Lincoln Assassination*, Vol. 1, III-19–III-21.

31. "The Assassins," *New York Observer*, July 20, 1865.

32. Doster, *Episodes of the Civil War*, 277–282.

33. "The Assassins Executed," *Boston Daily Advertiser*, July 8, 1865.

34. "The Dying Statements of Payne and Atzerodt," *North American and United States Gazette*, July 10, 1856. This article quotes an article from the *Washington Chronicle*.

35. Betty J. Ownsbey, *Alias "Payne": Lewis Thornton Powell, Mystery Man of the Lincoln Conspiracy* (Jefferson, NC: McFarland & Company, Inc., 2003), 137.

36. "End of the Assassins," *New York Times*.

37. Ownsbey, *Alias*, 138.

38. "The Clemency Plea Debate," in *The Lincoln Assassination: From the Pages of the Surratt Courier (1986–1999)*, Vol. 1 (Clinton, MD: The Surratt Society, 2000), VI-33.

39. "Pleaded for Pardon," *Washington Post*, July 21, 1901. Joseph George, Jr., "Support at the Last; The Efforts of John P. Brophy," in *The Lincoln Assassination: From the Pages of the Surratt Courier (1986–1999)*, Vol. 1 (Clinton, MD: The Surratt Society, 2000), VI-24–VI-25.

40. Chamlee, *Lincoln's Assassins*, 461.

41. "End of the Assassins," *New York Times*.

42. Gray, "The Fate of the Lincoln Conspirators," 635.

43. "The Great Execution. Full Details," *Washington Evening Star*, July 7, 1865.

44. Gray, "Fate of the Lincoln Conspirators," 635.

45. W. H. Cunnington, "The Hanging of the Lincoln Conspirators: Unpublished History by an Eyewitness," *Philadelphia Inquirer*, March 22, 1896.

46. "The Great Execution," *Washington Evening Star*, July 7, 1865.

47. Mary E. Trindal, "History at its Worst," in *The Lincoln Assassination: From the Pages of the Surratt Courier (1986–1999)*, Vol. 2 (Clinton, MD: The Surratt Society, 2000), VII-13.

48. "End of the Assassins," *The New York Times*.

49. Gray, "The Fate of the Lincoln Conspirators," 636.

50. Cunnington, "The Hanging of the Lincoln Conspirators."

51. See Cunnington, "The Hanging of the Lincoln Conspirators"; "Extra: The Execution," *Washington Evening Star;* "Particulars of the Execution of

the Conspirators"; *Macon Daily Telegraph,* July 13, 1865; "End of the Assassins," *New York Times;* and Harlow Randall Hoyt, "William Coxshall's Recollections," in *The Lincoln Assassination: From the Pages of the Surratt Courier,* Vol. 2 (Clinton, MD: The Surratt Society, 2000), VII-7–VII-10.

52. "The Great Execution," *Washington Evening Star.*

53. Hoyt, "William Coxshall's Recollections," VII-9.

54. James L. Swanson and Daniel R. Weinberg, *Lincoln's Assassins, Their Trial and Execution: An Illustrated History* (New York: William Morrow, 2006), 24–25.

55. Gray, "The Fate of the Lincoln Conspirators."

56. "The Case of Mrs. Surratt," *Daily Index,* July 17, 1865.

57. Hoyt, "William Coxshall's Recollections," VII-9. Trindal, "History at its Worst," VII-14.

58. "End of the Assassins," *New York Times.*

59. "The Great Execution. Full Details, the Last Scene," *Washington Evening Star,* July 7, 1865.

60. "End of the Assassins," *New York Times.*

Epilogue: American Tragedy or American Justice?

1. See Letter, P. H. Sheridan, Major-General to Lieut. Gen. U.S. Grant, New Orleans, November 20, 1865. "Correspondence, Etc., Union," in *The War of the Rebellion,* 1st Ser., 48: 1257.

2. "Mrs. Surratt's Mourners," *Chicago Tribune,* July 14, 1865.

3. "A Washington Story! What a Mr. Brophy Says," *Philadelphia Inquirer,* July 12, 1865.

4. Chamlee, *Lincoln's Assassins,* 425.

5. "Mrs. Surratt. Card from L. J. Weichmann," *Philadelphia Inquirer.*

6. "Mrs. Surratt. Card from L. J. Weichmann," *Philadelphia Inquirer.*

7. "Weichmann vs. Brophy!!" *Philadelphia Inquirer,* July 26, 1865.

8. "Statement of Gen. Hardie—The Interview between Himself and Rev. Mr. Walter—No Denial of Spiritual Consolation to the Prisoner," *New York Times,* July 21, 1865.

9. John T. Ford, "Behind the Curtain of Conspiracy," *North American Review,* April 1889, Vol. 148, Issue 389. John W. Clampitt, "The Trial of Mrs. Surratt."

10. See "Pleaded for Pardon," *Washington Post,* July 21, 1901; Rev. J. A. Walter, "The Surratt Case: A True Statement of Facts," *United States Catholic Historical Magazine,* Vol. III, 1890.

11. Noah Brooks, "Abraham Lincoln: The Close of Lincoln's Career," *Century; A Popular Quarterly,* May 1895, 27.

12. "Mary E. Surratt's Good Name," *New York Times,* March 24, 1895. "Was She a Martyr?" *Philadelphia Inquirer,* March 24, 1895.

13. Weichmann, *A True History,* xviii.

14. "From Washington. Surrender of Mrs. Surratt's Body," *Baltimore Sun,* February 9, 1869. "Reinterment of Mrs. Surratt," *Hagerstown Herald and Torchlight,* February 17, 1869.

15. "Daughter of Mrs. Surratt," *Washington Post,* October 26, 1904.

16. "Bury Isaac Surratt Here," *Washington Post,* November 5, 1907.

17. "Sale of Mrs. Surratt's Effects," *New York Times,* October 28, 1865.

18. "Mrs. Surratt's House Haunted," *Philadelphia Inquirer,* December 15, 1866.

19. "Who Hung Mrs. Surratt?" *Chicago Daily Tribune,* October 6, 1873. "Mrs. Surratt," *Chicago Daily Tribune,* August 27, 1873. "Andrew Johnson on the Execution of Mrs. Mary Surratt," *Chicago Daily Tribune,* September 14, 1872. Holt continued for years to convince everyone that he had shown Johnson those commutation papers. See, "New Facts about Mrs. Surratt: Correspondence of Judge Holt and Hon. James Speed," *North American Review,* Vol. 147, Issue 380, July 1888.

20. "New Books and New Additions," *Critic: A Weekly Review of Literature and the Arts,* November 9, 1895, 301.

21. "The Story of the Lincoln Conspiracy and the Conspirators," *Los Angeles Times,* December 12, 1902. W. H. Cunnington, "The Hanging of the Lincoln Conspirators: Unpublished History by an Eye Witness," *Philadelphia Inquirer,* March 22, 1896. Edward V. Murphy, "Lincoln Trial Court Reporter Tells His Story," *New York Times,* April 9, 1916. "Captain Charles Rath," *Daily Iowa State Press,* April 18, 1899. Smoot, *The Unwritten History* (Baltimore: Privately Printed by John Murphy Company for Orra L. Stone, 1908).

INDEX

255